America in the Twenties

The Beginnings of Contemporary America

PAUL GOODMAN
University of California, Davis

FRANK OTTO GATELL
University of California, Los Angeles

HOLT, RINEHART AND WINSTON, INC.

New York   Chicago   San Francisco   Atlanta
Dallas   Montreal   Toronto   London   Sydney

Preface

This brief volume attempts to interpret the history of the United States during the 1920s, a decade when the contours of contemporary America clearly emerged. It was a time of profound cultural change and social stress. An older, rural, religious culture gave way, not without struggle, to an urban and mechanized society whose fate, for better or worse, rested on faith in secular values. Nothing reveals more graphically the nature of the changes in progress during the Twenties than events in the schools and churches, in popular culture, and the mass anxieties which found outlets in Prohibition, the revival of the Ku Klux Klan, or the "Monkey Trial" in Dayton, Tennessee—all disturbing (sometimes traumatic) movements and incidents for Americans creating a Mass Society.

We have not sought to provide comprehensive treatments of events, favoring instead a more analytical approach which shifts the balance from narrative to interpretative history. And despite the requirements of brevity we have found it necessary to go back into preceding decades in order to explain a line of historical development that reached some point of crystallization in the 1920s. The focus of this volume is almost exclusively on the domestic scene. Following each chapter we have reprinted a representative document which will enable readers to probe more deeply into one of the major themes treated in the text.

P. G.
F. O. G.

Davis, California
Los Angeles, California
August 1971

Contents

Introduction

The Big Changes, 1900-1930

The common life-styles of present-day America emerged in the second and third decades of the twentieth century, the product of a hundred years of industrialization and urbanization. Turn-of-the-century Americans like William McKinley would have felt like aliens in the Roaring Twenties. By then the balance had shifted decisively from rural and small-town America to metropolitan America and the Mass Society that would shape the future.

In this new world, more than ever before, science and technology, applied by large organizations, became the masters. They produced unprecedented affluence and revolutionized older modes of living. America became a nation of consumers working to buy an endless variety of goods undreamed of by previous generations. The automobile, a triumph of mass production, came within the reach of a majority of American families in the 1920s. And other consumer durables, including an array of electric appliances from telephones to washing machines, promised to transform the American home.

The Age of Mass Consumption, spurred by a dramatic surge in national income, was also an Age of Leisure. Americans worked less, earned more, and played more often than in any time in their history. The advance and diffusion of technology meant also a simultaneous revolution in communications. Movies and radio brought inexpensive entertainment to the most remote places. And these new media, triumphs of the marriage between scientific research and Big Business, spread the culture of the city —its jazz and jokes, its folkways and foibles across a continent. This growth threatened to end regional, local and ethnic diversity. Main Street no longer nestled in the hills or on the plains, safely isolated from Broadway.

For over half a century people had been abandoning rural America for the cities. Now the metropolis began to spread its tentacles into the countryside. By 1930 almost 60 percent of the population lived in towns of 2500 or more. The auto enabled urban Americans to build suburban subdivisions ringing the cities. At the same time movies and radio reduced the cultural isolation of the hinterland. At last the nation was becoming one.

As in the past the price of social change proved high. Americans were torn between traditional values and new standards quickly adopted by young people. Now more than ever, science rather than religion promised to unlock the secrets of the universe, and with waning faith came moral attitudes that transformed interpersonal relations. Women seeking first-class citizenship tried to work out more satisfying roles in society. The family lost cohesiveness as its members made greater demands for autonomy that weakened the authority of the once all-powerful patriarch. And men and women experimented with new attitudes toward sexuality which made sensual pleasure an integral part of the pursuit of happiness, not the occasion for the growth of guilt complexes.

Yet as greater affluence and new technology were standardizing their lives, Americans reacted uneasily and with a sense of loss. Society changed more rapidly than ever and the country seemed fragmented. The gulf between old and new ways strained relations among Americans, raising unsettling questions about the nature of the national mission.

Wilson's war "to make the world safe for democracy" had ended in bitterness and cynicism. America's allies had toyed with Wilsonian principles of self-determination for all peoples, but were unwilling to make a peace that had a reasonable chance of preventing another bloodbath. Having entered the war supposedly to fulfill a global mission, the Treaty of Versailles, so at variance with this high expectation, left Americans bewildered and frustrated. Full of doubts about their role in history, they began to doubt themselves. Many turned against their neighbors and against historic traditions of generosity, idealism and tolerance. Convinced that in them alone reposed purity and virtue in a world dominated by corruption and evil, Americans sought to isolate themselves from sin.

This loss of confidence also bred distrust at home. Although Americans grasped at the fruits of modern society, especially its creature comforts, they felt threatened. Science undermined ancient faiths; new life-styles that emphasized leisure, consumption and pleasure flouted the tried-and-true virtues of hard work, thrift and self-denial. Metropolitan centers were now more than ever the wellsprings of the threatening new forces of modernism. In the cities lived hordes of immigrants and their ambitious, second-generation offspring, all alien in religions and habits, and all pushing for equal opportunity. Cities also housed the offices of the country's most powerful banks and corporations; they nourished Bolshevism and other frightening radicalisms, such as bohemianism, agnosticism, libertinism—in short, every *ism* but Americanism.

Fear bred hate, and hate bred repression. For a while hysteria gripped the country. Government, employing police state tactics, ran roughshod over individual liberties, while courts acquiesced. Dissenters went to jail, aliens were shipped back to Europe, and the gates clamped shut to keep out immigrant foreigners. A constitutional amendment banned all alcoholic beverages, a measure Prohibitionist forces urged as a powerful blow against immorality, poverty, and urban vice of every imaginable kind. Some state governments forbade the teaching of Darwinian evolution in the belief that in so doing they struck a mighty blow against science and modernist threats to the Old-Time Religion. For some, however, legal means of repression were too slow and gentle. A revivified Ku Klux Klan spread across the country, north and south, instilling fear in Catholics, Jews, blacks and nonconforming white folks whom the hooded vigilantes threatened with cross-burnings and beatings.

By the middle of the 1920s fear and anxiety were subsiding, due primarily to a very sharply improved standard of living. Americans became preoccupied with getting and spending, convinced more than ever that the business of America was business. The progressive spirit faded; attacks on Big Business and cries for social justice for the poor and weak went unheeded. Organized labor declined in the face of hostility from public opinion and government and sharp employer counterattacks stunted union growth. After two decades of prosperity, agriculture experienced a decline in the 1920s and farm organizations also encountered frustration in their fight for a larger share of national wealth.

For twelve years (1921–1933) the Republican party ruled the country—largely purged of its progressive elements and dominated by its eastern, business-oriented conservative wing. The GOP, accurately reflecting the national mood, met only token opposition from the disorganized and divided Democrats.

Millions of Americans did not share the comforts created by national affluence, but they were ignored. The complacent majority believed euphorically that the genius of American business would abolish poverty and assure permanent prosperity. Against these sentiments the skeptics and the distressed made little headway. Then, in October 1929, the Roaring Twenties ended. The Great Stock Market Crash ushered in the worst depression in American history, destroying confidence in business leadership and forcing Americans to search for new leadership and new directions. The pressures of intense crisis helped resolve many ambivalent attitudes toward modernity. Americans, even rural Americans, became more willing to discard repression, anti-intellectualism, bigotry and businessmen's folk wisdom and to rely on science and expertise, centralized power and political bureaucracies, pluralism and tolerance to restore prosperity.

For two decades the Progressives had preached the gospel of a new social morality. They had tried to reduce conflict and promote social stability but rhetoric alone did little to alter the central tendencies in American life that alarmed them—the loss of individual initiative, the fragmentation of society, the specter of class warfare, and the concentration of power in large business bureaucracies. Many knew that they could not turn back the clock to a simpler time, yet they groped ineffectively to redistribute power, to harness business in the public interest, to protect the weak, and to promote social cohesion. The failures of the middle-class reformers in the first two decades of the century, particularly their unwillingness to risk substantial changes in the system, meant the surrender of the 1920s to the complacent. Standpatters held on until overtaken by events beyond their control, events few Americans could fully comprehend. But knowledgeable or not, all shared responsibility in the new national disaster.

Suggestions for Further Reading

Suggestions for further reading following each chapter are highly selective. Works available in paperback editions are starred (*). Students should consult the bibliography in John D. Hicks, *Republican Ascendancy, 1921–1933* (1960)* and the footnotes in Burl Noggle's article "The Twenties," cited below, for additional references.

General Works on the Twenties

Frederick Lewis Allen, *Only Yesterday* (1931)*; William E. Leuchtenberg, *The Perils of Prosperity 1914–1932* (1958)*; John D. Hicks, *Republican Ascendancy, 1921–1933* (1960)*; Paul Carter, *The Twenties in America* (1968)*; Frederick J. Hoffman, "The Temper of the Twenties," *Minnesota Review*, Vol. I (1960), pp. 36–45; Henry F. May, "Shifting Perspectives on the 1920's," *Mississippi Valley Historical Review*, Vol. 43 (1956), pp. 405–427; Burl Noggle, "The Twenties: A New Historiographical Frontier," *Journal of American History*, Vol. 53 (1966), pp. 299–314.

Chapter One

The Age of Mass Consumption

The United States entered the twentieth century the world's richest nation. In the first thirty years of the new century (1900–1930), affluence transformed the daily lives of Americans more profoundly than in the preceding three hundred years. Technological advances created new industries and revolutionized existing ones. By 1930, Americans communicated by telephone, drove to work in cars, ate canned food, bought national brands under the hypnotic influence of multimedia advertising, and spent evenings beside the radio or in the movie theater. A generation earlier they had communicated by mail, traveled to work on foot or by streetcar, ate homemade food (even at lunch time), bought loose soap and crackers from the grocer's barrels, and looked forward to the infrequent visits of a traveling circus or vaudeville show. Good or bad, the Big Change had come.

This transformation of life-styles depended on enormous advances in basic industry in the late nineteenth century. In 1900 steel was the leading manufacturing industry; thirty years later, automobile making was king. But the mass production of consumer durables such as cars could not have come without existing capacity for the mass production of steel, rubber, glass, paint, and gasoline. Nor would the early car makers have found many customers had not rising family incomes created a mass market for their product. Yet new industries (like autos, electric power,

7

and telephones) themselves generated growth in national income. Detroit created enormous demand for all the products that went into automobiles, and it employed thousands of workmen who became customers for cars, electric appliances, movies and telephones. In this way technology, diffused by mass production at low cost, became a self-generating process that dramatically raised the standard of living in the United States.

These changes occurred unevenly. Periods of growth alternated with recessions, the most rapid advances coming after 1914. The outbreak of war in Europe generated a boom in the United States that lasted until a short, though severe postwar depression (1921–1922). Then the economy surged forward to new highs until toward the end of the decade the boom lost momentum and collapsed in 1929, plunging the country into a ten-year depression. Until then, people had marveled at a productive system that made Americans the first to enter the Age of Mass Consumption.

The Sources of Growth

For most of their history, Americans counted on a rapidly growing population to develop their virtually unpeopled but resources-rich continent. By 1900 there were seventy-five million Americans, making the country one of the world's most populous, and in the next thirty years the figure grew to almost 125 million. Until the outbreak of the First World War in 1914, immigrants kept flooding in. Then in the 1920s Americans abandoned unrestricted immigration. Henceforth, the country's growth would depend primarily on the birthrate of native-born stock, and that declined sharply between 1900 and 1930, falling by a third. Family size also shrank, the result of urbanization, the diffusion of new personal values and the spread of birth control.

Output grew much more rapidly than population. In 1900 gross national product per person was $800; by 1930 it reached $1100. The 1920s, a decade of pronounced economic progress, saw 60 percent of this advance. Developments in technology, and their widespread diffusion through mass production techniques, account in part for the economy's high performance. Manufacturing output led the way, growing three times faster than population. By 1920 the manufacturing sector generated almost three times the percentage of national income originating in agriculture. Yet despite this dominance by manufacturing, industry employed about the same percentage of the labor force—a fifth—in 1930 as in 1900, a percentage held steady by remarkable gains in labor productivity. A shift in occupational distribution became apparent in the 1920s, heralding future trends. By 1930 a smaller percentage of the work force found jobs in industry than a decade earlier, but expanded employment opportunities had emerged in various service industries—trade, finance, and government—industries which formed an increasingly large, lower middle class of white-collar workers.

Consumer durables and construction were the foundations of the boom in the 1920s. The dynamic role played by railroads and heavy industry in the late nineteenth century fell now to the cities. Urbanization continued to spark growth, with its endless demand for new residential housing, new office buildings and factories, sewage and water systems, and electric power. But in the Age of Mass Consumption, consumer durables—cars, household furnishings, appliances—also became one of the underpinnings of national prosperity, and automobiles led the way.

The Emergence of Detroit

In the 1890s a handful of companies began to manufacture automobiles powered by the recently developed internal-combustion gasoline engine. At first, cars were expensive playthings of the rich. Then in 1908, Henry Ford, an auto manufacturer who had begun by producing high-priced cars, reached out for the mass market with the famous Model T. Within a generation, autos had become America's leading manufacturing industry, transforming the national economy and its landscape.

At the outset, Ford explained his philosophy of building a car within the reach of the average family. "I will build a motor car for the multitudes," Ford announced. "It will be large enough for the family but small enough for the individual to run and care for. It will be constructed of the best materials, by the best men to be hired, after the best designs that modern engineering can devise. But it will be so low in price that no man making a good salary will be unable to own one—and enjoy with his family the blessings of hours of pleasure in God's great open spaces."

By exploiting the economies of standardization, division of labor, and mechanization through the introduction of the moving assembly line, Ford dramatically reduced the cost of manufacturing this highly complex product. By the 1920s, Ford made good his boast. The price of Ford's Model T had fallen from $850 to $310, and the Ford Motor Company became one of the most profitable business enterprises in history.

At the outset, many car manufacturers competed for the new markets. Initial capital requirements were small (Ford started with $28,000). Wall Street and Big Business all but ignored this small, unproved, risky business. By the 1920s, however, cars had become the biggest business of all. Three firms, then as now, dominated the industry—Ford, General Motors, and Chrysler—and Wall Street became deeply involved in their finance and management, especially with General Motors. The advantages of large-scale manufacture and enormous capital requirements now effectively excluded small manufacturers, a pattern that had developed earlier in heavy industry during the late nineteenth century.

Yet Ford's early methods proved inappropriate once the cars had become widely diffused. In the 1920s, General Motors seized the auto industry's leadership and has maintained it ever since. Founded in 1908 by William C. Durant, a manufacturer of horse-drawn carriages, General Motors started as a conglomeration of loosely integrated auto companies such as Buick, Oldsmobile and Chevrolet, and of several auto parts suppliers. Durant was a master salesman and empire builder but, like Ford, he failed to weld his company into an effectively administered unit. The postwar recession (1921–1922) severely hurt General Motors and brought in new management with fresh strategies, infusions of Wall Street money, and methods which soon made General Motors the industry leader.

By the mid-1920s the market for new cars was becoming saturated at existing levels and distribution of national income. The problem then was to sell cars to people who already owned them. General Motors began innovations in marketing. It developed a wide line of cars appealing to different tastes and pocketbooks, from the phenomenally successful and low-cost Chevrolet to the luxurious Cadillac. It stressed style and comfort, relying heavily on advertising, and offered customers annual model changes, trade-in allowances and installment credit. And General Motors developed efficient structures and procedures for administering a large corporation, realizing that it could no longer depend on expanding output to lower costs and assure satisfactory profit margins.

Because General Motors was so large and complex, top management freed itself from day-to-day operational responsibilities. It concentrated on coordinating product flow, maximizing use of resources, developing statistical and financial controls vital to planning intelligently for the future. Operational responsibilities, however, were decentralized in the various divisions involved in the manufacture of parts and accessories or assembly under the overall supervision of the general offices. These reforms of internal management provided the solution for efficiently managing this giant enterprise and they became a model for other Big Businesses.

Innovation meant profits for General Motors. Ford's failure to adjust to changing conditions had made that company No. 2. Previously, Ford succeeded by building a simple, standardized single product, the Model T. When few persons owned cars, everyone wanted the utilitarian Ford flivver which came in only one color—black. Ford's strategy was to achieve maximum cost-savings through standardization. In the 1920s, however, Americans became increasingly willing to sacrifice economy and utility for styling and glamor, but Henry Ford refused to change: "We want to construct some kind of machine," he insisted stubbornly, "that will last forever. . . . We never make an improvement that renders any previous model obsolete." Ford ruled his great empire single-handedly, but severe losses ultimately convinced him of the obsolescence of his own strategy. Ford finally changed and brought out new models; but not until after he died did the Ford Motor Company in the 1940s undergo the basic transformation that had helped make General Motors the world's largest corporation.

Ford became the greatest of the businessmen heroes. An amused but impressed British traveller observed: "Just as in Rome one goes to the Vatican and tries to get audience of the Pope, so in Detroit one goes to the Ford Works and endeavours to see Henry Ford." People listened to Ford's opinions and indulged his crotchets even on subjects he knew nothing about; and there were many of these, since Ford's genius did not extend beyond auto mechanics. His enormous wealth and status as folk hero assured him an audience for whatever ideas he wished to propound—including anti-Semitism. Ford was both naïve and shrewd, simultaneously the architect of the new technological America *and* the high priest of the American cult of nostalgia for a simpler, rural America. He spent millions on constructing a mythical small town, Greenfield Village, which when contrasted with his mammoth River Rouge assembly plant reveals him as a man of divided loyalties, a cultural schizophrenic. More than any other single individual, Ford helped to modernize America, yet this supreme innovator could lament with apparent sincerity: "It was an evil day when the village flour mill disappeared."

The automobile industry provides a dramatic example of a common process of economic development. New technologies increased productivity, reduced costs, and expanded markets in a self-generating cycle. New machines powered either by gasoline engines or run by electricity intensified and diffused the advantages of mechanization. A new textile loom enabled a worker to tend three times as many machines; new machinery mechanized bottle production, put farmers on tractors, and drastically reduced the cost of steel and cement. Between 1900 and 1930 urban America also became electrified, as new inventions sharply cut the costs of electricity.

Developments in one industry revolutionized others. The internal-combustion engine, for instance, transformed oil, rubber manufacturing, and agriculture. Entrepreneurs now systematically began to finance research to develop new products and manufacturing methods. Companies in the more advanced industries were the first to appreciate the possibilities of institutionalizing technological progress. Thus General Electric which began primarily as a manufacturer of electric motors, generating equipment and light bulbs, developed electric appliances, plastics and metal alloys. Du Pont moved from explosives into dyes, paint, and cellulose. In this way, divisions of research and development in the modern, large corporation systematized technological change upon which rapid economic growth depended.

The Structure of Mass Marketing

With manufacturing output growing three times faster than population, business had to develop new techniques of distributing and advertising products and, just as important, new ways to finance consumer purchases. Chain stores began garnering larger shares of the retail dollar, especially in foods and drugs. Woolworth's and other "five-and-dime" stores took business away from specialty shops, and the mail-order houses opened large retail outlets in the new suburban neighborhoods, at the expense of downtown department stores. As in manufacturing, so in retailing, Big Business could undersell small business because it enjoyed economies of scale. Sears, Roebuck & Company, for instance, manufactured some of the merchandise it sold or put its own label on goods while dictating the price and quality to its suppliers.

When food, clothing and rent had used up most of the consumer's budget, people needed little credit. By the 1920s, however, consumers were purchasing expensive, durable goods produced by the new industries, and they were buying them on time. Installment credit enabled people to buy now and pay later, instead of saving until they could afford a washing machine or a car. As people went into debt to acquire consumer durables, they had to allocate larger and larger portions of their income to pay their debts, rather than spend impulsively on small purchases at the grocery or clothing store.

Together with chain stores and installment credit, national advertising played a major role in creating a mass consumption society. Businessmen had begun to realize the advantages of advertising in the late nineteenth century but in the 1920s advertising expenditures tripled and Madison Avenue assumed its present-day importance. Manufacturers initially used national advertising to reach consumers directly and to stimulate demand without having to rely on jobbers and retailers to push their products. By familiarizing shoppers with the alleged advantages of national brands, manufacturers broadened their markets and tried to stabilize the market by cultivating brand loyalty. As consumers came to desire Brand X, for instance, retailers began to stock it; the stimulation and the demand reinforced each other.

At first advertising appeals were simple, though exaggerated. "Not truth but credibility," claimed an ad man, was the key to success. One manufacturer informed an unsuspecting but believing public that it had bad breath; California lemon growers claimed their product cleaned teeth, shampooed hair, removed stains, polished glass, and loosened cuticles for manicuring. As advertising men became more sophisticated, they added irrational appeals to exaggerated claims. Cars, they insisted, gave people status, and toothpaste gave them sex appeal. The successful ad man, J. Walter Thompson, revealing a basic assumption of the industry, explained that the average consumer had the mentality of a "fourteen-year-old human animal," a creature of whim, infinitely gullible and infinitely capable of being manipulated. George Washington Duke, irascible and shrewd founder of the American Tobacco Company, acknowledged that his firm relied on repetitive and annoying advertising.

A few people, alarmed by dishonesty in advertising and the difficulty of getting one's money's worth because of a bewildering variety of merchandise, demanded regulation of the business. These anxieties led to an organized consumers' movement to test goods scientifically and help people spend their money more rationally, but most consumers remained indifferent to such efforts and businessmen were hostile. Business denounced any interference with free enterprise as un-American and a communist plot. The second charge proved a convenient though preposterous way to discredit critics of advertising; the first charge may have had much validity in the America of the 1920s.

National advertising had become vital in an age of mass consumption. It created new desires, informed the public about existing products and most of all it persuaded people to buy a certain brand. Businessmen much preferred to compete through marketing appeals than through price wars, especially in industries such as soap, tobacco, cosmetics, and patent medicines in which little real difference existed among rival brands except the differences invented by the ad men.

Advertising served a larger function besides publicizing specific products. During the First World War the government used advertising to sell patriotism and Liberty Bonds, and in the 1920s Big Business turned to public relations to assure a favorable climate of opinion. Institutional ads depicted corporations as friendly, humane organizations, not soulless monsters. Americans learned that "Big Business is your Big Brother." But even more important, advertising trained people in new habits and values appropriate for a mass society. "Advertising," claimed one of its boosters, "is almost the only force at work against puritanism in consumption." It encouraged people "to live and enjoy— that is the basis of modern economics."

The Welfare of the American People

Economic growth produced remarkable improvements in the standard of living. The gains of productivity resulting from the achievements of basic industrialization and technological advance began to trickle down to working people. Real wages, which had grown slowly before 1914, surged ahead in the next fifteen years, while the average work week decreased from 60 hours in 1900 to just over 40 hours by 1930. As technology multiplied labor's efficiency, it simultaneously cut labor costs. Employers could improve wages and working conditions, and require fewer hours without cutting sharply into profits or raising prices. Both the climate of opinion generated by reformers and the pressure of unionization induced business to share more of the benefits of industrialization with the working classes.

No previous generation of Americans had experienced visible advances of such magnitude in its material well-being. Higher per capita income allowed people to spend a smaller portion of their income on food, clothing and housing. They could now afford more expensive items such as meat, dairy products, and fresh fruits and vegetables; and they had more money for medical care, entertainment, and gadgets. By the late 1920s many Americans spent more on cars than on clothing. At the same time family size was shrinking so that a larger family income supported a smaller household.

The health of the American people improved dramatically. Life expectancy increased more in the first three decades of the twentieth century than in the preceding one hundred years. Males born in 1900 could expect to live forty-eight years; by 1930 life expectancy had reached almost sixty. Infant mortality dropped sharply especially in the 1920s, and infectious diseases such as tuberculosis, diphtheria, and pneumonia took a much lower toll. Improvements in health resulted largely from better diet, housing, and sanitation. Cities purified water supplies and enforced requirements for pasteurization of milk. But as people lived longer, the afflictions of aging, such as cancer and heart disease, became increasingly important causes of death. And by 1930 automobile accidents joined the list of major killers.

The quality of medical care also advanced, especially through mass vaccination against infectious diseases. Until the latter half of the nineteenth century medical science remained relatively primitive. Competing schools of medicine confused the public and created a field day for what later generations regarded as quackery. As medicine became more experimental and empirical, and less theoretical and speculative, breakthroughs in fundamental knowledge occurred with increasing rapidity particularly after Louis Pasteur demonstrated the germ theory of disease. Discoveries of the specific causes and cures of many infectious diseases such as tuberculosis, yellow fever, malaria, diphtheria, typhoid and syphilis soon followed. At the same time the perfection of anesthesia opened up enormous new possibilities for the development of surgery. As the new knowledge seeped down, people became less inclined to accept disease and death as inevitable. They began consciously to conserve health, observe preventive measures, and seek professional care when illness struck.

An improvement in medical education had to precede the diffusion and wide application of this new knowledge. As medicine became more scientific, standards for practice tightened through tougher licensing requirements and radical improvement in the quality of medical schools. Although fewer medical schools and doctors per capita existed in 1930 than in 1900, the quality of medical care had advanced decisively. The number of hospital beds per capita almost doubled between 1900 and 1930, representing substantial investments in health facilities. And government, through city and county health departments, clinics and health centers, played a vital role. These agencies, together with philanthropic foundations and organizations such as the National Tuberculosis Association (1904), and the launching of industrial medicine by business, helped to diffuse new medical knowledge.

Yet advanced medical care remained too expensive or unavailable for most people. America, fast becoming a land of large-scale organizations of resources and services, still lived with a medical system largely in the hands of doctors maintaining individual practices—operating much like small businessmen. Health resources were unevenly distributed across the country, serving the city better than the country, the rich far better than the middle and lower classes. "We know how to do a lot of things which we don't do or do on a wretchedly small scale," complained Dr. William H. Welch, a medical reformer, in 1925. But organized medicine, speaking through the American Medical Association, fought, usually with success, the first, tentative steps towards bringing the benefits of modern medicine to all Americans regardless of wealth. Besides opposition from organized medicine to an adequate health care delivery system, millions of Americans were ignorant and even skeptical of modern medicine. "It's ridiculous to frighten people by talking about these millions of germs in our food, air, and water," said a midwesterner in the 1920s. "I went to school in a small room with lots of other children, and we were all rosy-cheeked and healthy and didn't know a thing about germs. There wasn't any of this foolishness of weighing children and frightening them to death because they may be underweight."

The Other Side of the Boom

Although most Americans fared better than ever before, economic gains had been distributed unevenly. Over half the income received by families and unattached individuals in 1929 went to the top 20 percent of the population, and only a quarter went to the bottom 40 percent. The Twenties produced *more* rather than less inequality in the distribution of income. Unemployment remained chronic. Between 1900 and 1930, the average annual rate of unemployment exceeded four percent (the currently "acceptable" minimum) in two out of every three years, and the average during the Twenties reached almost five percent. Since there was no unemployment insurance then, people thrown out of work often became destitute.

Millions of Americans lived below the poverty line. In 1915 the United States Industrial Commission reported that a third of the workers employed in mining and manufacturing lived at or below a subsistence level. A poor child was three times as likely to die before adulthood than a middle class child. And poverty and disease took a still greater toll among blacks, the poorest of the poor, than among poor whites. Two decades of progressive reform and three decades of rapid economic advance had not eliminated serious imbalances in the distribution of wealth. The contrast between those few enjoying the delights of affluence and the millions left in squalor was sharper than ever.

Imbalance characterized most of the booming Twenties. Some of the older industries, such as agriculture, soft-coal mining, and textiles experienced continuous hard times. In each case the markets for their products grew slowly in a maturing economy and an excess of supply over demand depressed prices. Nor were producers in these industries, made up of thousands of small units, able to adjust output to the market, whereas in steel and autos a handful of giants dominated and influenced supply and price.

The agricultural depression of the 1920s engulfed millions of Americans. The cities had been growing much more rapidly than rural America for decades but not until 1920 did the number of urban dwellers exceed the rural population. Although about 45 percent of the people still lived in rural areas in the 1920s, agriculture received only about 12 percent of the national income and its share continued to fall rapidly.

Farmers had traditionally lagged behind the urban sectors, where the *big* money could be made, but agriculture had enjoyed relative prosperity during the first two decades of the twentieth century (1900–1919). The depression of the 1890s and the closing of the frontier slowed the heady expansion of agricultural production that had resulted in supply outdistancing demand and plummeting prices. From 1900 to 1919 the terms of trade shifted. Domestic demand caught up with supply and pushed farm prices up more rapidly than the general price level. The outbreak of the First World War sustained and accelerated agricultural prosperity, as the United States became a major source of food for the Allies. Later, the government encouraged farmers to expand production with the patriotic slogan, "Food Will Win the War," and the even more convincing persuasion of guaranteed high prices.

Though rural America did not share in affluence to the same extent as urban America, agricultural productivity advanced in the early twentieth century. The gasoline engine promoted mechanization at a time when much of the countryside still had no electricity. By 1930 there were almost a million tractors and almost as many trucks on the farms, and the wealthier farmers had begun to buy grain combines, corn pickers and milking machines. But low farm income deprived small-scale farmers of the benefits of such mechanization.

Modernization of the American farm received an additional boost from the diffusion of scientific research. The normally conservative farmers at first resisted new methods, fearful of risking their resources on the advice of government officials, university experts and businessmen who were not themselves "dirt" farmers. But gradually, under prodding from the state agriculture colleges (which educated many of the farmers' sons) and businessmen who exerted economic pressure, the Agriculture Department officials gained their trust, and farmers began to innovate and achieve a modest growth in efficiency. Agriculture, however, did not benefit from lower prices, made possible by lower costs through expanded sales, to the same extent as other industries. Consumers who could already buy most of the food they wanted did not buy much more because prices fell.

Agriculture entered the 1920s with enlarged capacity but diminishing markets. Europe no longer relied as much on the

United States as during wartime and the domestic market grew too slowly to take up the slack. The decline hit hardest the wheat growers, hurt by the shift in consumer preference for more meat, and the cotton growers who supplied raw material for the "sick" textile industry.

These imbalances in the productive system, the widespread poverty amid plenty, the prevalence of "sick" industries in a rapidly growing economy, paralleled conflicting American life-styles. The ethic of production and work, the basis for the fast-receding rural society, now collided squarely with a new empha-sis on consumption and leisure as mass Society began to emerge in the 1920s.

Document: The Coming of the Automobile
Henry Ford, My Life and Work
Alfred P. Sloan, Jr., My Years with General Motors

Two of the great movers of modern America were Henry Ford and Alfred P. Sloan, Jr., founding fathers of the auto-mobile industry, keystone of the American economy in the twentieth century. Henry Ford was born on a Michigan farm in 1863. He left school at 15 to become an apprentice in a machine shop and later became chief engineer of the Edison Illuminating Company in Detroit in 1893. Experimenting with the design of automobiles in the 1890s, Ford founded the Ford Motor Com-pany in 1903. One of a number of early car manufacturers, Ford seized the leadership and transformed the industry by reaching out to capture a mass market with a car that sold for under $1,000. In the following selection, Ford describes the strategy that made his company in its heyday the most profitable busi-ness in history and moved the United States into the Age of Mass Consumption.

In the 1920s the Ford Motor Company lost the leadership in the automobile industry to General Motors, a large con-

glomerate of car companies and parts manufacturers put to-
gether by William C. Durant, who entered the auto industry
about the same time the Ford Motor Company was established.
General Motors, though it was to become the industry leader in
the 1920s and the largest corporation in the world, struggled
during its first decade with seemingly intractable problems of
internal management: could a large and complex business made
up of many companies be efficiently administered? One of
Durant's acquisitions was a parts manufacturing firm headed
by Alfred P. Sloan, Jr., (1875–1966) the man who became an
architect of GM's ascendancy. Sloan, unlike the largely self-
taught Ford, was a graduate of the Massachusetts Institute of
Technology. With help from his father, he purchased a roller
bearing company which became part of General Motors in 1916.
From the outset, Sloan demonstrated an original talent for
administration. He rationalized the management of the parts
division of GM and then turned his attention to creating an
efficient internal organization for the entire firm. Becoming
president of General Motors in 1923, Sloan presided over a
critical transformation in the company's administrative struc-
ture and in its production and marketing strategy which enabled
GM to displace Ford. In his memoirs, My Years with General
Motors, *a chapter of which is reprinted below, Sloan describes*
his strategy.

Henry Ford, My Life and Work

. . . From the day the first motor car appeared on the streets
it had to me appeared to be a necessity. It was this knowledge
and assurance that led me to build to the one end—a car that
would meet the wants of the multitudes. All my efforts were
then and still are turned to the production of one car—one
model. And, year following year, the pressure was, and still is, to
improve and refine and make better, with an increasing reduction in price. The universal car had to have these attributes:

Source: Henry Ford and Samuel Crowther, *My Life and Work*, (New York,
Doubleday & Co., 1923), 68–75, 78–79, 80–84, 145–149. Reprinted by
permission of Mrs. Samuel Crowther.

(1) Quality in material to give service in use. Vanadium steel is the strongest, toughest, and most lasting of steels. It forms the foundation and super-structure of the cars. It is the highest quality steel in this respect in the world, regardless of price.

(2) Simplicity in operation—because the masses are not mechanics.

(3) Power in sufficient quantity.

(4) Absolute reliability—because of the varied uses to which the cars would be put and the variety of roads over which they would travel.

(5) Lightness. With the Ford there are only 7.95 pounds to be carried by each cubic inch of piston displacement. This is one of the reasons why Ford cars are "always going," wherever and whenever you see them—through sand and mud, through slush, snow, and water, up hills, across fields and roadless plains.

(6) Control—to hold its speed always in hand, calmly and safely meeting every emergency and contingency either in the crowded streets of the city or on dangerous roads. The planetary transmission of the Ford gave this control and anybody could work it. That is the "why" of the saying: "Anybody can drive a Ford." It can turn around almost anywhere.

(7) The more a motor car weighs, naturally the more fuel and lubricants are used in the driving; the lighter the weight, the lighter the expense of operation. The light weight of the Ford car in its early years was used as an argument against it. Now that is all changed.

The design which I settled upon was called "Model T." The important feature of the new model—which, if it were accepted, as I thought it would be, I intended to make the only model and then start into real production—was its simplicity. There were but four constructional units in the car—the power plant, the frame, the front axle, and the rear axle. All of these were easily accessible and they were designed so that no special skill would be required for their repair or replacement. I believed then, although I said very little about it because of the novelty of the idea, that it ought to be possible to have parts so simple and so inexpensive that the menace of expensive hand repair work would be entirely eliminated. The parts could be made so cheaply that it would be less expensive to buy new ones than to have old ones repaired. They could be carried in hardware shops just as nails or bolts are carried. I thought that it was up to me as the designer to make the car so completely simple that no one could fail to understand it.

That works both ways and applies to everything. The less complex an article, the easier it is to make, the cheaper it may be sold, and therefore the greater number may be sold.

It is not necessary to go into the technical details of the construction but perhaps this is as good a place as any to review the various models, because "Model T" was the last of the models and the policy which it brought about took this business out of the ordinary line of business. Application of the same idea would take any business out of the ordinary run.

I designed eight models in all before "Model T." They were: "Model A," "Model B," "Model C," "Model F," "Model N," "Model R," "Model S," and "Model K." . . .

The "Model T" had practically no features which were not contained in some one or other of the previous models. Every detail had been fully tested in practice. There was no guessing as to whether or not it would be a successful model. It had to be. There was no way it could escape being so, for it had not been made in a day. It contained all that I was then able to put into a motor car plus the material, which for the first time I was able to obtain. We put out "Model T" for the season 1908–1909.

The company was then five years old. The original factory space had been .28 acre. We had employed an average of 311 people in the first year, built 1,708 cars, and had one branch house. In 1908, the factory space had increased to 2.65 acres and we owned the building. The average number of employees had increased to 1,908. We built 6,181 cars and had fourteen branch houses. It was a prosperous business.

During the season 1908–1909 we continued to make Models "R" and "S," four-cylinder runabouts and roadsters, the models that had previously been so successful, and which sold at $700 and $750. But "Model T" swept them right out. We sold 10,607 cars—a larger number than any manufacturer had ever sold. The price for the touring car was $850. On the same chassis we mounted a town car at $1,000, a roadster at $825, a coupé at $950, and a landaulet at $950.

This season demonstrated conclusively to me that it was time to put the new policy in force. The salesmen, before I had announced the policy, were spurred by the great sales to think that even greater sales might be had if only we had more models. It is strange how, just as soon as an article becomes successful, somebody starts to think that it would be more successful if only it were different. There is a tendency to keep monkeying with styles and to spoil a good thing by changing it. The salesmen were insistent on increasing the line. They listened to the 5 per cent, the special customers who could say what they wanted, and forgot all about the 95 per cent who just bought without making any fuss. No business can improve unless it pays the closest possible attention to complaints and suggestions. If there is any defect in service then that must be instantly and rigorously investigated, but when the suggestion is only as to style, one has to make sure whether it is not merely a personal whim that is being voiced. Salesmen always want to cater to whims instead of acquiring sufficient knowledge of their product to be able to explain to the customer with the whim that what they have will satisfy his every requirement—that is, of course, provided what they have does satisfy these requirements.

Therefore in 1909 I announced one morning, without any previous warning, that in the future we were going to build only one model, that the model was going to be "Model T," and that the chassis would be exactly the same for all cars, and I remarked:

"Any customer can have a car painted any colour that he wants so long as it is black."

I cannot say that any one agreed with me. The selling people could not of course see the advantages that a single model would bring about in production. More than that, they did not particularly care. They thought that our production was good enough as it was and there was a very decided opinion that lowering the sales price would hurt sales, that the people who wanted quality would be driven away and that there would be none to replace them. There was very little conception of the motor industry. A motor car was still regarded as something in the way of a luxury. The manufacturers did a good deal to spread this idea. Some clever persons invented the name "pleasure car" and the advertising emphasized the pleasure features. The sales people had ground for their objections and particularly when I made the following announcement:

> I will build a motor car for the great multitude. It will be large enough for the family but small enough for the individual to run and care for. It will be constructed of the best materials, by the best men to be hired, after the simplest designs that modern engineering can devise. But it will be so low in price that no man making a good salary will be unable to own one— and enjoy with his family the blessing of hours of pleasure in God's great open spaces.

This announcement was received not without pleasure. The general comment was:

"If Ford does that he will be out of business in six months."

The impression was that a good car could not be built at a low price, and that, anyhow, there was no use in building a low-priced car because only wealthy people were in the market for cars. The 1908–1909 sales of more than ten thousand cars had convinced me that we needed a new factory. We already had a big modern factory—the Piquette Street plant. It was as good as, perhaps a little better than, any automobile factory in the country. But I did not see how it was going to care for the sales and production that were inevitable. So I bought sixty acres at Highland Park, which was then considered away out in the country from Detroit. The amount of ground bought and the plans for a bigger factory than the world has ever seen were opposed. The question was already being asked:

"How soon will Ford blow up?"

Nobody knows how many thousand times it has been asked since. It is asked only because of the failure to grasp that a principle rather than an individual is at work, and the principle is so simple that it seems mysterious.

For 1909–1910, in order to pay for the new land and

buildings, I slightly raised the prices. This is perfectly justifiable and results in a benefit, not an injury, to the purchaser. I did exactly the same thing a few years ago—or rather, in that case I did not lower the price as is my annual custom, in order to build the River Rouge plant. The extra money might in each case have been had by borrowing, but then we should have had a continuing charge upon the business and all subsequent cars would have had to bear this charge. The price of all the models was increased $100, with the exception of the roadster, which was increased only $75 and of the landaulet and town car, which were increased $150 and $200 respectively. We sold 18,664 cars, and then for 1910–1911, with the new facilities, I cut the touring car from $950 to $780 and we sold 34,528 cars. That is the beginning of the steady reduction in the price of the cars in the face of ever-increasing cost of materials and ever-higher wages.

Contrast the year 1908 with the year 1911. The factory space increased from 2.65 to 32 acres. The average number of employees from 1,908 to 4,110, and the cars built from a little over six thousand to nearly thirty-five thousand. You will note that men were not employed in proportion to the output.

We were, almost overnight it seems, in great production. How did all this come about?

Simply through the application of an inevitable principle. By the application of intelligently directed power and machinery. In a little dark shop on a side street an old man had labored for years making axe handles. Out of seasoned hickory he fashioned them, with the help of a draw shave, a chisel, and a supply of sandpaper. Carefully was each handle weighed and balanced. No two of them were alike. The curve must exactly fit the hand and must conform to the grain of the wood. From dawn until dark the old man labored. His average product was eight handles a week, for which he received a dollar and a half each. And often some of these were unsaleable—because the balance was not true.

To-day you can buy a better axe handle, made by machinery, for a few cents. And you need not worry about the balance.

They are all alike—and every one is perfect. Modern methods applied in a big way have not only brought the cost of axe handles down to a fraction of their former cost—but they have immensely improved the product. . . .

The more economical methods of production did not begin all at once. They began gradually—just as we began gradually to make our own parts. "Model T" was the first motor that we made ourselves. The great economies began in assembling and then extended to other sections so that, while to-day we have skilled mechanics in plenty, they do not produce automobiles— they make it easy for others to produce them. Our skilled men are the tool makers, the experimental workmen, the machinists, and the pattern makers. They are as good as any men in the world— so good, indeed, that they should not be wasted in doing that which the machines they contrive can do better. The rank and file of men come to us unskilled; they learn their jobs within a few hours or a few days. If they do not learn within that time they will never be of any use to us. These men are, many of them, foreigners, and all that is required before they are taken on is that they should be potentially able to do enough work to pay the overhead charges on the floor space they occupy. They do not have to be able-bodied men. We have jobs that require great physical strength—although they are rapidly lessening; we have other jobs that require no strength whatsoever—jobs which, as far as strength is concerned, might be attended to by a child of three. . . .

The first step forward in assembly came when we began taking the work to the men instead of the men to the work. We now have two general principles in all operations—that a man shall never have to take more than one step, if possibly it can be avoided, and that no man need ever stoop over.

The principles of assembly are these:

(1) Place the tools and the men in the sequence of the operation so that each component part shall travel the least possible distance while in the process of finishing.

(2) Use work slides or some other form of carrier so that when a workman completes his operation, he drops the part al-

ways in the same place—which place must always be the most convenient place to his hand—and if possible have gravity carry the part to the next workman for his operation.

(3) Use sliding assembling lines by which the parts to be assembled are delivered at convenient distances.

The net result of the application of these principles is the reduction of the necessity for thought on the part of the worker and the reduction of his movements to a minimum. He does as nearly as possible only one thing with only one movement.

The assembling of the chassis is, from the point of view of the non-mechanical mind, our most interesting and perhaps best known operation, and at one time it was an exceedingly important operation. We now ship out the parts for assembly at the point of distribution.

Along about April 1, 1913, we first tried the experiment of an assembly line. We tried it on assembling the flywheel magneto. We try everything in a little way first—we will rip out anything once we discover a better way, but we have to know absolutely that the new way is going to be better than the old before we do anything drastic.

I believe that this was the first moving line ever installed. The idea came in a general way from the overhead trolley that the Chicago packers use in dressing beef. We had previously assembled the fly-wheel magneto in the usual method. With one workman doing a complete job he could turn out from thirty-five to forty pieces in a nine-hour day, or about twenty minutes to an assembly. What he did alone was then spread into twenty-nine operations; that cut down the assembly time to thirteen minutes, ten seconds. Then we raised the height of the line eight inches—this was in 1914—and cut the time to seven minutes. Further experimenting with the speed that the work should move at cut the time down to five minutes. In short, the result is this: by the aid of scientific study one man is now able to do somewhat more than four did only a comparatively few years ago. That line established the efficiency of the method and we now use it everywhere. The assembling of the motor, formerly done by one man, is now divided into eighty-four operations—

those men do the work that three times their number formerly did. In a short time we tried out the plan on the chassis.

About the best we had done in stationary chassis assembling was an average of twelve hours and twenty-eight minutes per chassis. We tried the experiment of drawing the chassis with a rope and windlass down a line two hundred fifty feet long. Six assemblers travelled with the chassis and picked up the parts from piles placed along the line. This rough experiment reduced the time to five hours fifty minutes per chassis. In the early part of 1914 we elevated the assembly line. We had adopted the policy of "man-high" work; we had one line twenty-six and three quarter inches and another twenty-four and one half inches from the floor—to suit squads of different heights. The waist-high arrangement and a further subdivision of work so that each man had fewer movements cut down the labour time per chassis to one hour thirty-three minutes. Only the chassis was then assembled in the line. The body was placed on in "John R. Street" —the famous street that runs through our Highland Park factories. Now the line assembles the whole car.

It must not be imagined, however, that all this worked out as quickly as it sounds. The speed of the moving work had to be carefully tried out; in the fly-wheel magneto we first had a speed of sixty inches per minute. That was too fast. Then we tried eighteen inches per minute. That was too slow. Finally we settled on forty-four inches per minute. The idea is that a man must not be hurried in his work—he must have every second necessary but not a single unnecessary second. We have worked out speeds for each assembly, for the success of the chassis assembly caused us gradually to overhaul our entire method of manufacturing and to put all assembling in mechanically driven lines. The chassis assembling line, for instance, goes at a pace of six feet per minute; the front axle assembly line goes at one hundred eighty-nine inches per minute. In the chassis assembling are forty-five separate operations or stations. The first men fasten four mud-guard brackets to the chassis frame; the motor arrives on the tenth operation and so on in detail. Some men do only one or two small operations, others do more. The man who places a part does not fasten it—the part may not be fully in place until after several operations later. The man who puts in a bolt does not put on the nut; the man who puts on the nut does not tighten it. On operation number thirty-four the budding motor gets its gasoline; it has previously received lubrication; on operation number forty-four the radiator is filled with water, and on operation number forty-five the car drives out onto John R. Street.

Essentially the same ideas have been applied to the assembling of the motor. In October, 1913, it required nine hours and fifty-four minutes of labour time to assemble one motor; six months later, by the moving assembly method, this time has been reduced to five hours and fifty-six minutes. Every piece of work in the shops moves; it may move on hooks on overhead chains going to assembly in the exact order in which the parts are required; it may travel on a moving platform, or it may go by gravity, but the point is that there is no lifting or trucking of anything other than materials. Materials are brought in on small trucks or trailers operated by cut-down Ford chassis, which are sufficiently mobile and quick to get in and out of any aisle where they may be required to go. No workman has anything to do with moving or lifting anything. That is all in a separate department—the department of transportation.

We started assembling a motor car in a single factory. Then as we began to make parts, we began to departmentalize so that each department would do only one thing. As the factory is now organized each department makes only a single part or assembles a part. A department is a little factory in itself. The part comes into it as raw material or as a casting, goes through the sequence of machines and heat treatments, or whatever may be required, and leaves that department finished. It was only because of transport ease that the departments were grouped together when we started to manufacture. I did not know that such minute divisions would be possible; but as our production grew and departments multiplied, we actually changed from making automobiles to making parts. Then we found that we had made another new discovery, which was that by no means all of the parts had to be made in one factory. It was not really a discovery—it was something in the nature of going around in a circle to my first manufacturing when I bought the motors and probably ninety per cent of the parts. When we began to make our own parts we practically took for granted that they all had to be made in the one factory—that there was some special virtue in having a single roof over the manufacture of the entire car. We have now developed away from this. If we build any more large factories, it will be only because the making of a single part must be in such tremendous volume as to require a large unit. I hope that in the course of time the big Highland Park plant will be doing only one or two things. The casting has already been taken away from it and has gone to the River Rouge plant. So now we are on our way back to where we started from —excepting that, instead of buying our parts on the outside, we are beginning to make them in our own factories on the outside. . . .

. . . Instead of giving attention to competitors or to demand, our prices are based on an estimate of what the largest possible number of people will want to pay, or can pay, for what we have to sell. And what has resulted from that policy is best evidenced by comparing the price of the touring car and the production.

YEAR	PRICE	PRODUCTION
1909–10	$950	18,664 cars
1910–11	$780	34,528 "
1911–12	$690	78,440 "
1912–13	$600	168,220 "
1913–14	$550	248,307 "
1914–15	$490	308,213 "
1915–16	$440	533,921 "
1916–17	$360	785,432 "
1917–18	$450	706,584 "
1918–19	$525	533,706 "
(The above two years were war years and the factory was in war work).		
1919–20	$575 to $440	996,660 "
1920–21	$440 to $355	1,250,000 "

. . . Our policy is to reduce the price, extend the operations, and improve the article. You will notice that the reduction of price comes first. We have never considered any costs as fixed. Therefore we first reduce the price to a point where we believe more sales will result. Then we go ahead and try to make the price. We do not bother about the costs. The new price forces the costs down. The more usual way is to take the costs and then determine the price, and although that method may be scientific in the narrow sense, it is not scientific in the broad sense, because what earthly use is it to know the cost if it tells you you cannot manufacture at a price at which the article can be sold? But more to the point is the fact that, although one may calculate what a cost is, and of course all of our costs are carefully calculated, no one knows what a cost ought to be. One of the ways of discovering what a cost ought to be is to name a price so low as to force everybody in the place to the highest point of efficiency. The low price makes everybody dig for profits. We make more discoveries concerning manufacturing and selling under this forced method than by any method of leisurely investigation.

The payment of high wages fortunately contributes to the low costs because the men become steadily more efficient on account of being relieved of outside worries. The payment of five dollars a day for an eight-hour day was one of the finest cost-cutting moves we ever made, and the six-dollar day wage is cheaper than the five. How far this will go, we do not know.

We have always made a profit at the prices we have fixed and, just as we have no idea how high wages will go, we also have no idea how low prices will go, but there is no particular use in bothering on that point. The tractor, for instance, was first sold for $750, then at $850, then at $625, and the other day we cut it 37 per cent. to $395.

The tractor is not made in connection with the automobiles. No plant is large enough to make two articles. A shop has to be devoted to exactly one product in order to get the real economies.

For most purposes a man with a machine is better than a man without a machine. By the ordering of design of product and of manufacturing process we are able to provide that kind of a machine which most multiplies the power of the hand, and therefore we give to that man a larger rôle of service, which means that he is entitled to a larger share of comfort.

Keeping that principle in mind we can attack waste with a

definite objective. We will not put into our establishment anything that is useless. We will not put up elaborate buildings as
monuments to our success. The interest on the investment and
the cost of their upkeep only serve to add uselessly to the cost of
what is produced—so these monuments of success are apt to
end as tombs. A great administration building may be necessary.
In me it arouses a suspicion that perhaps there is too much administration. We have never found a need for elaborate administration and would prefer to be advertised by our product than
by where we make our product.

The standardization that effects large economies for the
consumer results in profits of such gross magnitude to the pro-
ducer that he can scarcely know what to do with his money.
But his effort must be sincere, painstaking, and fearless. Cutting
out a half-a-dozen models is not standardizing. It may be, and
usually is, only the limiting of business, for if one is selling on the
ordinary basis of profit—that is, on the basis of taking as much
money away from the consumer as he will give up—then surely
the consumer ought to have a wide range of choice.

Standardization, then, is the final stage of the process. We
start with consumer, work back through the design, and finally
arrive at manufacturing. The manufacturing becomes a means to
the end of service.

It is important to bear this order in mind. As yet, the order
is not thoroughly understood. The price relation is not understood. The notion persists that prices ought to be kept up. On the
contrary, good business—large consumption—depends on their
going down.

And here is another point. The service must be the best you
can give. It is considered good manufacturing practice, and not
bad ethics, occasionally to change designs so that old models will
become obsolete and new ones will have to be bought either because repair parts for the old cannot be had, or because the new
model offers a new sales argument which can be used to persuade a consumer to scrap what he has and buy something new.
We have been told that this is good business, that it is clever
business, that the object of business ought to be to get people to
buy frequently and that it is bad business to try to make any-

thing that will last forever, because when once a man is sold he will not buy again.

Our principle of business is precisely to the contrary. We cannot conceive how to serve the consumer unless we make for him something that, as far as we can provide, will last forever. We want to construct some kind of a machine that will last forever. It does not please us to have a buyer's car wear out or become obsolete. We want the man who buys one of our products never to have to buy another. We never make an improvement that renders any previous model obsolete. The parts of a specific model are not only interchangeable with all other cars of that model, but they are interchangeable with similar parts on all the cars that we have turned out. You can take a car of ten years ago and, buying to-day's parts, make it with very little expense into a car of to-day. Having these objectives the costs always come down under pressure. And since we have the firm policy of steady price reduction, there is always pressure. Sometimes it is just harder! . . .

Alfred P. Sloan, Jr., My Years with General Motors

(Transformation of the Automobile Market)

By the middle of the 1920s General Motors had accomplished some things, but apart from survival and reorganization, they were more in the realm of the mind than of reality. We knew, as I have related, the strategy with which we proposed to approach the car business, how we proposed to manage the enterprise financially, and the relationships we wanted to establish among persons in different roles. But by the end of 1924 little of this was reflected in our activities in the automobile market. That our volume of business had increased after the slump of 1921—and especially in 1923—could be attributed less to our own wits than to the improvement in the general economy and the rising demand for automobiles. While internally we had made much progress, externally we had marked time. But the time had come to act.

Now it so happened—luckily for us—that during the first part of the 1920s, and especially in the years 1924 to 1926, certain changes took place in the nature of the automobile market which transformed it into something different from what it had been all the years up to that time. (Seldom, perhaps at only one other time in the history of the industry—that is, on the occasion of the rise of the Model T after 1908—has the industry changed so radically as it did through the middle twenties.) I say luckily for us because as a challenger to the then established position of Ford, we were favored by change. We had no stake in the old ways of the automobile business; for us, change meant opportunity. We were glad to bend our efforts to go with it and make the most of it. We were prepared, too, with the various business concepts which I have described, though I must say we saw them as merely *our* way of doing business and not as having any general application or logical involvement in the future of the industry.

To set the scene, let me divide the history of the automobile, from a commercial standpoint, into three periods. There was the period before 1908, which with its expensive cars was entirely that of a *class* market; then the period from 1908 to the mid-twenties, which was dominantly that of a *mass* market, ruled by Ford and his concept of basic transportation at a low dollar price; and, after that, the period of the mass market served by better and better cars, or what might be thought of as the *mass-class* market, with increasing diversity. This last I think I may correctly identify as the General Motors concept.

All three of these periods have in common the long-expanding American economy, the horizon of each period having been formed by the respective degrees of that rise and its spread through the population. The willingness of the relatively few who could afford them to buy expensive though unreliable cars—by today's standards—enabled the industry to get going. Then when a large number of individuals were able to afford a few hundred dollars of expenditure, they made possible the development of the inexpensive Model T (it is possible that such a market was long waiting for the offering of a car like the Model T). As the economy, led by the automobile industry, rose to a new high level in the twenties, a complex of new elements came into existence to transform the market once again and create the watershed which divides the present from the past.

These new elements I think I can without significant loss reduce to four: installment selling, the used-car trade-in, the closed body, and the annual model. (I would add improved roads if I were to take into account the environment of the automobile.) So imbedded are these elements in the nature of the industry today that to conceive of the market without them is almost impossible. Before 1920 and for a while thereafter the typical car buyer was in the situation of buying his first car; he would buy it for cash or with some special loan arrangement; and the car would be a roadster or touring car, most likely of a model which was the same as last year's and could be expected to be the same as next year's. This situation was not to change for some years and the change would not be sudden except at its climax. For each of the new elements of change had a separate beginning and rate of development before they all interacted to cause complete transformation.

Installment selling of automobiles in regularized form first appeared in a small way shortly before World War I. This form of borrowing, or inverse saving, when placed on a routine basis, enabled large numbers of consumers to buy an object as expensive as an automobile. The statistics of installment selling in those days were very poor, but it is clear that it grew from some very low level in 1915 to around 65 per cent for new cars in 1925. We believed that with rising incomes and the expectation of a continuance of that rise, it was reasonable to assume that consumers would lift their sights to higher levels of quality. Installment selling, we thought, would stimulate this trend.

As the first car buyers came back for the second round and brought their old cars as down payments, the custom of trading was established. That the industry was engaged in a trading business had revolutionary significance not only for dealer arrangements but for manufacturing and the whole character of production, since dealers usually had to sell to a man who already had a car with mileage left in it.

The statistics for used-car trade-ins before 1925 are as poor as those for installment selling. It stands to reason, however, that there was some kind of upward curve in used cars traded from World War I on, if only because there were relatively few cars in existence before that time. Until some unknown date in the early 1920s, the majority of car buyers were buying their first car. The total number of passenger cars in operation in the United States from 1919 through 1929 rose by years in millions approximately as follows: 6, 7.3, 8.3, 9.6, 11.9, 13.7, 15.7, 16.8, 17.5, 18.7, 19.7. The industry, on the other hand, produced in those years passenger cars for domestic and export markets in approximate millions as follows: 1.7, 1.9, 1.5, 2.3, 3.6, 3.2, 3.7, 3.7, 2.9, 3.8, 4.5.[1] This production was enough to cover both the growth in numbers and the scrappage. The used car was traded perhaps two or three times on the way to the scrap heap. So I assume there must have been a rising curve of used-car trade-ins.

The closed body was a specialty and mainly a custom-job affair before World War I. In the years 1919 through 1927, in round numbers by years, the industry sold closed cars in the following uninterruptedly rising percentages: 10, 17, 22, 30, 34, 43, 56, 72, and 85.

Of the annual model I shall say more later; suffice it to say here that in the early twenties it was not a formal concept as we know it today, except as it was negatively expressed in Ford's concept of a static model.

We were not unconscious of the unfolding of these four elements when the administration of General Motors changed in 1921. We started GMAC in the installment financing field in 1919. We had an interest in Fisher Body, which made closed bodies. As large sellers of medium- and high-price cars, we met the used-car trade-in early. And we tried to make our models more attractive each year. Yet we did not see the movement—especially the interaction—of these elements in the whole automobile market as I can see it today looking back. We saw them then as uncertainties, unknowns, and trends, in the form of

[1] The figures above are for passenger cars only. The full production of all vehicles, cars and trucks, for 1919 through 1929, was as follows: 1.9, 2.2, 1.6, 2.5, 4, 3.6, 4.3, 4.3, 3.4, 4.4, 5.3.

figures to study at a desk. However, the plan of campaign laid down in the product program of 1921 logically fitted better and better the unfolding situation.

It was that plan, policy, or strategy of 1921—whatever it should be called—which, I believe, more than any other single factor enabled us to move into the rapidly changing market of the twenties with the confidence that we knew what we were doing commercially and were not merely chasing around in search of a lucky star. The most important particular object of that plan of campaign, which followed from its strategic principles, was, as I have said, to develop a larger place for Chevrolet between the Ford car below and the medium-price group above, a case of trying to widen a niche. That was all, in the beginning, despite the completeness of the plan with regard to the whole market.

There was the pause while we settled the copper-cooled-engine matter, in which we gave up the commercial-mindedness of our original strategic plan to pursue an engineering dream. We were rescued from that folly by the four-million car-and-truck year of 1923, which absorbed some 450,000 Chevrolets, and we saw the illusions of the upward swing of that year dashed in the recession of 1924. It was thus made clear to us that the plan of 1921 would have meaning only if meaning were given to it in the design of the product itself.

Certain facts of failure in particular were impressed upon us. During the year 1924, while the industry's passenger-car sales in the United States fell 12 per cent, General Motors' sales fell 28 per cent. Of the industry's decline in sales of about 439,000 car units, almost half was represented by the decline in General Motors' car sales. Our share of the passenger-car market in units dropped from 20 per cent to 17 per cent, while Ford's share went up from 50 per cent to 55 per cent. Some of the General Motors decline was in Buick and Cadillac, as was to be expected of higher-priced cars in a period of economic recession. (Olds increased, Oakland was unchanged.) But most of it was in sales of the Chevrolet, which fell 37 per cent while sales of its opposite number, the Ford, fell only 4 per cent. Of course, what happened was not due entirely to the events of 1924, including some bad management, but to the recession of that year combined with earlier events. The lag between automotive design and production is a peculiar feature of the automobile industry. The events in a current year are always in part due to decisions taken from one to three years earlier. Hence the extent of the Chevrolet slump of 1924 could properly be laid to the retarded development of Chevrolet's design during the previous three years. Among other things, it had an infamous rear end; but there is no use specifying its deficiencies. The curious thing was that there we were with a plan that rested upon the concept of better and better cars, with a bigger package of accessories and improvements beyond basic transportation, and the concept of a Chevrolet at a higher price that would be so compellingly attractive as to draw buyers away from the Model T. It would be difficult to find a wider margin between aspiration and realization than that represented by the plan of 1921 and the Chevrolet of 1924. Nevertheless, we did not alter the original plan, perhaps because we knew better than anyone the causes of our decline.

Indeed from the time the copper-cooled-engine program was abandoned, in the summer of 1923, Chevrolet's engineers, headed by Mr. Hunt, had worked intensively on redesigning the old car into a new model, known as the K Model, for the 1925 model year. The K Model had among its new features a longer body, increased leg room, a Duco finish, a one-piece windshield with automatic wipers on all closed cars, a dome light in the coach and sedan, a Klaxon horn, an improved clutch, and a sound rear-axle housing in place of the old one which had given so much trouble. It was far from being a radically new car but it was much better than it had been, and in the particulars noted above it gave the first real expression of what we had in mind to do. The K Model came on a rising market in 1925 and recovered Chevrolet's position sharply with factory sales of 481,-000 cars and trucks, a 64 per cent gain over 1924 and a level 6 per cent above the 1923 peak.

Ford's sales held about even in 1925 with a volume of about two million cars and trucks. But since the market as a whole in that year rose substantially over 1924, Ford's share declined relatively from 54 to 45 per cent, a sign of danger, if

Mr. Ford had chosen to read it. Yet he still held almost 70 per cent of the low-price field, and his touring car, priced at $290—without a starter or demountable rims—seemed unbeatable in that area. The Chevrolet touring car in 1925 was selling at $510, though with its extras it was not exactly comparable with the Ford. The Ford sedan—with starter and demountable rims—then sold at $660; the Chevrolet K Model at $825. Chevrolet's dealer discount was larger than Ford's, which made a difference in trading.

Chevrolet's internal statement of policy at this time was that it was our objective to get a public reputation for giving more for the dollar than Ford. As a matter of fact, when the Ford and Chevrolet were considered on a comparable-equipment basis, the Ford price was not far below that of Chevrolet. On the quality side we proposed to demonstrate to the buyer that, though our car cost X dollars more, it was X plus Y dollars better. Too, we proposed to improve our product regularly. We expected Ford, generally speaking, to stay put. We set this plan in motion and it worked as forecast.

Nevertheless, despite the success of the K Model Chevrolet, it was still too far from the Ford Model T in price for the gravitational pull we hoped to exert in Mr. Ford's area of the market. It was our intention to continue adding improvements and over a period of time to move down in price on the Model T as our position justified it.

As we said in our product policy of 1921, any given car was related to other cars that impinged upon it below and above in price and engineering design. Hence when looking at the Chevrolet in relation to the Ford below it, it was logical to consider equally what might happen to Chevrolet as a result of similar actions by competitors above it. This question was very much on our minds while the Chevrolet 1925 K Model sedan was being prepared during the year 1924, and for good reason.

A glance at the General Motors price list that year shows that we had still to realize the ideal or theoretical list set up in the 1921 plan. The list for the still-dominant touring cars in 1924 was as follows: Chevrolet, $510; Olds, $750; Oakland, $945; Buick "4," $965; Buick "6," $1295; and Cadillac, $2985.

The most obvious gaps in this line were between the Cadillac and Buick "6" at the top and between the Chevrolet and Olds at the bottom. To fill the gap between the standard Cadillac and the Buick "6," I proposed that Cadillac study the possibility of making a family-type car to sell at about $2000, which eventually resulted in the famous La Salle car, introduced in 1927. From the strategic standpoint at that time, however, the most dangerous gap in the list was that between the Chevrolet and the Olds. It was big enough to constitute a volume demand and thereby to accommodate, on top of Chevrolet, a competitor against whom we then had no counter. It was therefore an important gap to fill both offensively and defensively; offensively because there was a market demand to be satisfied there, and defensively because competitive cars could come in there and come down on Chevrolet as we planned for Chevrolet to come down on Ford. On this reasoning, we made one of the most important decisions in the history of General Motors, namely to fill the gap above Chevrolet with a brand-new car with a new six-cylinder engine. We had come to believe from an engineering standpoint that the future favored sixes and eights. However, to make the strategy effective, it would be necessary to fill the gap with a car that also had some volume economies. Otherwise, because the new car would draw some volume away from Chevrolet, reducing its economies, a loss would result for both cars. We concluded, therefore, that the new car must be designed in physical co-ordination with Chevrolet so as to share Chevrolet's economies, and vice versa.

The idea for such a car was first discussed by Mr. Hunt, Mr. Crane, and myself a few months after I became president. We had learned something of value in trying to make dual-purpose bodies and dual-purpose chassis for the copper-cooled and water-cooled engines in the period of uncertainty in those matters. We talked now about the development of a six-cylinder car based on the use, if possible, of such Chevrolet body and chassis parts as would fit the new design. As a "6," it would be a smoother-running car than the Chevrolet "4" and would require a longer wheel base, greater engine displacement and horsepower, and increased car weight. A longer and deeper frame, a

heavier front axle, and a short-stroke six-cylinder L-head engine, proposed by Mr. Crane, were the principal new units in the
design.

While the corporation's engineering committee worked on
the design, I remained uncertain where to place the car in the
divisional picture. Mr. Hannum, general manager of Oakland,
wrote to me proposing that his division undertake the development phase of the work. My reply to him, on November 12,
1924, shows how I felt about the new car then, from the point
of view of co-ordination with Chevrolet and of competition. I
quote:

> Your letter of October 11th reached me in Detroit but I
> did not have, you will remember, a clear viewpoint with rela-
> tion to the so-called Pontiac car. I have been, in a way, up in the
> air on the Pontiac car development and did not reply to your
> letter although I read it over several times very carefully pend-
> ing a crystallization of a viewp[o]int on what happened to be the
> best policy to pursue.
>
> I am thoroughly convinced, and have been from the begin-
> ning, that there was a place for such a car and, second, that if
> General Motors didn't go in there someone else sooner or later
> would. If the whole field was left to General Motors I do not
> know as I would be so anxious about it but, of course, fortu-
> nately for us, I presume it is not, therefore, we must give weight
> to what the other fellow is likely to do.
>
> One very difficult thing has developed in all the discussions
> there have been and that is the tendency to get away from the
> Chevrolet part of the idea. Every time it comes up some one
> wants to make something different and the result of that is that
> if everybody had their way we would have a second Olds or
> probably an Oakland car, more likely a second Buick or Cadil-
> lac. In other words, we are never going to make a success I
> think you will agree with me unless we st[i]ck to the principle,
> namely, a Chevrolet chassis with a six-cylinder engine.
>
> That being the case, I have definitely come to the conclu-
> sion that the only thing to do in order to work along the lines of
> least resistance is to have the development undertaken by the
> Chevrolet Engineering organization, because in so doing there
> will be every tendency to use what we can of Chevrolet as
> against the other method—the tendency to use something dif-

ferent, due to the natural and very proper tendency of an independent engineer to inject his own personality and ideas into the
picture, perhaps to the detriment of the car but certainly not to
the detriment of this particular development, which must follow
along Chevrolet lines if we are going to capitalize Chevrolet
components, plants and assembly plants, either at the beginning
or at some future date when volume justifies same.

Therefore, I have been discussing the matter with Mr.
Knudsen and feel that we should turn over to Mr. O. E. Hunt,
his Engineer, all that we have accomplished, let him weigh it
carefully, let him undertake to work out for us a six-cylinder
engine along constructive lines, recognizing, as he does, what
the picture has got to be. As a matter of fact, Chevrolet should
be experimenting with engine developments on its own account
and these two things should work along concurrently . . .

On the same day, I crystallized my thoughts on the subject
in a report to the Executive Committee under the title, "Status
of the Pontiac Car So-Called." I quote from this report the pas-
sages relating to costs, competition, co-ordination, and assign-
ment in the corporation, these being the final questions to be resolved in a decision:

Mr. Brown has had his Staff develop some costs which, although not in any way conclusive, appear to demonstrate what
we have felt was reasonable, namely, that even loading the cost
with such overhead as it should logically carry, that is, on a
basis of equal distribution with other items, there remains con-
sidering a list price of something like $700, a profit which will
give us a very excellent return on the capital employed. This
data has been laid down using figures on the Olds engine, the
cost of which we know to be excessive and which for that reason will probably not be used. Looking at the development from
the standpoint of the economic cost or real profit to the stock-
holders, the result is very satisfactory and of such a nature as
really requires us to go ahead.

In addition to the above, information not conclusive seems
to indicate that one or two of our competitors are going to attempt the same thing which brings us to the consideration that
although this development will probably take business from both
Olds and Chevrolet, it will be better that we take business from

our own Divisions than have competitors do so. It looks now as
if both things would ultimately happen.

We have been working on this proposition for about a
year and I am frank to say we have made little headway. It
seems as if every time we bring it up for discussion that an
uncertainty develops in the minds of the Executive Committee
as to its practicability. I have come to the definite conclusion
that we are never going to get anywhere along the lines we
must proceed to make it a success if we have it developed by an
independent engineering department or by the Oakland Division
where it was originally started. I am further definitely of the
opinion that the only chance for success is to have it developed
in the Chevrolet Division. Under such auspices coordination as
to the chassis will come about as a natural course of events
and there will be no tendency to introduce this and that difference simply because the engineer wishes very naturally and
properly to inject his own personality into the picture. In other
words, it will logically follow a development it has got to follow
if we are to come through at all.

The thing especially worth noting in this report is the consideration given to the question of co-ordinating the manufacture of one car with another. For the Pontiac represented the
first important advance in co-ordinating the physical product in
manufacturing. Physical co-ordination in one form or another
is, of course, the first principle of mass production, but at that
time it was widely supposed, from the example of the Model T,
that mass production on a grand scale required a uniform product. The Pontiac, co-ordinated in part with a car in another
price class, was to demonstrate that mass production of automobiles could be reconciled with variety in product. This was again
the opposite of the old Ford concept, which we persistently met
and opposed at every turn. For General Motors, with its five
basic price classes by car makes and several subclasses of models, the implication of the Pontiac idea was very great for the
whole line. If the cars in the higher-price classes could benefit
from the volume economies of the lower-price classes, the advantages of mass production could be extended to the whole car
line. This gave new significance to the product plan of 1921, and
was in fact eventually applied in varying degrees by all the General Motors car divisions.

The proposed Pontiac was assembled and road tested at Chevrolet and then assigned back to Oakland with full responsibility to that division for its final development, production, and ultimate sale as a companion car to the Oakland. We scheduled it for the model year 1926.

During the time of this development, another more or less independent event took place which was profoundly to influence the fortunes of the Pontiac, the Chevrolet, and the Model T. In 1921 Roy Chapin of the Hudson Motor Company had introduced the Essex coach at a price of $1495, or $300 above the Essex touring car. This was a relatively smaller price difference for the closed body than had been the case for the lines of other manufacturers. By 1923 the Essex "4" coach had been reduced to $1145. Early in 1924 the Essex "6" superseded the "4" and came on the market at a price of $975 for the coach model, which was $125 over the touring-car price. In June of that year prices were increased to $1000 for the coach and $900 for the touring car. Then, beginning in 1925, Mr. Chapin cut the price of the coach model to $895, or $5 below the touring-car model. Nothing like that had ever been seen before in the automobile industry, and the Essex coach had a considerable vogue. This suggested that closed cars, priced on a volume basis, could in the future dominate even the low-price field.

Such a development doubtless was inevitable, but in fact the Essex competition stimulated us in two matters at once, first our general closed-body development, and second, our preparations for the forthcoming Pontiac car.

General Motors had already been changing over to closed bodies. On September 18, 1924, the Executive Committee "expressed the sentiment that our Managers should be cautioned to be very careful about open car schedules as the trend seems to be very rapidly turning to closed jobs." In October we raised the proportion of our production of closed cars from about 40 per cent, where it had been for most of that year, to 75 per cent for November. A year later, at the end of 1925, the proportion of closed-car production for the corporation as a whole was up to almost 80 per cent.

I do not recall that the Essex coach influenced the Pontiac program directly, but the Essex and the future Pontiac were clearly to be competitors, and in point of fact we designed our first Pontiac cars exclusively with closed bodies, a coupe and a coach.

In the Executive Committee meeting of September 30, 1925, I reported confidently: ". . . when the 'Pontiac' car comes out in December it will give us everything for which we have been working, namely, the lowest priced 6-cylinder car that is possible, constructed with Chevrolet parts."

At the Executive Committee meeting of October 21, 1925, I reported on the over-all situation of growing tension in the market. From the minutes of the meeting I glean the following: "Attention was called to the fact that the Essex is attacking the Chevrolet market from the top while the Ford Company (whose policy now seems to be that of improving the quality of its car rather than reducing the price) is a strong competitor on the other side."

The Pontiac went on the market on schedule for the model year 1926 with the coach priced at $825, that is, about halfway between the Chevrolet coach, priced at $645, and the Olds coach, priced at $950; and the gap in our car line was closed.

That event settled General Motors' basic car positions for many years. The Cadillac and the Buick were first and second from the top of the price pyramid. Chevrolet was always the base of the pyramid. The Oakland organization, which produced the Pontiac car, later became the Pontiac Division, and the manufacture of Oakland cars was discontinued. The Pontiac became a distinctive car in its own right while maintaining its original economies. That put Olds between Pontiac and Buick, making the basic price line: Chevrolet, Pontiac, Olds, Buick, and Cadillac, more or less as it is today.

I shall not deal here with the evolution of all the cars in the line in the 1920s. I observe only that Olds and Oakland were not very lively lines. Buick, though always basically strong, had its ups and downs. Cadillac, as always, was strong in its price class, though it was superseded as sales leader for a time, beginning in 1925. I pass over the interesting record of these divisions to concentrate upon the most important changes that took place in that period, namely, those in the low-price, high-volume area where we were seeking a position against Ford.

The last decisive element in this competition, I believe, was the closed body, which itself was by far the largest single leap forward in the history of the automobile since the basic car had been made mechanically reliable. The closed body expanded the use of the automobile by making it a comfortable all-year-round vehicle, and added substantially to the price of the product. The 1925 Model K Chevrolet coach sold for 40 per cent and the sedan for 57 per cent more than the roadster.

As the closed body developed rapidly from 43 per cent of the industry in 1924 to 72 per cent in 1926 and 85 per cent in 1927, Chevrolet's percentage of closed-body production rose from about 40 per cent in 1924 to 73 per cent in 1926 and on to 82 per cent in 1927. A big change in every respect.

The rise of the closed body made it impossible for Mr. Ford to maintain his leading position in the low-price field, for he had frozen his policy in the Model T, and the Model T was pre-eminently an open-car design. With its light chassis, it was un-suited to the heavier closed body, and so in less than two years the closed body made the already obsolescing design of the Model T noncompetitive as an engineering design. Mr. Ford, nevertheless, put closed bodies on the Model T and sold 37.5 per cent of his production in this form in 1924. Although the market for closed bodies rose sharply in the next three years, he sold only 51.6 per cent in 1926 and only 58 per cent in 1927, while Chevrolet's sales of closed bodies during that period rose to 82 per cent.

From 1925 to 1927 the Chevrolet, as its cost position justi-fied a lower price, became more competitive with Ford, as we had hoped, the Chevrolet two-door coach going in that period progressively from $735 to $695 to $645 to $595, while the Ford Tudor Model T went from $580 in 1925 to $565 in June 1926, and to $495 in 1927. Thus the old strategic plan of 1921 was vindi-cated to a "T," so to speak, but in a surprising way as to the par-ticulars. The old master had failed to master change. Don't ask me why. There is a legend cultivated by sentimentalists that Mr. Ford left behind a great car expressive of the pure concept of cheap, basic transportation. The fact is that he left behind a car that no longer offered the best buy, even as raw, basic transportation.

It was not difficult to see in 1925 and 1926 that Chevrolet was closing in on Ford. In 1925 Chevrolet had about 481,000 U.S. factory sales of cars and trucks, while Ford had approximately two million factory sales. In 1926 Chevrolet moved up to about 692,000 factory sales of cars and trucks, while Ford moved down to about 1,550,000. His precious volume, which was the foundation of his position, was fast disappearing. He could not continue losing sales and maintain his profits. And so, for engineering and market reasons, the Model T fell. And yet not many observers expected so catastrophic and almost whimsical a fall as Mr. Ford chose to take in May 1927 when he shut down his great River Rouge plant completely and kept it shut down for nearly a year to retool, leaving the field to Chevrolet unopposed and opening it up for Mr. Chrysler's Plymouth. Mr. Ford regained sales leadership again in 1929, 1930, and 1935, but, speaking in terms of generalities, he had lost the lead to General Motors. Mr. Ford, who had had so many brilliant insights in earlier years, seemed never to understand how completely the market had changed from the one in which he made his name and to which he was accustomed.

Go back for a moment to the first four-million car-and-truck year, 1923. From then to 1929, setting aside variations in the years, there was a seven-year plateau in new-car sales. And yet the total number of cars in use, as I have shown, continued to rise. While the total market, including used cars, expanded, the new-car market leveled off, and, as I have said, the role of the new car was to cover scrappage and growth in car ownership. Meanwhile the used cars at much lower prices dropped down to fill the demand at various levels for basic transportation. Mr. Ford failed to realize that it was not necessary for new cars to meet the need for basic transportation. On this basis alone Mr. Ford's concept of the American market did not adequately fit the realities after 1923. The basic-transportation market in the United States (unlike Europe) since then has been met mainly by the used car.

When first-car buyers returned to the market for the second round, with the old car as a first payment on the new car, they were selling basic transportation and demanding something more than that in the new car. Middle-income buyers, assisted by the trade-in and installment financing, created the demand, not for basic transportation, but for progress in new cars, for comfort, convenience, power, and style. This was the actual trend of American life and those who adapted to it prospered.

It was thus that the four elements with which I began the discussion in this chapter, installment selling, the used-car trade-in, the closed-car body, and the annual model, interacted in the 1920s to transform the market. But I have not completed the picture. What of the annual model?

The annual model was not a declared policy of General Motors, or of anyone, I believe, in the 1920s. It was, however, inherent in the policy of creating a bigger and better package each year. With this concept necessarily went the need for salesmanship. . . .

General Motors in fact had annual models in the twenties, every year after 1923, and has had them ever since, but as the discussion above shows, we had not in 1925 formulated the concept in the way it is known today. When we did formulate it I cannot say. It was a matter of evolution. Eventually the fact that we made yearly changes, and the recognition of the necessity of change, forced us into regularizing change. When change became regularized, some time in the 1930s, we began to speak of annual models. I do not believe the elder Mr. Ford ever really cared for the idea. Anyway his Model A, which he brought out in 1928, as fine a little car as it was in its time, it seems to me was another expression of his concept of a static-model utility car.

At the time when Ford's plants were shut down for lack of a new model design, I thought that both his and our policies would survive—Ford's in the form of the new car, which would express the old policy adapted to the then higher state of the art. In other words, I had no idea in 1927 that the old Ford policy was washed out and that the General Motors policy of ungraded cars had won in a much larger sense than was reflected in the rise in sales of Chevrolet.

Suggestions for Further Reading

General

George H. Soule, *Prosperity Decade . . . 1917–1929* (1947)*; Joseph Schumpeter, "The American Economy in the . . . Twenties," *American Economic Review*, Vol. 36 (1946), pp. 1–10.

The Sources of Growth

Solomon Fabricant, *The Output of Manufacturing Industries, 1899–1937* (1940); Simon Kuznets, *National Income and Its Composition, 1919–1938* (2 vols., 1941); Harold Barger, *Outlay and Income in the United States, 1921–1938* (1942).

The Emergence of Detroit

John B. Rae, *The American Automobile* (1965)*; Keith Sward, *The Legend of Henry Ford* (1948)*; Allan Nevins and Frank E. Hill, *Ford: The Times, the Man, the Company* (3 vols., 1954–1963); Alfred P. Sloan, Jr., *My Years With General Motors* (1964).

The Structure of Mass Marketing

Adolph A. Berle, Jr. and Gardiner G. Means, *The Modern Corporation and Private Property* (1932); Peter Drucker, *The Concept of the Corporation* (1946); Harry W. Laidler, *Concentration of Control in American Industry* (1931); Alfred D. Chandler, Jr., *Strategy and Structure: Chapters in the History of Industrial Enterprise* (1962); Otis Pease, *The Responsibilities of American Advertising . . . 1920–1940* (1958).

The Welfare of the American People

Richard H. Shryock, *Medicine in America* (1966); Clarke A. Chambers, *Seedtime of Reform; American Social Service and Social Action, 1918–1933* (1963)*.

National Tea Store, Minneapolis, c.1923.
Courtesy of the Minnesota Historical Society.

The crowd that gathered outside the Warner Theatre to see the opening of the first sound motion picture, August 6, 1926.
Courtesy of Culver Pictures, Inc.

Mr. and Mrs. John Morton listening to the radio with ear phones, 1924.
Courtesy of the Minnesota Historical Society.

Autos parked on the sand at Nantasket Beach, Mass., Fourth of July
holiday, early 1920s.
Courtesy of Culver Pictures, Inc.

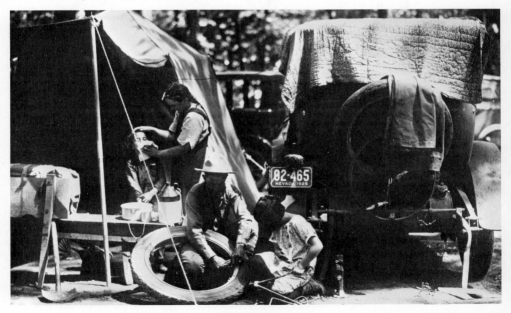

Park guide changing tire for girl in Minnehaha tourist camp, c.1925.
Courtesy of the Minnesota Historical Society.

"The Battle of the Century," 1927. Alfred P. Sloan (left) and Henry Ford (right).
All photos on this page, courtesy of Culver Pictures, Inc.

Chapter Two

Emerging Life Styles in Mass Society

Greater affluence generated new life-styles. Mass society, rooted in an advanced, industrial economy and in urbanization, put its trust in large organizations and science rather than in individual enterprise and animistic religions. The process of constructing a secular "religion" began before the 1920s, but in that decade its consequences spread so widely that few Americans escaped its impact. New patterns of family life, interpersonal relations, and leisure, as well as new cultural directions and codes, reflected changes in American thought and life. Science and technology, schools and universities, movies and radio challenged the validity of older beliefs and the power of institutions nourished by them, especially the churches whose traditional pieties flourished in a rural society.

People left family farms and small towns for the exciting, impersonal city. They now lived far from relatives and old friends, working for unseen bosses, performing endlessly repetitive tasks as the clerks and production workers required by a complex division of labor. They thereby lost a sense of personal achievement, and the dignity and self-esteem that came from running a farm or small business, or practicing a craft.

Two decades of "reform" left unsolved the problems of humanizing an industrial society, and the disillusioning experience of the First World War left the United States and the rest of the world less safe than ever for democracy. Americans, in their pursuit of happiness, became confused and bewildered. Nothing seemed the same; even one's neighbors had changed. "I have no best friends," complained the wife of a working man in a medium-size midwestern town, one of thousands of such hamlets fabled in song and story for their friendliness. "It doesn't pay to be too friendly," warned another woman. People worked hard to buy things but, reported sociologists, they "seem to be running for dear life in the business of making money." Desires always outpaced means and "everyone seemed to run intent upon his own business as though one feared to stop lest those behind trample him down."

Artists, writers, architects and musicians were the most sensitive barometers of change. They, more than others, lived at the intersection of old and new cultures. They probed critically and experimented ingeniously to find fresh ways of expressing authentically what life meant in an emerging mass society. They spoke for the silent millions experiencing the painful process of social change which undermined the old and nourished new life-styles, a process which betrayed the verities of the past yet seemed irresistibly attractive.

Men, Women, and Children: Shifts in Interpersonal Relations

The family underwent changes that altered its function and redefined the relationship of its members. While most Americans lived on farms, the family functioned as a cohesive economic unit. On the farm, large families were an advantage, and women worked all day. The children's responsibilities in helping their fathers run the homestead made a strong patriarchal authority essential. Farm families before the age of the automobile were isolated; they spent most of their time at home, working, with little but the visits of neighbors and peddlers to relieve the monotony.

Urbanization weakened the family's economic function. Men worked in factories and offices and sometimes their wives and older children had to find jobs to supplement the bread-winner's wages. In the city large families became more of an economic burden than a blessing. A child a year meant more mouths to feed, whereas on the farm children enlarged the labor force. Living space was scarce and expensive in the city whereas on the farm there had always been room for more children and dependent, older relatives, such as aged grandparents. Though the urban working classes in the late nineteenth century continued to raise large families, the urban middle classes began to curb family size, and by the 1920s the limiting trend had spread to other groups. Between 1900 and 1930 the size of the average household fell from 4.6 persons to 3.8, though people now married younger. Contraception allowed for earlier marriage and smaller family size, and contributed to the rising standard of living. The middle classes, fearful of loss of status, were especially eager to ensure that their children had ample opportunity to "get ahead" by means of a "good education."

The reduction in the size of families depended on the adoption of birth control and of new attitudes towards sexuality. Some people approached sex with fear and guilt, most with ignorance. Conventional morality based on the teaching of the churches, Protestant and Catholic, insisted that procreation, not pleasure, was the sole legitimate function of sex, and urged the repression of sexual appetites. Sexual intercourse was moral only within marriage and for purposes of procreation. Sex itself was a forbidden subject, unfit for frank discussion among the decent and upright. "I believe children ought to be taught such things," said a midwestern mother of a sixteen-year-old in the 1920s but "I'm not much for talking about them. I've never talked to my daughter at all, though I suppose she knows more than I think she does. She's the only one I've got and I just can't bear to think of things like that in connection with her. I guess I wouldn't even talk to her if she was going to get married—I just couldn't!"

Yet birth control and new attitudes toward sex continued to spread, first among the middle classes, and then among the working classes. Techniques of contraception were as old as antiquity. Their widespread adoption, however, waited upon the industrialization and urbanization which made many people wish to limit family size. Self-appointed guardians of public morality, especially the Protestant clergy, tried to block change. In 1873 Congress barred contraceptives from interstate commerce and birth control information from the mails, and states such as Connecticut adopted repressive policies making it illegal to use contraceptives.

Court decisions eventually liberalized federal law, the medical profession encouraged birth control for reasons of health, and a militant movement led by Margaret Sanger organized to spread the new gospel and to fight government repression. Science lent the weight of its growing authority, especially the discoveries of Sigmund Freud, father of psychiatry. Freud's ideas, once popularized, undermined the view that sex was "dirty" or that a sensual appetite was normal among beasts but not among men. Freud interpreted the sex drive as natural and healthy, one that required satisfaction; repression of the sex drive only produced guilt, anxiety, and mental illness. The new outlook regarded sex as a means of expressing love and it needed neither the shelter of marriage nor the aim of procreation to give it moral legitimacy.

During the first three decades of the twentieth century, millions of Americans moved haltingly toward the new sexual morality. The continued decline of orthodox religion weakened the most powerful moral force standing in the way of such change. And the anonymity of urban life and the convenience of the automobile facilitated experimentation, especially among the young. Meanwhile the mass media, especially sensational magazines, newspapers and movies, diffused and glamorized naturalistic attitudes toward sex. Hollywood particularly catered to the climate of opinion and produced movies like *Sinners in Silk, Women Who Give, The Price She Paid* and other films "with burning heart interest" such as *Alimony* about "brilliant men, beautiful jazz babies, champagne baths, midnight revels, petting parties in the purple dawn, all ending in one terrific smashing climax that makes you gasp." Popular magazines chipped in with stories of "The Primitive Lover" who "wanted a caveman husband," and advice about "How to Keep the Thrill in Marriage."

Thus began a sexual revolution stimulated by the availability of more leisure. People worked less hard and thus had more time and more energy to channel into other outlets. For millions this led to more premarital sexual activity and a consequent decrease in the frequency with which men resorted to prostitutes. For the first time, American women were becoming sexual partners, not merely sexual objects—a process of emancipation still largely uncompleted, but which was transforming the life of the American woman.

The New Woman

American morality put women on a pedestal. The special function of females was to uphold virtue, serve as guardians of culture, and restrain the animal instincts of their mates. Men regarded wives as creatures not only "purer and morally better" than themselves, but as "relatively impractical, emotional, unstable, . . . incapable of facing facts or doing hard thinking." Man's arena was the factory and the marketplace, where aggressiveness and drive paid off. The home, the woman's responsibility, provided a refuge from the harsh, workaday world ruled by force and power. It was a civilized and genteel atmosphere. Women were so idealized that they faced the danger of becoming unreal. "There is a being," said one typical celebrator of womanhood, "the image and reflection of whom is ever present in the mirror of my soul. Her works are like charmed echoes in a beautiful dell and her laughter like the sweetness of the bursting magnolia and her beauty like the smiling violets and the laughing morning glory . . . heaven's divinest gift to the world— womanhood."

Until the twentieth century, nearly all women accepted their role. Child rearing and housekeeping in large families absorbed their energies. With both partners preoccupied with work, within and outside the home, marriage was less a setting for intimate companionship than a practical arrangement. Women regarded sex as an obligation, associating it with the endless cycle of child bearing that wore them out and killed thousands. Twentieth century mores, however, redefined the role of women. A century earlier married women had almost no legal rights. During the nineteenth century they acquired rights to their own property, even after marriage, and in 1919 after almost a century of struggle they won the right to vote under the Eighteenth Amendment, a victory that symbolized the changes occurring in the status of women.

When the founding fathers in 1776 proclaimed that "all men are created equal" they did not see fit to include women. At the beginning of the nineteenth century wives were legal wards of their husbands and they had few legal rights over their property or their earnings. In practice, however, women were better treated in America than in Europe because there were relatively more men, and women were indispensable for running a farm household. But this demographic advantage did not immediately improve women's legal status nor open educational opportunity. Regarded as inferior to men, in mind as well as in body, women were declared unsuited for intellectual development. Instruction in painting, music and embroidery seemed sufficient. Women, unfit for "the turmoil and battle of public life," should merely exert a "mild, dependent, softening influence upon the sternness of man's opinion."

A few especially gifted women and their male sympathizers thought otherwise. "Remember," Abigail Adams reminded her husband, John, the revolutionary leader who professed to oppose tyranny from whatever source, "all men would be tyrants if they could." Women, barely educated, appeared mentally inferior because—as Dr. Benjamin Rush, the scientist-statesman of the revolutionary era, explained—they were denied a chance to develop their minds and personalities; men were "taught to aspire, but women were early confined and limited."

Eventually a few women began to insist that a nation founded on the principles of human equality respect their humanity too. The early feminists established grammar schools, then colleges, so that at least a few women could develop their potential. A small cadre of educated women became the shock troops in the struggle for female rights, a struggle that flourished after the 1850s as one of the galaxy of reforms, including antislavery and temperance, that sought to rescue the weak and oppressed. Women advanced their own cause as they became prominent in crusades for the rights of others, especially the

slaves. They forged alliances with males, learned skills in organization and in molding public opinion, and by expressing themselves on public issues, the reformers demonstrated their moral
fitness for civic responsibility.

Women's entrance into man's world—schools, colleges,
and finally the political arena—alarmed conservatives who saw
a threat to society's most basic institution, the patriarchal family. Ignoring critics, feminists and suffragists by the middle of
the nineteenth century had won improvements in their legal
status, an advance achieved in part because the wealthy wished
to protect female heirs from husbands who might squander their
wife's inheritance. The struggle for freedom and equality for the
black man in the 1860s encouraged women to press further but
the Civil War enfranchised Negro males, not women.

Meanwhile, industrialization and urbanization more effectively changed the status of women than revolutionary ideology
and protest, the principal forces of change until then. During the
late nineteenth century in the cities of America and Europe,
thousands of women left the home to work in factories and
shops. By 1880 women constituted 15 percent of the American
labor force, and by the 1920s over 20 percent. Mechanization
created jobs which required less physical strength, jobs as suit-
able for women as men, and women were willing to work for
less money. The growing importance of service industries and
communications also created thousands of jobs for women as
office workers, retail clerks, and telephone operators. At the
same time the diffusion of mass education enlarged the demand
for teachers; by 1890 a quarter million women were staffing
the nation's schools. A few also began to find careers in other
professions, including medicine and social work.

At the same time that women entered the labor force, increasing technological changes especially by the 1920s were
revolutionizing housekeeping. Electric lighting, gas cooking and
new household appliances such as refrigerators, electric irons,
and washing machines lightened household chores in middle-
class and some working-class homes. So too did the shift to
factory-made clothing, store-bought bread and canned foods
which came into wide use during the 1920s.

Once women became an integral part of the work force, they gained new status. As working wives they helped support the family, or they could be self-supporting though unmarried. Spending much of their time outside the home, economically they formed part of a previously all-male world. Eventually, they joined the reformers in demanding the political and social rights appropriate to first-class citizens.

The leadership in the movement for women's rights received fresh impetus from the growing number of educated, middle-class women who were the first to benefit from the new leisure and the newer permissible forms of female behavior. In the late nineteenth century women played a more important role than ever in national reform movements. The Women's Christian Temperance Union, for example, stood at the forefront of the crusade against liquor; and women were active in campaigns to clean up politics and improve living conditions in the slums.

During the progressive period a favorable climate existed for renewal of the struggle for the right to vote. "Suffragettes" argued that women would strengthen the moral forces in American politics in the battle against the liquor interests, urban squalor and political corruption. Their organizations, resembling professional political machines, won the vote in enough states by 1916 to create a female bloc vote in national elections. The final push came during the First World War. Reluctantly, President Wilson accepted the inevitable: "Democracy means that women shall play their part in affairs alongside men and upon an equal footing with them. . . . We have made partners of the women in this war; shall we admit them only to a partnership of suffering and not to a partnership of privilege and right?" Resistance stiffened, especially among southerners, the liquor interests, the Catholic church, and eastern industrialists who feared that women social workers would strengthen the movement to curb business. To the charge that giving women the vote would rob them of femininity, Rose Schneiderman replied: "We have women working in the foundries, stripped to the waist, if you please, because of the heat. Yet the Senator says nothing about these women losing their charm. . . . Women in the laundries . . . stand for thirteen or fourteen hours in the terrible steam and heat with their hands in hot starch. Surely these women won't lose any more of their beauty and charm by putting a ballot in a box once a year. . . ."

The Amendment carried in 1919, but the outcome of the battle for the vote proved disappointing. Women's suffrage had little immediate effect on American politics since wives tended to be politically uninformed and few exercised a political judgment independent of their husbands. Nor did the vote resolve the tensions in the American family. Leisured, middle-class women wanted to be more than homemakers but they were not attracted to the physically tiring and intellectually unchallenging jobs then available to working women. These women insisted that they, no less than men, had a right to happiness through freedom for personal development and individual expression.

Women began to breach the double standard. They smoked and drank in public; they alternately shimmied and slithered as they danced the charleston and the tango; and they insisted upon greater satisfactions (even romantic love!) in marriage as well as liberation from the endless cycle of child rearing that birth control made possible. In the past women had suffered through unhappy marriages. Now couples separated more often when marriage failed to offer emotional fulfillment and companionship. At the same time that women were demanding more of marriage than in the past, many men were unable or unprepared to adjust to the women's new demands and attitudes. As a result the divorce rate soared. In the 1920s the United States had the highest divorce rate in the world, except possibly for the Soviet Union.

In the 1920s widespread anxiety existed over the stability of the American family. Not only the high divorce rate, but also the changing relationship between parents and children, generated those fears. "We seem to be drifting away from the fundamentals in our home life," a midwesterner complained in the 1920s. "The home was once a sacred institution where the family spent most of its time. Now it is a service station except for the old and infirm." Members of the family spent less time with one another and more with their peers outside the home. Poverty had driven tens of thousands of children into the factories—almost 20 percent of the male population between 10 and 15 worked in 1900—but after 1910 child labor declined as rising family income levels eliminated some of the need.

Compulsory school attendance laws, longer school terms, and the diffusion of secondary education on a mass scale meant that children spent much of their time during their formative years in the classroom. The child's peer group—his fellow students and friends—competed with his parents for his attention and loyalty. In the densely packed cities, children were far less isolated from one another than they had been on the farm. As a result young people born into an urbanized, mass society began to form a "youth culture" with distinctive life-styles. Their parents still cherished many of the values and attitudes of the past and the Old World, but these youngsters were more prone to experiment. Especially among the middle classes, the automobile gave teen-agers new privacy and intimacy, and the telephone put them in instant communication with one another. Thus the young were more open in their attitudes toward sex and pleasure, and they often found themselves in conflict with the traditional mores of their parents.

The social life of the family centered around the evening meal but the rest of the time family members were off in different directions: children at school, fathers at their jobs, mothers doing the household chores. Not only did they work separately, they played separately as well. Each had his routine of leisure-time activities, especially clubs, sports, and other entertainment. "Folks today want to eat in a hurry," complained a butcher in the 1920s, "and get out in the car." The family car, a convenience and source of recreation, became something more, too. "I never feel as close to my family as when we are all together in the car," confided a midwesterner in the 1920s. "We save every place we can and put the money into the car," another explained hopefully. "It keeps the family together." People mortgaged their homes to buy autos before they had acquired bathtubs. "I'll go without food before I'll see us give up the car," was a common attitude. The car became a family symbol, often a pathetic and counterproductive one, and since families without autos did not amount to much, people desperately sought them—but the car could not supply the cohesion missing in family life in mass society. As the family became less important in the urban setting, formal education came to mean more to young people.

The Expansion of Education

The coming of the common school during the two decades preceding the Civil War (1840–1860) made basic education available to most white Americans. But quality trailed far behind educational quantity and until this century few received more than eight years of primary schooling. During the first three decades of the twentieth century, however, developments already under way earlier began to bear fruit. Americans stayed in school longer. Over 80 percent of the population between the ages of 5 and 17 attended schools in 1930, a considerable jump since 1890. The school year lengthened, increasing almost forty days between 1890 and 1930, and compulsory school attendance laws began to ensure that potential pupils were not kept home or sent to work prematurely.

Advances in educational participation also came through the spread of high schools. In 1890 few but the children of the rich and upper middle class could study beyond elementary school. By the 1930s the sons and daughters of farmers and working people joined them. As the high school became nearly universal, colleges became the next target for the educational explosion. The percentage of people 18 to 21 enrolled in colleges and universities quadrupled in the period from 1890 to 1930, much of the growth occurring during the 1920s. At the end of that decade a million students attended institutions of higher learning, compared to half that number a dozen years earlier. While these extraordinary advances in the diffusion of education took place, other changes occurred which altered the style and substance of learning in primary and high schools and transformed the old colonial college into the modern university.

The expansion and extension of public education stemmed from several interrelated pressures. Urban growth shifted responsibilities for the socialization and education of children from the home to the school because city families counted less on the labor of their children than did rural families. The management of large numbers of children in crowded urban settings created problems. There was less room for play than rural children had, and overcrowding strained family life, producing demands that the state assume more of the burden of child rearing. Industrialization also made new demands on the schools to train a labor force in the habits and skills of factory and office. And in the late nineteenth and early twentieth centuries, social reformers looked to the schools to promote more equal opportunity for the disadvantaged, to equalize conditions of life, abolish child labor, and to instill social discipline in a society increasingly divided by the tensions of labor violence and urban unrest. The cities filled up with "exotic" immigrants with their different customs and beliefs, their "un-American" styles of life. Some thought they threatened the dominant position of the WASPS, the native-born Anglo-Saxon elements, and they expected the schools to Americanize the newcomers.

Until the twentieth century, high schools and private academies, catering mainly to more prosperous families, prepared adolescents for admission to college. By the 1920s the mission of high schools had changed as their enrollments soared and their doors opened to all income levels. High schools still prepared some for college, an ever-growing percentage, but most of their graduates went directly to work. Vocational training edged its way into the curriculum, under pressure from businessmen for practical courses in typing, bookkeeping, business English and arithmetic, homemaking, and the mechanical arts such as carpenty and auto repair. To make room for these new subjects, students spent less time studying the traditional classical curriculum which had emphasized Latin, mathematics, and history. By the 1920s science also had made heavy inroads into the academic course of study, reflecting the growing tendency for a society, so obviously enjoying the fruits of applied technology, to value scientific knowledge and its applications.

The new curriculum was one of several changes instituted by educational reformers seeking to transform the beleaguered schools. In the 1890s discontent first emerged in sustained form in muckraking attacks on the quality of common schools. Overwhelmed by hundreds of thousands of students, inadequately financed, committed to a socially conservative mission of imposing on children "a life of order, self discipline, civic loyalty, and respect for private property," the nineteenth-century school system turned to the bureaucratic principles of centralization and standardization. The result was the graded school, frequent examinations, mass-produced textbooks, standardized buildings and salary schedules for teachers. School facilities were run-down, classes overcrowded, teachers overworked and poorly paid, and rote learning the norm. There was little regard to individual differences among children and little attempt to motivate learning by exploiting student interests and unleashing their imaginations. Above all, fear and repression pervaded the classroom. "Why should they look behind when the teacher is in front of them" insisted a principal, explaining why his school did not permit students to move their heads during recitation. "How can you learn anything with your knees and toes out of order," scolded another educator.

Educational progressives believed there were better ways the schools could serve the needs of an industrial society than as "grim factories deadened by routine." They attempted to break down the wall between the school and society by enlarging its functions. In addition to providing vocational instruction, incorporating the pioneering work of settlement houses in the urban ghettoes, the schools broadened their mission and looked after children's health, instructed them in hygiene, cultivated taste for music and the fine arts, introduced nature study and organized recreational activities. In these ways reformers thought education could better serve the needs of an urban society. The millions of immigrants arriving from Europe and the rural Americans who now lived in crowded cities had to be schooled in "proper"—that is, middle class—standards of morality, behavior, and deportment. Reformers thus invested the schools with responsibilities for accommodating potentially disruptive elements into the existing order.

A philosopher, John Dewey, pioneered in constructing a theory of progressive education. The schools, he urged, must undertake what the family, neighborhood, shop and farm had previously done. They must train citizens to assume civic responsibilities for improving society through the application of science and intelligence to social problems, while trying to cultivate the fullest potential for human development in every child. Exploiting new psychological insights, progressive educators insisted that children be regarded, not as miniature adults, but as a distinctive age group with needs which educators must understand and adapt to. Traditional educational doctrine held that subjects such as Latin and mathematics disciplined the mind and personalities of children. The progressives insisted that mathematics did not train people to think more logically, nor did memorization of Latin or English grammar teach students how to write and speak grammatically.

Dewey and other advocates of progressive education inspired dozens of experiments to exploit the student's natural curiosity and encourage learning as a means of self-gratification instead of arbitrarily imposing on children a body of subject matter which—like it or not—they had to assimilate. Thus a student's natural curiosity about experiences in his own life would provide a springboard into the study of nature and society, and the cultivation of the arts. At the same time, progressives tried to replace the coercive atmosphere of the classroom with a more informal, spontaneous environment that encouraged student initiative. Teachers were to become guides rather than taskmasters, and would pay greater attention to individual differences among children.

Progressive education promised more than it delivered. As Dewey's ideas became translated into popular practice only a few teachers had the knowledge, imagination and training to make progressivism work fully. Nor would conservatives tolerate Dewey's idea that the schools should turn out citizens who would become social critics and social reformers, rather than conformists. And few communities were willing to finance the schools with the generosity necessary to implement a truly progressive system. Yet a marked improvement took place in the schools: the classroom atmosphere did became less repressive, the curriculum was broadened, and teachers received better training and better salaries. Education, if not revolutionized, had at least been revitalized—and the country spent a greater share of its income on education in 1930 than thirty years earlier.

The Emergence of the University

A revolution in higher education paralleled the developments in basic and secondary education. Although in the 1930s only 12 percent of Americans between 18 and 22 were in college, enrollment between 1890 and 1925 had grown almost five times faster than the population. An advanced, industrial economy generating ever higher per capita income required more professionally trained people: doctors, lawyers, engineers and teachers. The colleges and universities provided them, but to do so required an overhaul in the structure of higher education, a process that occurred in the half-century following the Civil War.

Seven hundred colleges were founded in America before 1860, partly because of the competitive enterprise of the religious denominations which controlled most of them. Established to promote the interests of a particular denomination by training future ministers and providing an appropriate sectarian environment for the sons of the upper classes, the colleges served the few. As conservators and transmitters of traditional culture, the colleges relied on the classical curriculum and neglected science and other modern disciplines. Most also rejected free inquiry and expensive research, since these might threaten established doctrine. Their mission was to promote sound morals, not to stimulate intellectual inquiry or the advancement of knowledge.

The teachers, mostly clergymen, taught piety. But young men seemed more interested in "getting on" in the world, and in Greek letter fraternities. Originating in the 1820s and 1830s, these clubs filled a gap in college life and "institutionalized various escapes—drinking, smoking, card playing, and seducing" as well as "the new prestige values of worldly success, for they recognized good looks, wealth, good family, income, clothing, good manners." Officially, however, the colleges remained committed to the preeminence of spiritual values.

After the Civil War, science, secularism, and utilitarianism transformed the old liberal arts college into the modern university. Before that, the great scientific advances of the preceding two centuries had made limited inroads in higher education. The triumph of Darwinism in the late nineteenth century opened the way for change. Darwinism did more than substitute the theory of evolution for the biblical account of creation. It fostered the feeling that science held the key to the universe. This break-through in human knowledge also represented a triumph for the scientific method. It assumed that truth was not fixed, but some-thing man discovered by formulating tentative explanations of puzzling phenomena and then testing the theories experimen-tally. At the same time that naturalistic explanations of creation were challenging supernatural accounts, medical science discov-ered the causes of several killer diseases such as tuberculosis. As a result, a dramatic, visible improvement in human welfare took place, giving science enormous prestige among ordinary Americans, further strengthened by such applications of scien-tific knowledge as the use of electricity in lighting.

In the late nineteenth century, Americans learned that sci-ence meant power, and the university became the center for the diffusion and advancement of scientific knowledge. Though some managed to reconcile religion and science, Darwinism convinced many that man, through the use of the scientific method, could understand the impersonal forces governing the world. This belief undermined the religious character of the American college and redefined its mission.

Leading colleges became universities by emphasizing the centrality of research and providing scholars with the resources and conditions to engage in free inquiry. Harvard led the way in 1869 when it chose a scientist, Charles W. Eliot, rather than a clergyman as president. Eliot placed science on an equal footing with the humanities in the curriculum, and he introduced the elective system, giving students considerable leeway in choosing their course of study. The elective principle proved revolution-ary because it reawakened intellectual curiosity: undergraduates could pursue their interests and professors could offer special-ized instruction in areas in which they did research and had gained expertise.

The old colleges had been financed on a shoestring but the

new universities were far more expensive to run. The university required laboratories and libraries—and a large faculty, many of whom spent much of their time engaged in research and in training apprentice faculty. Increasing knowledge resulted in fragmentation and ushered in the age of the academic specialist. Science split into separate disciplines, such as physics, chemistry, zoology and geology, and specialization eventually reached the more traditional disciplines as well. History, for example, also became "scientific" and specialized. Historians became experts by concentrating on a particular period such as ancient, medieval or modern history, or the history of a particular country.

While science worked to transform the college, new wealth, generated by the industrial development of the late nineteenth century, provided the money. Tycoons such as John D. Rockefeller (benefactor of the University of Chicago) donated millions as tokens of their philanthropic spirit and as a means of winning public approval.

Paralleling an enormous increase in private support for higher education was the emergence of the state university. The first state universities were founded before the Civil War in the South and West, where private colleges were much weaker than in the East. The Morrill Act (1862) created the land-grant state university and provided federal funding for state institutions that offered instruction in agriculture and in the mechanical arts. As the state universities enlarged in the late nineteenth century, they imitated the older institutions but they also developed new functions to serve the people on whose support they depended. They engaged in agricultural research and also established professional schools. Free from sectarian control, the state universities were hospitable to science and to modern curriculums and together with the leading private universities they established graduate schools. Their special contribution was to make college available to thousands who could not afford private institutions and to make public service, together with research and the transmission of liberal education, one of the missions of the modern university.

A precondition of the modern university was academic freedom—the freedom of students and faculty to search for the truth, wherever it might lead. The old colleges had no room for such freedom, since truth was deemed fixed and already discovered, embodied in the theology of the sponsoring church and the values of influential laymen. In the new universities an accepted truth was never safe from critical scrutiny, for science had demonstrated that knowledge could advance only as men subjected all accepted beliefs to the test of scholarly inquiry. Inevitably scholars challenged many accepted beliefs and provoked criticism of the university by angry citizens and alumni. Some professors who espoused unconventional or unpopular views lost their jobs; others had to remain silent. The battle for academic freedom was hard-fought but by 1915 professors felt sufficiently strong to demand, through the newly organized American Association of University Professors, that universities voluntarily respect the need for free inquiry. At first college presidents and trustees refused, but by the 1920s the leading institutions accepted the principle of academic freedom though they sometimes violated it in practice.

By the 1920s the modern university had evolved. It still transmitted culture and moral values to undergraduates but at the same time it incorporated science into the curriculum and the scientific method into the spirit of the university. Graduate and professional schools trained the highly skilled personnel modern America needed, and large-scale private philanthropy together with public support of state institutions financed the expansion of higher education.

At the same time, the university engaged in a new activity, peripheral to its central concerns, but which provided entertainment for millions every Saturday afternoon—college football. The rise of football as a mass spectator sport in the 1920s satisfied the need of an emerging mass society for organized diversion that was inexpensive, frequent, and easily accessible. Spectator sports—college and high school football and professional baseball—and the new industries of movies and radio reshaped the way Americans spent their leisure time in the twentieth century.

Entertainment for the Masses

Mass society created the mass media and mass entertainment. Newspapers were older than the republic, but in the twentieth century, journalism took a new turn. Newspapers became big business and went after the largest market possible. Tabloids exploiting sensationalism catered to the urban masses and provided them with cheap, daily entertainment which they read to and from work each day. Magazine editors also learned the popular touch and found that there was more money in entertaining than in edifying. As in other businesses, the most successful entrepreneurs, such as newspaper magnate William Randolph Hearst, built huge publishing empires that made them a power in the republic. People looked to the press for information but they also insisted on being entertained—something the newspapers and magazines accomplished with great cleverness, through muckraking, comic strips, crossword puzzles, crimes of violence reported daily in gory detail, and gossip columns.

Mass entertainment was also the function of professional sports. The popularity of professional baseball and college football (which was amateur only in name) depended only partly on the skill of the athletes or the excitement of the games themselves. Professional sports had still another appeal: people identified with teams and athletic heroes. Cities rooted for the home club and basked in the glory of their victories. Following the exploits of a favorite team added interest and excitement to otherwise drab and dull lives. The triumphs of the baseball star "Babe" Ruth or a football hero like "Red" Grange enabled people who felt (and to a great extent were) like cogs in the industrial machine to identify with the individual achievements of heroic men. College football went even further in strengthening the loyalty of alumni to their alma mater, and inducing both alumni and state legislators to finance higher education more generously.

Professional sports thus catered to the need for entertainment and escape in an urban society but, like the theater and the circus, they were not readily accessible to or within the means of everyone; movies and radio were, however, and they transformed the way Americans spent the increasing leisure time created by affluence. These media relied on new technology and the marketing techniques and financial resources of Big Business to bring cheap entertainment into residential neighborhoods via thousands of local movie houses and into the homes through millions of radio receivers.

The commercial production and exhibition of movies began early in the twentieth century, first as peep shows and then with film projected on theater screens where many people could watch simultaneously. The first movies were primitive in technique, with inexperienced actors and directors. Shown in "nickleodeons," these short films depicted familiar scenes of city life—the pool hall, the ghetto, the pawnshop, and police and fire departments in action.

Crude though they were, the early films proved enormously popular. This attracted businessmen who built theaters and production companies turning out hundreds of short films. Fierce competition among producers and exhibitors, resembling the early competition in the railroad, steel, and oil industries, led to consolidation of many firms into a few powerful companies. The movie moguls gained control over the distribution system, acquiring hundreds of theaters across the country which assured them a steady outlet for their films. When movies became a profitable Big Business, Wall Street financiers in the 1920s and 1930s supplied capital and gained control.

At first New York City reigned as the center of moviemaking, but by 1920 the industry had shifted to Hollywood, California. Independent producers located there so they could easily escape across the border to Mexico when the movie trust (located in New York) attempted to enforce its control over key patents. Southern California also offered a climate that made year-round production possible. The concentration of moviemaking in Hollywood led to the development of a community of filmmakers which was highly competitive but which also encouraged the cross-fertilization of ideas.

The moviemakers repeatedly misjudged both the financial and artistic possibilities of the new medium. At first actors were ashamed to work in motion pictures. Those who did, appeared anonymously in dozens of movies ground out like automobiles from a factory production line. When the public took a fancy to some of the early actors, producers feared that popular performers would demand higher salaries. Eventually, however, they realized the potential of the star system. Similarly, early movies were short, since no one thought people would watch a film for more than half an hour. The successful Italian full-length spectacle, *Quo Vadis* (1912), helped to convince them otherwise. Theaters could charge more for feature films and Hollywood thus made more money. The industry also resisted the introduction of sound. In 1927, Warner Brothers introduced talkies in a desperate bid to stave off bankruptcy. Convinced that talkies were a fad that would pass, fearful that sound would undermine the huge investments in silent film stars, and reluctant to invest the millions of dollars conversion to sound would require, the leading studios held back until the popularity of talkies forced them to go along.

The star system, the feature film, and the sound track were three essential developments in the emergence of movies. In addition, the audience had broadened from the working classes to include the middle classes who caught the moviegoing habit by the 1920s. The first movie houses were built in working class neighborhoods but in the 1920s luxurious movie "palaces" rose in the big-city downtown districts, and impressive if less imposing theaters appeared in residential areas. In small towns the principal movie house was often the most impressive building in the community. By 1927 there were 17,000 movie houses and new plush theaters helped make moviegoing genteel and respectable. Finally, a shift in the thematic content of films captured the interest of the middle classes. The early silent films had realistically exploited scenes of urban life. They were crude social documents, sympathetically depicting the experiences of the poor and the downtrodden—as in the great films of Charlie Chaplin, who won the hearts of millions around the world with his portrayal of the tramp, the symbol of the underdog.

Middle class audiences wanted something else. As the technical quality of movies improved, leading Broadway actors went to Hollywood. Films began to cater to the interests and anxieties of the new audience. Prewar movies, reflecting prewar optimism, assumed that love and honesty made for happiness, that poverty ennobled men because wealth corrupted them. In the 1920s, however, movies became preoccupied with the foibles of the rich, depicting them as restless, unhappy and faithless—but glamorous. The audience sought vicarious pleasure for a few hours by escaping into a world inhabited by people who enjoyed luxury and who indulged in romantic exploits denied to most people. The movies thus exploited a fascination that derived from middle-class envy of the upper crust, ocean-liner set, an envy often accompanied by fear and disdain for those who repudiated conventional mores.

Movies could be more than a business and a form of mass entertainment. In the hands of creative people, movies became an art. Directors and cameramen slowly mastered their technique. They learned how to use the camera, edit film, and to light the set to create an aesthetic experience unique to films. D. W. Griffith was the great pioneer director whose films, such as *Birth of a Nation* (1915) and *Intolerance* (1916), explored the technical and artistic possibilities of the motion picture. But Hollywood never fully realized its potential. Movies remained first and foremost a business; commercial pressures, especially the need for rapid production of many movies, restricted the art of moviemaking. Some directors were little more than glorified foremen grinding out their prescribed footage, using formula actors whose box office appeal mattered much more than acting talent. Customers wanted to see their favorites play the same role in movie after movie. Hollywood obliged. In the 1920s the center of artistic filmmaking shifted to Europe, and there it has remained. The combination of mass production, new technology, and Big Business created the modern American movie industry, and made inexpensive entertainment available to millions every week (U.S. films were as popular overseas as at home), but the pressures of the marketplace stunted the film's development as an art.

Radio, like movies, represented a triumph of the new technology and Big Business. Radio broadcasting began in the early 1920s and quickly became popular. Mass production allowed millions to buy radio sets and stations multiplied to fill the airwaves with sound. At first, the financing of radio programming remained unclear. Set manufacturers might broadcast programs to stimulate sales or set owners might pay a fee. But the idea of government transmission smacked of socialism, and the notion of selling radio time to advertisers struck many as undesirable. Secretary of Commerce Herbert Hoover warned in the 1920s: "It is inconceivable that we should allow so great a possibility for service . . . to be drowned in advertising matter," and the code of the National Association of Broadcasters in 1929 banned radio commercials between 7 and 11 P.M.

But just as commercial pressures shaped the development of movies, advertising determined the destiny of radio. In the 1920s business had come to appreciate the power of advertising, and radio offered an unparalleled medium for selling brand-name products nationally. To attract large audiences radio stations hired leading entertainers. This raised costs but advertisers willingly bought expensive radio time because millions could be reached instantly and repeatedly across the entire country. The initiation of radio networks such as NBC (1926) and CBS (1927) hooked together hundreds of local stations and cleared prime evening time, nationwide, for popular programs originating from New York. The public quickly became addicted to radio. In millions of homes Americans tuned in their favorite weekly programs, at virtually no expense. Radio seemed like a free service, since the cost was hidden in the prices people paid for nationally advertised brands. Advertisers, wishing to reach the largest possible audience, geared programming to the lowest common denominator of popular taste. The public, however, seemed generally satisfied, and the addiction spread from the programs to the commercials, as consumers dutifully bought the products which the radio stars assured them "make this program possible."

Culture in a Mass Society

At the same time that radio, commercial sports, and movies were providing entertainment for millions, writers, artists, architects, and musicians expressed the feelings of those sensing most keenly, often most painfully, the strains that altered people's lives in modern America. The first three decades of the twentieth century saw the birth of modern American "high" culture, following a generation of incubation. After 1900, a galaxy of great artists produced a distinctively American spirit in the creative arts. From provincials, American writers and artists became cosmopolitans, the best of them acknowledged world masters.

As in the first American Renaissance of 1830–1860—the burst of literary excellence that sprang from the pens of Hawthorne, Emerson, Whitman, and Melville—literature provided the most important vehicle through which Americans gave expression to their creative imagination. Emily Dickinson, Edwin Arlington Robinson, Robert Frost, Carl Sandburg, Ezra Pound and T. S. Eliot, to mention a few, brought powerful, fresh voices to poetry. Among prose writers, Mark Twain, Henry James, and William Dean Howells in the last decades of the nineteenth century, followed in the next generation by Edith Wharton, F. Scott Fitzgerald, Theodore Dreiser, Ernest Hemingway, Sherwood Anderson, Thomas Wolfe, Sinclair Lewis, and John Dos Passos, transmuted experience into art in a series of classic modern novels.

Long in the making, modern American culture burst into full bloom in the 1920s, a decade of unprecedented vitality in the history of the creative arts in America, and of unprecedented alienation among intellectuals at odds with the ruling precepts and practices of their society. This achievement stands in sharp contrast to the situation thirty years earlier. In 1888 Matthew Arnold, an English man of letters and arbiter of culture, surveyed the American scene and delivered a negative verdict. "Let us take the beautiful first, and consider how far it is present in American civilization," he began. "Evidently, this is that civilization's weak side. There is little to nourish and delight the sense of beauty there. . . . What people in whom the sense for beauty and fitness was quick could have invented, or could tolerate, the hideous names ending in *ville*, the Briggesvilles, Higginsvilles, Jacksonvilles, rife from Maine to Florida. . . ." By 1930, European judgments on American small town culture had remained constant, but there was a new respect for

American literature. In that year, the Nobel Prize for literature went, for the first time, to an American, Sinclair Lewis.

Yet this American cultural flowering, what Lewis called in 1930 a "second coming of age," differed from the awakening of the 1840s and 1850s. Before the Civil War, most important creative artists had been isolated; isolated from one another, from the literary world abroad, and from a large, appreciative audience at home. Their successors in the twentieth century, not only poets and novelists, but playwrights, architects, and musicians reached larger audiences and won recognition far beyond American shores. And most significant, they were artistic revolutionaries, rejecting established conceptions of the nature of art and its place in life. Despite intense hostility and, what was worse, indifference, they ultimately overcame both, giving powerful expression to a counterculture which repudiated much of what most Americans cherished.

The imaginative writers reveal most clearly the roots of cultural modernity. In the late nineteenth century, literature, like the other arts in America, fell under the sway of the Genteel Tradition. Most Americans regarded the arts as artificial, far from the central concerns of a busy people. "Essentially we were taught to regard culture," explained the literary critic Malcolm Cowley, "as a veneer, a badge of class distinction—as something assumed like an Oxford accent or a suit of English clothes." The colleges where the young middle-class men and women received the finishing touches were "sales rooms and fitting rooms of culture," remote from real life, rather than "ground-floor shops" that opened one "to the life of the street." As custodians and transmitters of official culture, the colleges destroyed "whatever roots we had in the soil," setting up foreign aesthetic models and maintaining that whatever was sordid was unfit for a work of literature. Literature in general, and art and learning in particular, Cowley reminisced, "were things existing at an infinite distance from our daily lives."

"Good" literature, insisted the pundits of the Genteel Tradition, had to be ennobling and "pure." Dwelling on the sordid, or anatomizing the underside of life had no place in books intended for the chaste living rooms of middle-class

America or for the eyes of the female readers who dominated the fiction audience. The function of art was to adorn, uplift, and entertain. Against such socially imposed constraints, such narrowing limits that smothered vision and feeling, such prissiness, two generations of American writers struggled.

A few cracks were formed in the Genteel Tradition's Great Wall during the three decades after the Civil War which coincided with the heyday of industrialization. Writers, like other Americans, were alarmed by the social dislocations accompanying American growth. Eventually the malaise seeped into their work. Literary "realists" sought to discover in fiction life as it was. "Let fiction cease to lie about life," commanded William D. Howells, "let it portray men and women as they really are, actuated by the motives and the passions in the measure we all know." Howells led the way himself in *A Hazard of New Fortunes* (1894) writing about class conflict and the dilemma of the individual facing an increasingly collectivized society; Frank Norris described how corporations crushed the weak in *The Octopus* (1901); while Stephen Crane re-created, with extraordinary poignancy, the impact of war on a young man in *The Red Badge of Courage* (1895) and the impact of urbanization on a young woman in *Maggie, A Girl of the Streets* (1892).

Yet even before realism became a literary movement, Mark Twain was writing stories so deceptively simple and popular that many readers and critics never realized their real literary worth or their critical significance. Ernest Hemingway later described *Huckleberry Finn* (1884) as the source of all modern American fiction. Twain, one of a group of regionalist writers, wrote about the southern half of the Mississippi Valley, and about Americans everyone could recognize. He employed a vernacular style rooted in the speech of the people, and masked his savage satire and growing pessimism behind irresistible humor and a folk manner that won him huge audiences. Few puzzled over the larger meaning of the adventures of Huck Finn who runs away from civilization, befriends an escaped slave, and when the moment comes to decide whether to do his civic and Christian duty and turn the black man over to the law, decides otherwise. "All right," Huck declared, "I'll *go* to Hell"—hardly the destination American boys were supposed to prepare themselves for. Acclaimed in his own day as America's leading writer, Twain received the highest accolade his audiences could bestow, being classified as a writer of juvenile fiction by a generation that did not understand him. No wonder Twain died a bitter, old man with hardly a good thought for the human race.

Twain's contemporary Henry James was as different from the Hannibal, Missouri master as one could imagine. The product of an eastern, elite family of culture and means, James spent most of his career in Europe, the setting for many of his novels. Alienated from a society that deified self-made businessmen devoid of taste or refinement, James wrote a series of complex stories that explore men's minds, striving for psychological realism in an effort to illuminate the human condition. Though he separated himself physically from the United States, James often wrote about Americans in Europe, all very rich, very impressed by a superior civilization, very uncultured, but sincere. In *Daisy Miller*, a young American girl, "an inscrutable combination of audacity and innocence," is victimized not by corrupt European suitors, but by her own innocence. Unlike Twain who employed vernacular style, James developed a highly self-conscious concern for form and language which made his work inaccessible to a wide audience.

William D. Howells, Mark Twain, and Henry James, together with Stephen Crane, Frank Norris and others, acted as pathbreakers preparing the way for the next generation that pushed into the promised land. Despite a desire to free artists to confront social reality, Howells, for example, could never fully escape from his middle-class gentility that insisted that the good in life was more real than the evil. The next generation of writers, for whom the chaos and brutality of industrial America were formative experiences, felt no such constraints.

Three outstanding "liberated" writers were Frank Norris, Jack London, and Theodore Dreiser, men whose novels had terrific impact though as literary stylists they fell far below the mark of James, Howells, or Twain. Influenced profoundly by the work of France's Émile Zola, the father of naturalism in literature, they strove to write objective yet searing accounts of

American men and institutions, of a system crushing individuality, of an affluent society ignoring a hungry proletariat. Norris's *The Octopus* (1901), and *The Pit* (1903), laid bare two "monster" institutions, California's Southern Pacific Railroad, and Chicago's grain exchange. Jack London achieved considerable popularity with novels that tried unsuccessfully to mix Social Darwinism with Marxism. The greatest of the naturalists was Theodore Dreiser.

Beginning with *Sister Carrie* (1900) and reaching the peak of his power in *An American Tragedy* (1925), Dreiser spoke for the new generation of naturalists who lifted the curtain on every corner of American experience, especially the corrupting influence of the business world. Unlike the comfortable Howells, Dreiser came from the other side of the tracks: poor and Catholic, his parents had been crushed by the struggle for survival. Dreiser's method was to pile detail upon detail (sometimes too many), drawn from life both in the lower depths and at the heights, to re-create a thickly-textured, believable picture of how life in America really was. Seeking a scientific objectivity without distortion of reality, Dreiser nonetheless could not hide his compassion for the victims of a society he found essentially self-destructive. At the heart of the American tragedy stood Clyde Griffiths, the hero whose material success required a girl's death, a price he was ready to pay until chance unexpectedly did the job for him. *An American Tragedy* is a Horatio Alger story with the morality turned around. Dreiser discovered that the truth hurt. Censorship temporarily silenced him; *Sister Carrie* suppressed shortly after publication in 1900, did not appear again for twelve years.

Yet during the years of Dreiser's enforced silence, powerful underground forces were at work that were to burst forth by the 1920s and destroy the Genteel Tradition. Everywhere a young generation of writers, painters, and musicians, were experimenting and creating something new in America: an artistic community. Little magazines, with tiny circulations but big ideas, opened their pages to experimental writers whose unorthodox works would not otherwise have seen publication. In 1913, a mammoth art show brought modern painting to America, not only from the studios of the young masters in Paris but from their counterparts in the United States. "Everywhere young men and women were coming up," reported John Butler Yeats, an Irish Painter, "who felt themselves the appointed children of the twentieth century." One of those children, Mabel Dodge Luhan, who ran the most successful *salon* in Greenwich Village, later looked back with exhilaration to a time when it seemed "as though everywhere, in that year of 1913, barriers went down and people reached out to each other who had never been in touch before." Young artists were most likely to meet in New York City's Greenwich Village. Creative people from all over the country flocked there to find a community inhabited by others like themselves who stimulated, supported and often savaged one another.

Perhaps the greatest contribution of "The Village" was to house small, experimental theaters operating on shoestrings which gave unknown playwrights such as Eugene O'Neill a chance to present their works. On the eve of the First World War, the American theater had shown few signs of maturation. A dismal parade of mindless melodramas and insipid musical comedies monopolized the productions on Broadway. The theater had adopted the star system—producing a system duplicated later by the movie industry. Ignoring Shakespeare's dictum, "the play's the thing!," the handful of producers who controlled Broadway put all their energies (and their dollars) into showing off their stars. The general public seemed satisfied, unconcerned over the lack of a national repertory company, or of experimental theater. But American intellectuals could not allow so powerful a vehicle of communication, the theater, to be lost by default. In 1915 the Provincetown Players shifted their yet unheralded operations from Cape Cod to Greenwich Village, producing among other things translations of European "new wave" drama and some short plays by Eugene O'Neill.

O'Neill, the son of an alcoholic, actor father and a drug-addicted mother, had wandered as a youth, working for a while as a merchant seaman and finding at last in theater a means for personal expression. When in 1920 a Village theater group moved "uptown" to perform his *Emperor Jones*, O'Neill had arrived, beginning a career without peer among American dramatists. He wrote extensively, and won three Pulitzer prizes for drama in the 1920s.

Though not a member of the Lost Generation of the 1920s, since his damnation was a *personal* problem, O'Neill nevertheless kept in tune with what was modern in literary experience. As much an interior and psychological writer as Henry James, O'Neill's dramas still employed the innovations of the realistic and impressionistic European drama masters. Far from painting a rosy picture of human nature and of life in America, this brooding and brilliant man always flirted with but kept a short step away from despair, as in his greatest play, produced late in his career, *The Iceman Cometh* (1947). Yet he did not blame "the system" for human tragedies, but human nature itself, an attitude which made him an ideological loner. A Nobel Prize in 1936 reconfirmed that with Eugene O'Neill, the American theater had come of age.

The trail to bohemia started typically in the villages and small towns of mid-America. To the rebels who departed, according to Sinclair Lewis, Main Street was "an unimaginatively standardized background . . . a rigid ruling of the spirit by the desire to appear respectable." It was "contentment . . . the contentment of the quiet dead . . . prohibition of happiness . . . slavery self-sought and self-defended . . . dullness made God." Its inhabitants were "savorless . . . gulping tasteless food, and sitting afterward coatless and thoughtless . . . listening to mechanical music, saying mechanical things about the excellence of Ford automobiles, and viewing themselves as the greatest race in the world."

Bohemia was another world. Convinced that "each of us at birth," as Malcolm Cowley put it, affirmatively if a bit romantically, "has special potentialities which are slowly crushed and destroyed by a standardized society," it sought to liberate people from repression so that a new generation might arise where children could "develop their own personalities, to blossom freely like flowers. . . ." Anticipating the gospels of the Beatniks and Hippies, Bohemians rejected conventional careers and insisted that people could only achieve "full individuality through creative work and beautiful living in beautiful surroundings." They turned inward to proclaim that "the body is a temple in which there is nothing unclean, a shrine to be adorned for the ritual of love." One lived for momentary gratifications and broke "every law, convention or rule of art that prevents self-expression or the full enjoyment of the moment."

Whereas Main Street had been built on deferred gratifications, repressed feelings, and preoccupation with money-making, the new morality of Bohemia denounced all forms of puritanism as the enemy of life. It stunted the possibilities for human happiness, they charged. Its prototype—the successful American businessman—like others who became the victims of materialism, led in Bohemian eyes a life that was "joyless and colorless . . . tawdry, uncreative, given over to the worship of wealth and machinery." And none paid a higher price than women. The businessman's wife, Malcolm Cowley argued, "finds him so sexually inept that she refuses to bear him children and so driveling in every way except as a money getter that she compels him to expend his energies solely in that direction while she leads a discontented, sterile, stunted life," seeking compensation "by making herself empress of culture."

The First World War, which ended a hundred years of peace and material progress in the Western World, helped to intensify and crystallize the revolution against the old morality. War's brutality and irrationality made the charges of men like Dreiser and others more plausible. A young novelist of the 1920s, F. Scott Fitzgerald, recounted the shock of discovery: "Here was a new generation shouting the old cries, learning the old creeds, through a revery of long days and nights; destined finally to go out into that dirty gray turmoil to follow love and pride; a new generation dedicated more than the last to the fear of poverty and the worship of success; grown up to find all Gods dead, all wars fought, all faiths in man shaken." Ernest Hemingway was another of a group of young Americans who enlisted in the First World War as a volunteer ambulance driver in Italy to exchange the safe life at home, for the danger, adventure, courage and fatalism of men in war. "I was always embarrassed by the words 'sacred', 'glorious', and 'sacrifice', and the expression 'in vain'," Hemingway remembered. "We had heard them . . . and read them, on proclamations . . . for a long time, and I had seen nothing sacred, and the things that were glorious had no glory and the sacrifices were like the stockyards at Chicago if nothing was done with the meat except to bury it."

At war's end, a stream of intellectuals abandoned America, including Greenwich Village, convinced that a nation whose ideal was Warren Harding and which responded to the call to liberate the human spirit with Prohibition, could not be redeemed. How could they stay, explained Malcolm Cowley, when "hardly anyone seemed to believe in what he was doing— not the workmen on the production line, or the dealer forced to sell more units each month to more and more unwilling customers . . . or the underpaid newspaperman kidding historians . . . and despising his readers—not even the people at the head of the system, the bankers and stock promoters and politicians in the little green house on K Street; everybody was in it for the money, everybody was hoping to make a killing and get away."

Exiles of the Lost Generation of the 1920s went to Europe, escaping to Paris, one of them explained "to recover the good life and the traditions of art, to free themselves from organized stupidity, to win their deserved place in the hierarchy of the intellect." But they found that though America was richer than other nations, it was not much different: the spirit of Main Street and of George F. Babbitt was abroad in the capitalist nations of Europe, and the spirit of statist repression was abroad in the totalitarian dictatorships, fascist and communist. Nor could the artists and intellectuals of the Old World offer the eager Americans "stable intellectual leadership and esthetic values." Abroad as at home, Americans "found only chaos and shifting values." In the end, art became their only hope for personal salvation. "I know myself but that is all," said Fitzgerald. As for man's destiny, he concluded—"so we beat on, boats against the current, borne back ceaselessly into the past." In words such as these Fitzgerald and Hemingway forged a popular literary style that heightened then released the anguish and alienation of a generation that felt cut off from the past and without an acceptable future. All that remained was to perfect the craftsmanship of their art so that they might convince others and themselves, in Alfred Kazin's words, "that in writing the story of their generation, they were in some sense describing the situation of contemporary humanity. . . ."

Music, Art, and Architecture

Like the English from whom they derived so much of their culture, nineteenth-century Americans showed only meager gifts for making music—except for American blacks who poured their souls into spirituals. When Americans tried their hand at composing symphonic music, their tepid imitations of European masters revealed both lack of inspiration and rudimentary technique. In the early twentieth century, however, Americans began making their own music. First, jazz began moving upstream along the Mississippi from New Orleans to Chicago, again relying on black musical genius for sustenance. Then came the rise of Tin Pan Alley, a professional stable of New York song writers that ground out new tunes weekly, but still created sounds that gave urban America an authentic and popular voice. American music, popular tunes and jazz, became exportable.

Popular music flourished by exploiting the musical heritage of the American Negro. The first such borrowings took place before the Civil War with the rise of minstrelsy. The minstrel show, *very* freely adapting plantation banjo music, remained popular throughout the nineteenth century. In the 1890s the combination of such banjo music and the minstrel's versions of black strutting rhythm, or the cakewalk, became known as ragtime and swept the country. The piano replaced the banjo as ragtime's characteristic instrument. An aggressive popular music industry turned out ragtime songs by the hundreds, forever changing the nature of American social dancing. After the turn of the century, the cocky, rapid-fire urban musical comedy triumphed, especially in the Broadway productions of George M. Cohan, establishing a particularly American form of musical culture which would flourish in the Twenties and beyond.

Despite their origins, minstrelsy and ragtime had had very little to do with Negroes. The more direct line of black music extended from the planation spirituals and work chants and urban songs of blacks, elements fused together around 1890–1900 in blues. New Orleans, with its slightly freer racial mores, and its high concentration of black musicians, provided the setting. In the clubs and "houses" of the French Quarter, black groups played ragtime (and anything else popular in order to earn a living) while they began developing other forms much closer to Negro folk songs. The music began spreading slowly north from New Orleans, to St. Louis and then Chicago. By about 1915, the word jazz entered the national vocabulary.

White America found jazz attractive but "immoral." The word itself had sexual connotations, perhaps from its French Quarter origins, or from its association with supposedly sensual blacks. But the music could not be ignored, as proved by the success of W. C. Handy's *St. Louis Blues* (1912) and "Dixieland" jazz bands. White musicians quickly tried their hand at the jazz idiom, and large jazz bands (such as Paul Whiteman's) further tamed the music to make it more acceptable to the mass, white audience. Black jazz musicians responded to these pressures, as the solo (as opposed to continuous ensemble playing) and the bigger band began to predominate. The jazz influence was clear in the works of George Gershwin, *Rhapsody in Blue*, and *An American in Paris*, as in his later opera *Porgy and Bess* (1935). What became popular in the Twenties was not authentic New Orleans jazz, but a new American music unmistakably influenced by jazz. It would maintain its hold on America, and most of the world.

At the same time that popular music took off, America produced its first major composer of "classical" music. Charles Ives, a Connecticut Yankee, was a partner in one of the largest insurance agencies in New York City. He also wrote strange music which employed American folk materials in a style that flouted the conventions of classical composition. Isolated from direct contact with the musical world, working alone and in his spare time, Ives attempted to forge a new musical language—in ways that anticipated the next wave of European masters of modern music. Ives's music remained unplayed for decades, too difficult for musicians to perform, too unconventional for audiences to comprehend. Yet he caught in sound, better than any other American composer, the sense of innocence and its loss, the nostalgic longing for a simpler past into which one could escape from the anguish, uncertainty, and confusion of the present.

America's painters could not match its music makers in originality. America exported music but it imported its art. What Americans lacked in original creativity in painting they more than made up for in imitating the European masters and acquiring samples of their best work. Capitalists who accumulated fortunes in industrial America became avid collectors. With money to burn, they ravaged Europe for paintings by Rembrandt, Rubens, Titian and other great masters. When they patronized American artists they preferred imitations of European masters to anything original. Most American artists obliged. Leading American painters received their training in Europe and some of the best of them such as James M. Whistler and Winslow Homer spent much of their career in the Old World, close to the centers of artistic creativity. The most original of the late nineteenth-century artists, Alfred Ryder, composed dark, mystical canvases which few understood and even fewer appreciated. Like Charles Ives, Ryder's work did not find an audience until after he was no longer around to bask in its admiration.

At their best, American artists skillfully imitated styles which were popular in Europe. When Impressionism became the vogue, some Americans joined the movement. When European painters turned to rendering realistically the seamier sides of life, Americans, too, turned their gaze on life in all its rawness. In the fifteen years before the First World War, this so-called "Ash Can" school rejected the false gentility, sentimentality and social sterility of the older pictorialists and society portraitists who flattered the rich and comfortable.

In 1913 a bombshell exploded in the American art world. New York City became the scene of the "Armory Show," an exhibition of some 1600 works of art that included examples of the latest achievements of Europe's avant-garde—Postimpressionists, cubists, surrealists and futurists. The show attracted a large attendance and great public interest, and it generated heated controversy. But it did not immediately redirect American art. The traditionalists stood firm and conservative critics dismissed modern art as "unadulterated cheek."

In the 1920s the pace of American artistic activity cooled down after the fever-pitch of the pre-Armory days. Most American artists remained basically realists, despite considerable experimenting in abstract forms. Typically the decade produced Daniel Chester French's heroic statue of Lincoln, and placed it in its neo-classical setting in the Lincoln Memorial in Washington, D.C. Not until the 1950s did America become the center of an artistic vision—abstract expressionism—which became one of the central forces in contemporary art.

Between 1880 and 1930, American painting lacked originality but American architecture more than compensated for this failing. Like painting, architecture after the Civil War was at first imitative. Architects borrowed from the past and ground out pseudo-classical, Gothic, and Renaissance buildings which their patrons deemed "artistic," because they thought them appropriate monuments to their wealth and importance. Only rarely did an architect such as Henry H. Richardson take an old style— the Romanesque—and infuse it with new life through powerful simplicity and apt design.

In the generation after Richardson, modern American architecture was born. The traditionalists still dominated, designing structures in which there was little relationship between form and function, whose façades were more important than the way they worked. Greek and Roman temples went up in the guise of customs houses and music halls, and twenty-five story office buildings sported gargoyles, flying buttresses and Corinthian columns somewhere between the eighteenth and twenty-first floors.

But new forces redirected American architecture. Technology revolutionized building and enabled man to construct tall buildings made of steel and concrete, utilizing elevators. The skyscraper posed new artistic challenges and the technology that made them possible gave architects new materials with which to build. Not until after the Second World War did a new international architectural style become the norm in America's large cities, but already two generations earlier a group of first-rate architectural innovators were pointing the way. At their center was Louis H. Sullivan and his pupil, Frank Lloyd Wright. In 1901 Wright told a Hull House audience in Chicago what he thought was wrong, namely, everything:

> Chicago in its ugliness today becomes as true an expression of the *life* lived here as is any center on earth where men come together closely to live it out or fight it out. . . . We must walk blindfolded through the streets of this, or any great modern American city, to fail to see that all this magnificent resource of machine-power and superior material has brought to us, so far, is degradation.

Sullivan and Wright devoted their careers to designing buildings that authentically rendered in steel, concrete, and glass a modern architectural vision. What is the essence of an office building, Sullivan once asked? ". . . At once we answer, it is lofty. . . . It must be tall, every inch of it tall . . . It must be every inch a proud, soaring thing, rising in sheer exultation that from bottom to top it is a unit without a single dissenting line." This meant that a building's form must be adapted to its function and must express that function. "All things in nature have a shape," he proclaimed, "that tells us what they are. . . . Unfailingly in nature these shapes express the inner life . . . of the animal, tree, bird, fish, that they present to us." Buildings must do no less. Sullivan and Wright made good on their promise. Each commission they accepted proved a fresh problem to be solved according to the doctrine that form follows function. And they began designing structures that could be found nowhere else and which seemed a natural part of the landscape or cityscape.

In time, Sullivan and Wright won recognition as America's greatest architects but not in the decades between 1890–1930. Preferring the "imperial architecture" of traditional styles that supposedly made buildings impressive, the major patrons entrusted few commissions to Sullivan or Wright. Compare, for example, the Chicago *Tribune* skyscraper (1923–1925), with its Gothic towers, by Raymond H. Hood and John Mead Howells with the daring simplicity and beauty of Frank Lloyd

Wright's design for the Press Building in San Francisco, a design that never came to life. Or compare the New York mansion Richard M. Hunt designed for William K. Vanderbilt with the bold but simple beauty of Sullivan and Wright's James M. Charnley House, or Wright's F. C. Robie House. Sullivan, who died destitute, once bitterly observed: ". . . the unhappy, irrational, heedless, pessimistic, unlovely, distracted and decadent structures which make up the bulk of our contemporaneous architecture point with infallible accuracy to qualities in the heart and soul of the American people."

The new music, the new literature, and the new American architecture, all gave expression to the feelings and dreams of sensitive and imaginative artists growing up in modern America. Most Americans passed them by, preferring the familiar and the nostalgic. The artists of early twentieth-century America, however, were creating a modern High Culture in the United States out of their alienation from the prevailing values and the central tendencies of a nation whose folk heroes were successful businessmen like Henry Ford, and popular politicians like Warren Harding and Calvin Coolidge.

Document: The New Morality
The Literary Digest, *"Is the Younger Generation in Peril?"*

In the 1920s a youth culture began to emerge whose life-styles conflicted with those of an older generation brought up according to the puritanical standard of Victorian morality. Most members of the younger generation did not rebel, but the minority that flouted convention—mostly among the urban upper middle classes—attracted a great deal of attention from scandalized traditionalists. "Flaming Youth" or the Flapper Generation, searched for a new code of personal values because they could no longer believe in the values of their parents. After a century of peace and material progress, the world had plunged into the

Source: "Is the Younger Generation in Peril?," *The Literary Digest*, Vol. LXIX (May 14, 1921), pp. 9–12, 58, 61, 63–64, 66–67, 69–70, 72, 73.

First World War, brutally shattering optimism and complacency, as had the Progressive generation's discovery of social injustice a decade earlier. The war made a mockery of faith in human progress: it proved to be a tragic, bloody struggle that sacrificed the flower of a whole generation of European youth on the altar of nationalism, greed, and power politics. The outcome was the more unsettling because all sides, the British, the French, the Germans, but especially the Americans, cloaked their participation and justified the immense human sacrifice by professing to be fighting for noble ideals. In the United States, the war also marked the end of the Progressive quest for social justice and the restoration of conservative business interests to nearly undisputed leadership.

As a result of the failure of domestic reform and a crusade overseas that in retrospect appeared to serve no humane, rational purpose, a segment of the younger generation sought joy in living through private experience, through exploration of the self, hedonistic experimentation, and cultivation of the arts. This search for heightened personal experience resulted in manners and mores that shocked many Americans and generated public concern and controversy, reflected in the following selections from The Literary Digest, *a widely read news magazine in the 1920s.*

Is "the old-fashioned girl," with all that she stands for in sweetness, modesty, and innocence, in danger of becoming extinct? Or was she really no better nor worse than the "up-to-date" girl—who, in turn, will become "the old-fashioned girl" to a later generation? Is it even possible, as a small but impressive minority would have us believe, that the girl of to-day has certain new virtues of "frankness, sincerity, seriousness of purpose," lives on "a higher level of morality," and is on the whole "more clean-minded and clean-lived" than her predecessors?

From Pope Benedict's pronouncement against "the present immodesty and extravagance in women's dress," to the widely copied protests of a Brown University student-editor against girls who wear too few clothes and require too much "petting," the press of the world in general, and of America in particular, is having much to say about "the present relaxation of morals and manners among young men and women." College presidents, famous divines, prominent novelists, and grave professors of sociology have joined the controversy. Thus, Franklin H. Giddings, author and Professor of Sociology at Columbia University, emits a counterblast to the many indictments of present conditions in the perhaps extreme pronouncement that "whether. girls wear their skirts long or short makes as much difference as whether a man parts his hair in the middle or on the side." He concludes that "our moral tone is no lower than it was in the days of our mothers or our grandmothers, or even in the days of our great-grandmothers." The Professor does not question, however, the generally exprest opinion that the young people of to-day live in a more "free-and-easy" social atmosphere than surrounded their mothers. "We can't have anything without having too much of it," said William James, and Alexander Black, the novelist, quotes his philosophy in admitting that, in specific times and places, we may be having "too much" of this relaxation. The point of greatest disagreement comes up with the question of morality in general. "Do modern modes in dressing, dancing, and social intercourse," as an Eastern college paper phrases the question, "really mean that the present generation is less moral than the preceding one?" The answers, as given by college and school authorities, religious editors, the editors of student magazines, and the general press seem to be fairly evenly divided between attack and defense. It has been called the most two-sided question of the hour.

In the midst of the discussion, pro and con, a good deal is being done to check the tendency toward laxity among boys and girls of high-school age, where, in the belief of many observers, the greatest danger, or the only real danger, lies. We are reminded that supervision is always necessary here, and even so convinced a champion of modern ideas in manners and morals as the New York *Morning Telegraph* is stirred to protests by a report from Chicago that co-educational institutions in Illinois will not be responsible for the moral conduct of their girls. *The Telegraph* objects:

Girls, when away from home, should not be thrown upon their own resources at an age when their judgment is unripe and their ability to steer their own course at best undeveloped. We are further informed that hereafter college dances will be unchaperoned and that self-reliance will be preached instead. This may make it easy on the deans of women, but it also may result disastrously in particular cases. Parents will hesitate before committing their daughters to institutions which, in striving to be up to date, have overlooked one of the most obvious truths in nature.

Aside from the usual protective measures, however, a number of organizations are unusually active on the ground that there is an unusual amount of immodest dressing and conduct. The Y. W. C. A. is conducting a national campaign among high-school girls. . . . [It] is also, through its press department, supplying newspapers with material which appears under such suggestive head-lines as "Working Girls Responsive to Modesty Appeal"; "High Heels Losing Ground Even in France"; and "It Isn't What the Girl Does; It's Just the Way She Does It." Photographs, pointing morals in dress and conduct, are also supplied. . . .

. . . The Woman's Auxiliary of the Episcopal Church has entered upon a nation-wide campaign, reports the New York *Times*, and it has "definite progress to report." It is conducting a series of meetings for girls throughout the country, to discuss the problem of "upholding standards." The Catholic Archbishop of the Ohio diocese has issued a warning against the "toddle" and "shimmy" and also against "bare female shoulders." A bill which has passed both the New York Assembly and Senate gives the Commissioner of Licenses in New York the right to act as a censor of dances. In a number of State legislatures, bills have been introduced aiming at regulation of women's dress, reports the New York *American:*

In Utah a statute providing fine and imprisonment for those who wear on the streets skirts higher than three inches above the ankle is pending. The Philadelphia "moral gown," with its seven and a half inches of "see level," as one visitor called it, would cease to be moral in Utah if this law goes through.

A bill is before the Virginia legislature which would raise the *décolletage*—front and back. It provides that no woman shall be permitted to wear a shirtwaist or evening gown displaying more than three inches of her throat. She must not have skirts higher than four inches above the ground or any garment of "diaphanous material."

In Ohio a bill has been drafted prescribing that no *décolleté* shall be more than two inches in depth and that no garment composed of any transparent material shall be sold, nor any "garment which unduly displays or accentuates the lines of the female figure."

"And no female over fourteen years of age," says this same measure, "shall wear a skirt which does not reach to that part of the foot known as the instep."

Similar legislation, differing only in the inches above the ground and the inches below the neck, has been offered in New Jersey, South Carolina, Kansas, Iowa, Pennsylvania, and a full dozen other States.

From the three bills actually cited it would seem that, were these to become laws, the dress with its four-inch-high skirt which would be moral in Virginia would be immodest in Utah, while both the Utah and Virginia skirts would be wicked enough in Ohio to make their wearers subject to fine or imprisonment. Undoubtedly, other State laws would add to this confusion, and therefore a standardization acceptable to all is something that might ultimately be welcomed by women.

In Philadelphia a Dress-Reform Committee of prominent citizens decided to attack the problem in a businesslike way, and settle from the mouths of the critics themselves, once and for all, just what is immodest dress. A questionnaire was sent to 1,160 clergymen of all denominations in and near Philadelphia. Replies were received from them all, but examination, we are told, revealed that the clergy "were absolutely at odds themselves. There was far from a unanimous verdict even on the preliminary query as to whether the modern extreme styles are harmful to the morals of the wearers and to masculine observers." The Dress Committee adopted the device of striking an average of the answers and building a dress upon these averages, after sub-

mitting specifications and sketches to the clergymen. The design
. . . was accepted by the majority, "altho there still remained two
fairly strong minority parties, one of which thought the dress
was not yet conservative enough, while the other thought it was
too conservative."

Denunciation and defense center more specially, however,
about modern dances and the conditions that surround the associations of boys and girls at these affairs. Conditions are
"appalling," declares one critic who may be expected to speak
with authority, a dean of women in a Midwestern college.
"There is nothing wrong with the girl of to-day," insists another
dean of women, also stationed at a Midwestern college, and
speaking on the basis of a wide acquaintance with practically
the same set of conditions. It is the perennial case of the "youngsters *versus* the oldsters," a Princeton College wit remarks, but
the line-up of opinion somewhat disarranges his idea, for many
"oldsters" are found championing the new and freer ways of the
present generation, while numerous uncompromising enemies
of the modern dance, abbreviated clothes, and "relaxed morals
and manners" are to be found among those whose years classify
them with the youngsters. The Digest, by way of gathering national sentiment on the whole question, lately addrest a circular
letter to the religious editors of the country, to the presidents of
colleges and universities, and to the editors of college papers,
asking for their opinions upon the charges of "lax standards"
which have been freely made throughout the country, and for
remedial suggestions, in case conditions seemed to demand
remedies. These replies have been correlated with material on the
same subject collected from newspapers and magazines in The
Digest office.

The comment, as received from religious editors, editors of
student papers, and college deans and presidents, shows a sur-
prizingly even division of opinion between those who believe
that conditions are unusually bad and those who believe that
they are not. The editors of college papers, themselves distinctly
to be classed with the youngsters, show a larger proportion of
"moral alarmists," as one of their number calls the reformist
element, than do the presidents and deans of colleges. In round
numbers, 55 college student-editors believe that conditions are

unusually bad as against 38 who believe that they are not. Of the college presidents and deans, the proportion stands 52 against 43. The religious press, as might have been expected, shows a larger ratio of condemnation. Fifty-three religious editors believe we are having something like an immorality wave, as against six who believe that we are not. Fifteen of the replies in this category are difficult to classify, unless the writers be placed with the defenders of modernity on the ground that they do not consider present conditions worse than usual. Allowance must be made in these replies for a considerable number of editors of denominations which oppose dancing in any form. In forty-two of the colleges whose presidents replied, dancing is prohibited. Of the total number of replies received, counting out those religious editors who condemn dancing *per se*, without expressing any opinion as to the present conditions, counting out also the college professors who reply merely that dancing is prohibited in their institutions, the writers divide on the question in the order of 130 to 102, the first figure representing those who believe that we are in the midst of a dangerous moral decline, especially as it affects the younger generation. Including all the opponents of dancing, the figures would stand 202 to 102. . . .

Dividing the replies roughly into those which attack and those which defend modern manners and morals, the student-editors of the country, most of them young men, are found to furnish quite as severe an indictment as is presented by their elders. The defense, while not numerically so well represented, is strongly presented by student-editors chiefly representing the larger colleges. The attack, which will be presented first, comes almost entirely from the smaller institutions. This, of course, raises the old question whether the big or the little college has the more brains and character, which is another story. The Hobart College *Herald* (Geneva, N. Y.) sums up the arguments of many of the attackers in this thoughtful fashion:

> The outstanding objection to the modern dance is that it is immodest and lacking in grace. It is not based on the natural and harmless instinct for rhythm, but on a craving for abnormal excitement.

And what is it leading to? The dance in its process of its degradation has passed from slight impropriety to indecency, and now threatens to become brazenly shameless. From graceful coordination of movement it has become a syncopated embrace.

Even the most callous devotee of modern dancing can not think with unconcern of the danger involved in any further excess. For American morals have undoubtedly degenerated with the dance.

It can not be denied that many who indulge in modern dancing do not realize the nature of the incentive which leads them to do so. They like to dance; it becomes a habit, a fascinating obsession. Continual debauches of highly emotional character weaken the moral fiber. When a newer and more daring dance is introduced it is immediately accepted without question.

Were this thoughtless immodesty restricted to the ballroom the danger would be great enough, but it is unconsciously carried into every-day life. Truly, then, it is imperative that a remedy be sought to arrest the development of the modern dance before this perilous state gets beyond control.

In spite of the gallant remark of the Michigan Agricultural College *Holcad*, in an editorial entitled "Haven't We Gone a Bit too Far?" that "the men are just as much to blame as the girls," a great many student-editors, mostly, as one of them points out, men, avail themselves of the Adamic tradition to point an accusing finger. From the New York University *News* we quote the following:

Overlooking the physiological aspects of women's clothing, there is a strong moral aspect to this laxity of dress. When every dancing step discloses the entire contour of the dancer, it is small wonder that moralists are becoming alarmed. The materials, also, from which women's evening dresses are made are generally of transparent cobweb. There is a minimum of clothes and a maximum of cosmetics, head-decorations, fans, and jewelry. It is, indeed, an alarming situation when our twentieth-century débutante comes out arrayed like a South Sea Island savage. . . .

The University of Maryland *Review* finds some of the dances "mere animal exhibitions of agility and feeling. There is nothing of grace in them, and such dances serve as an excuse for actions that would be severely censored anywhere but on the modern dance floor." The Mercer University *Cluster* considers that "the young people who take part in them can not fail to lose their fine sense of decency and propriety. No boy who has high ideals would allow his sister to take part where such dances are tolerated." *The Round Up*, of the New Mexico College of Agriculture and Mechanic Arts, believes that dancing such as is being done there "will lead to certain degeneration of decent society, and it is our understanding that this part of the country is no worse than any other." The writer objects further:

> To glide gracefully over a floor, keeping time to the rhythm and harmony of music, is a pleasant recreation and is pleasing to witness, but to jig and hop around like a chicken on a red-hot stove, at the same time shaking the body until it quivers like a disturbed glass of jell-o, is not only tremendously suggestive but is an offense against common decency that would not be permitted in a semirespectable road-house.

The University of Illinois *Siren* explains for these objectors: ". . . if bow legs and thick ankles won't curb the present patent indecency in women's dress, morality surely hasn't any chance."

This same publication, however, furnishes a vivid arraignment of the modern dance, in the comments of a musician who played for college dances. The musician decided, one day, that he would play for no more such dances, and he gives his reason in these words:

> The girls—some of them, not all of them, of course—dance by me with their eyes closed, their cheeks inflamed, a little line of passion across their brows. They cling to their partners; they cling and clutch. They are like Madonnas, some of them, and yet they dance . . . that way. The men who use us for an audience are not capable—quite—of being terrible. They are exhibitors, rather. They show us the closed eyes and dusky-red cheeks of their partners—they wink at us, they turn their eyes heavenward, as if to say, "You birds will know me, I wager, when next you see me. See what a state this girl is in. Hasn't she fallen for me, tho? Look at her; look at her!"—then they toddle out of sight. . . .

. . . The Dartmouth *Jack-o'-Lantern* attacks the subject in this frivolous manner, somewhat characteristic of the more sophisticated student papers:

> We're a dizzy people. The shimmy proves that, without the ghost of a need for further proof. We—any of us—will travel for miles on a black night through mud and rain, we will endure any discomfort, eventually to arrive at a place where the shimmy is being shaken. Young girls, pretty girls, vivacious girls trust themselves to come safely through the identical experiences many of their wartime sweethearts were enduring in France. They will shimmy for hours, indefinitely, undergoing the pangs of hunger and increasing bodily fatigue. The mental side probably is not very much taxed. The effect seems merely to be that next night and thereafter they are ready to shimmy wherever the shimmy is being vibrated. All this doesn't prove anything, except that we're a dizzy lot!

The Cornell *Widow*, known in the periodical world as one of the cleverest and best-edited of student publications, presents this rimed review of the changes that dancing has undergone:

> Times have waxed and waned a lot, as old-timers can recall, and the dancing now is not what it used to be at all; only awkward rubes and hicks execute the bows and kicks that were clever parlor tricks when our *paters* threw a ball. Our progenitors took pleasure in a slow and solemn way; they would tread a stately measure that was anything but gay, and the orchestra would render sentimental stuff and tender which the folks of either gender wouldn't listen to to-day. With a flock of flutes and cellos, plus a harp and silver horn, these accomplished music fellows would play on till early morn; they could keep "Blue Danube" flowing without letting up or slowing, till the bantams started crowing and they'd leave to hoe the corn. . . .

And as for the maids of yesterday and of to-day, says *The Widow*:

> They used to wrap their hair in knobs fantastic, high, and queer; but now they cut it short in bobs or curl it round their ears. The skirts they wore would scrape the street, and catch the dust and germs; they're now so far above their feet, they're not on speaking terms. The things they do and wear to-day, and

never bat an eye, would make their fogy forebears gray, they'd curl right up and die. . . .

(The "Flapper Problem" in the Newspapers)

The same general moral, that the greatest danger is to be found among girls of high-school age, is pointed by a series of widely advertised full-page articles in the Boston *Sunday Advertiser.* "The girl of fourteen is the problem of to-day," we are told, in large, black-faced letters, in the introduction to one of the pages of exposure and criticism. Among the "modern conditions" assigned as causes of trouble are:

"1. Auto 'pickups.'
"2. Modern dances and commercialized dance halls.
"3. Modern fashions.
"4. The pocket-flask habit, an outgrowth of prohibition.
"5. The occasional unclean movie.

"But the first blame is being placed on the mother—the child-girl's first guardian." . . .

Perhaps half of the several hundred recommendations received are summed up in a letter from President Gaines, of Agnes Scott College, Decatur, Ga. He suggests as remedies.

> First, the influence of the home. I am informed that in many places parents themselves indulge in modern dances. What can be expected of their daughters but to follow their example? I am also informed that frequently mothers approve of the way in which their daughters dress. Can we not secure the cooperation and influence of the home in correcting these deplorable evils?
>
> My second suggestion is to secure the influence of the press.
>
> My third suggestion is that the entire influence of religion shall be exerted against these great evils. I suggest that all church papers, the influence of the pulpits of all the churches, should be brought to bear against these evils.
>
> My fourth suggestion is to enlist the colleges. In the colleges of the country are the future leaders. If they can be enlisted even while they are in college they may be able to begin

a crusade against these evils which will be most effective. Especially should this be true of the colleges for women.

These four great centers of influence could do much toward creating a healthy public sentiment which would counteract the evils of which you speak—namely, the home, the press, the church, and the college.

The college press, by and large, consider it a hopeful sign that the movement for reform should come, as is the case in so many colleges, from the students themselves. The immediate methods may vary somewhat, but in scores of institutions, the student-editors testify, various student governing associations have been able to do away with suggestive dancing and clothing. The Oberlin College *Review* states that the objectionable dances have been banned by the influence of the recreational director and some of the students. The daily *Nebraskan* says that they have not been bothered much by "the Eastern dances," but does admit that "the knee-length dresses of the modern girl have cast modesty from the dictionary," and says that recently some of the girls in the upper classes, "who are by no means the prudes at this school," at a large mass-meeting "passed resolutions to the effect that an era of simple dress for co-eds should be launched at Nebraska University," and advises:

> If our country is to return to normalcy again in regard to dress, we must not look on with a critic's eye and take on the guise of reformers, but we must wear sensible clothes ourselves. If we start this as the "fad" of the day, it will not be long until everybody is wearing simple garments because it is "being done." . . .

The Smith College *Monthly* writes that Smith College students have taken a decided stand in favor of dress reform and are conducting a vigorous campaign against immodest clothing. In an editorial in that paper an attempt is made to explain the "petting" youngsters in a way both kindly and keen:

> So long as the older generation "views with alarm," so long will the younger generation glory in its naughtiness and invent prodigious reasons.
>
> The real reason is, I believe, simply this: young people are

forced by the exigencies, customs, and inventions of modern life—such as newspapers, magazines, "movies," telephones, and facilitated modes of travel—to be cognizant at an early age of the world about them. Formerly, the family was a child's world till he left it for the larger one of school or business; nowadays, he comes in contact with persons, facts, and problems not at all connected with family affairs almost as soon as he can read and can run about by himself. He has to make up his mind for himself by himself; and he early learns the value of experiment.

Young men and women discover and face the idea of love by themselves; they experiment in that as in other things—not reckless, as is commonly supposed, but cautious.

As for remedy—well, gone long ago are the days when an evil might be checked by crying "Wicked!" Passing now is the detracting influence of "Danger!" and coming soon, I hope, the days when the only warning necessary will be "Foolish!" The "wild young people of to-day" are not fools, and do not want to be considered so. They will change their ways as soon as they have proved to themselves that their ways are—not wrong, not dangerous, but—unnecessary.

("There Is Nothing Wrong with the Girl of To-day")

A thoroughgoing optimist appears, ready to try conclusions with practically every real pessimist on the girl question. "There is nothing wrong with the girl of to-day," asserts the Dean of Women of Northwestern University, and she finds plenty of authorities, with excellent opportunities for observation, who agree with her. Several critics, not satisfied with denying the allegation that we are experiencing "an immorality wave," declare that, in spite of much talk and certain appearances, the younger generation of to-day is actually better, "more clean-minded and clean-lived," than its predecessors. Such is the view of President Sills, of Bowdoin College, Brunswick, Maine, who writes:

Ever since the time of Horace at least each generation has thought the succeeding generation worse than anything that has gone before, in manners and morals, and in criticising the youth of the present day we ought, I think, to keep this in mind. It is my opinion that the influence, to quote from your letter, "exercised upon our young people by some of the new dances and the costumes worn by those attending them" is much more patent on the side of manners than on the side of morals. The undergraduate of the present day is, I am sure, as good as any of his predecessors, probably more clean-minded and clean-lived. If he can be taught to avoid what is vulgar and cheap, and also be made to see that some of the new dances are very silly, some good might result.

"There has been some gain for women in the newer modes of dress which give them greater freedom of action and tend to better health," President Wilbur, of Stanford University, points out. "The oncoming generation will have grown accustomed to the exposure of limbs and neck and will not react as does the passing generation." President Smith, of Washington and Lee University, Lexington, Va., after admitting that abuses of the freer modern manners may have occurred, presents the following considerations which, he says, "may serve to comfort those inclined to pessimism":

1. Ignorant innocence is not true purity nor is prudery true modesty. Freedom of intercourse and constant association of boys and girls does not increase but rather diminishes sex-consciousness and immorality. And I have long since come to the conclusion that the suggestiveness of any mode of dress disappears entirely as soon as we become thoroughly accustomed to it. To the orthodox Persian a woman's uncovered face is shamelessly indecent and suggestive.

2. I have spent a lifetime in constant association with young people, and I am fully convinced that, surprizing as it may seem, in view of present social laxity, the level of sexual morality is higher to-day than formerly in those localities with which I am familiar.

3. The present dancing mania and general social laxity is probably a passing 'craze,' due to exceptional present conditions, which is already awakening universal condemnation, and like most epidemics will prove temporary and self-limited. . . .

(College Editors in Defense of the Modern Girl)
    If some college student-editors have taken the lead in speaking harshly to and about the short-skirted, free-acting, free-

talking girl of to-day, others of the youthful brotherhood present defenses equally pungent and pointed. Thus *The Tartan*, the newspaper of the Carnegie Institute of Technology at Pittsburgh, rises up to defend the girl of to-day:

> Just at present it seems to be the custom for every college paper to take a slam at the girls. It would appear that the younger generation is going to rack and ruin unless a halt is called in the terrible downward trend of the fashions. No ray of hope lightens the gloom which is, in the minds of most of our contemporaries, descending upon our colleges in the form of an assurance that all the young women are going from bad to worse. They not only wear clothes which would shock the most sophisticated of a few years back, but they dance—well, they dance simply awful.
>
> Of course girls are wearing shorter skirts than they have ever worn before. But what wholesome, clean-minded men would not rather see a woman in a sane, short skirt, with plenty of freedom to move as nature intended she should, than in one of the "sheath" creations which emphasized her every contour while hobbling her movements almost beyond endurance, sweeping the ground in an attempt to trip her at every step. And yet we are supposed to have become so much more immodest with the innovation of the sensible short skirt.
>
> Yet the gentler sex must be reformed before it is too late, say our virtuous youth. We have attended several dances during the last week, and no shocking décolletées were noticed except possibly on matrons who should have known better. The débutantes were even conservative in their manner of covering the throat. . . .

The Columbia *Spectator*, of Columbia University, New York, speaks for the metropolitan college:

> The day is past when trusting parents confine their offspring to convents and monasteries, bringing them forth in due season, mature, worldly innocent, unsophisticated, and still none the less educated. Living as the college student of to-day does, in the heart of New York, Chicago, Boston, or San Francisco, in direct touch with city life—in fact, a part and parcel of it—that the scholar should conduct himself any differently from those about him is impossible. . . .

The *Spectator*'s colleague, the Columbia *Jester,* with the liberty traditionally permitted to cap and bells, declares that it stands—

> Unequivocally and irrevocably for the continuance of "petting" as a national institution, in order to guarantee sufficient contributions to bring out one magazine a month. We fail to take a more serious view of the situation, because we feel that the situation exists largely in the minds of bloodthirsty reformers and copy-by-the-inch hounds. They always have and they always will—which refers to fretting as well as petting. . . .

Two of the largest and best-known women's colleges in the East, Wellesley and Bryn Mawr, reply that their own dances have given them little concern, since, in the words of Wellesley's director of publicity, "objectionable and extreme dances are so comparatively rare."

(Journalists and Authors Who See No "Moral Decline")
"Salvation this new generation doubtless needs—like every other. But it has its virtues and they are large ones, we are convinced—candor, frankness, sincerity, seriousness of purpose, for a few items." So an editorial writer in the New York *Tribune* takes issue with the present "prophets of evil" in the social world. . . .

. . . Gertrude Atherton, the novelist, writing in *The Forum,* is similarly indignant with traducers of the new social freedom. "Take it all in all, it seems to me that if the United States of America is conquered by internal or external enemies," she writes, "it will not be from bad morals but smug stupidity." An editorial writer in *The Nation* also has this fear that we will be injured, not by immorality growing out of relaxed manners, but rather by the reaction that is likely to follow our present little taste of frankness and naturalness in the social relationships. Taking a historical view, he says:

> The rank and file of the virtues have not greatly changed, so far as we can see, during the comparatively few years in the life of the race over which the memory of man runs. All that appears is a certain pendulum swing from one repression or

indulgence to another, reaction setting in whenever the virtues or vices of an age begin to bore it. Instead of repining that the present generation is unmitigably naughty, we observe that drunkenness throughout the world is pretty certainly on the decline and that the improving status of women bids fair to make them able to look out for themselves—a condition which we candidly prefer to all the chivalry that ever was invented. What worries us is not the age itself but the fear that its hilarities portend a reaction in the direction of insipid, smug propriety.

Suggestions for Further Reading

General

Robert S. and Helen M. Lynd, *Middletown: A Study in Contemporary American Culture* (1929)*; Blake McKelvey, *The Emergence of Metropolitan America, 1915–1966* (1968); Roy Lubove, *Community Planning in the 1920's* (1963)*.

Men, Women and Children

Arthur W. Calhoun, *A Social History of the American Family, From the Civil War* (1919)*; Sidney Ditzion, *Marriage, Morals, and Sex in America* (1953); Paul H. Jacobson, *American Marriage and Divorce* (1959).

The New Woman

Aileen S. Kraditor, *The Ideas of the Woman Suffrage Movement, 1890–1920* (1965); Anne Firor Scott, "The 'New Woman' in the New South," *South Atlantic Quarterly*, vol. 61 (1962), pp. 473–483; Anne Firor Scott, "After Suffrage: Southern Women in the Twenties," *South Atlantic Quarterly*, vol. 62 (1963), pp. 92–106; Carl N. Degler, "Revolution Without Ideology: The Changing Place of Women in America," in Robert Jay Lifton (ed.), *The Woman in America* (1967)*.

The Expansion of Education

R. Freeman Butts and Lawrence A. Cremin, *A History of Education in American Culture* (1953); Merle Curti, *Social*

Ideas of American Educators (1935); Lawrence A. Cremin, *The Transformation of the School: Progressivism in American Education, 1876–1957* (1961)*.

The Emergence of the University

Richard Hofstadter and C. DeWitt Hardy, *The Development and Scope of Higher Education in the United States* (1952); Laurence R. Veysey, *The Emergence of the American University* (1965); Richard Hofstadter and Walter P. Metzger, *The Development of Academic Freedom in the United States* (1955)*.

Entertainment for the Masses

Albert McLean, *American Vaudeville as Ritual* (1965); Lewis Jacobs, *The Rise of the American Film* (1939)*; L. C. Rosten, *Hollywood* (1941); Arthur Knight, *The Liveliest Art* (1957)*; G. N. Fenin and William Everson, *The Western* (1962); Kelton Lahue, *Continued Next Week: A History of the Movie Serial* (1964); Paul Schubert, *The Electric Word: The Rise of the Radio* (1928); Eric Barnouw, *A History of Broadcasting in the United States* (2 vols., 1965–1968); Russel B. Nye, *The Unembarrassed Muse: The Popular Arts in America* (1970); Foster Rhea Dulles, *A History of Recreation: America Learns to Play* (1965)*.

Culture and Mass Society

Alfred Kazin, *On Native Grounds* (1942)*; Maxwell D. Geismar, *The Last of the Provincials: The American Novel, 1915–1925* (1947)*; Maxwell Geismar, *Writers in Crisis: The American Novel, 1925–1940* (1942)*; Frederick J. Hoffman, *The Twenties: American Writing in the Postwar Decade* (1955); Roderick Nash, *The Nervous Generation: American Thought, 1917–1930* (1970); Carolyn F. Ware, *Greenwich Village 1920–1930* (1935)*; Ernest Hemingway, *A Movable Feast: . . . Life in Paris in the Twenties* (1964); Arthur Mizener, *The Far Side of Paradise: A Biography of F. Scott Fitzgerald* (1951)*; Mark Schorer, *Sinclair Lewis* (1961)*; Edmund Wilson, *The American Earthquake* (1958); Matthew Josephson, *Life Among the Surrealists* (1962); Malcolm Cowley, *Exile's*

Return: A Literary Odyssey of the 1920's (1934)*; Arthur and Barbara Gelb, *O'Neill* (1962)*.

Oliver P. Larkin, *Art and Life in America* (1960); John Burchard and Albert Bush-Brown, *The Architecture of America* (rev. edition, 1966)*; Irving Sabolsky, *American Music* (1969)*; Sigmund Spaeth, *A History of Popular Music in America* (1948); Isaac Goldberg, *Tin Pan Alley* (1930); Roland Gelatt, *The Fabulous Phonograph* (1955); Barry Ulanov, *A History of Jazz in America* (1952); Gunther Schuller, *Early Jazz* (1968).

Chapter Three

The Anxieties of Mass Society, 1900-1930

The shift from a rural society of individual entrepreneurs to an urban, mass society of workers, managers, and bureaucrats and the new life styles of mass society bewildered and frightened millions of Americans. They seemed powerless to check or control the unsettling forces of change which swirled around them. Rapid social change reawakened old anxieties and stirred new ones. The self-confidence that fueled the progressives' earnest though ineffective attempts to achieve stability and social justice gave way to repressive apprehensions in the second and third decades of the twentieth century.

For those holding fast to the vision of an older America, the enemy lurked everywhere. The cities, they thought, were cancerous growths, spawning radicals, foreigners, and the sexually liberated Bohemians. In these cesspools of all that was "un-American," people danced to jazz music, raucous and lascivious new tunes created by black musicians in New Orleans. "Does Jazz put the Sin in Syncopation?" asked *The Ladies Home Journal* suggestively. Prominent clergymen rushed to denounce jazz as "a sensual teasing of the string of physical passion." Sinful or not, the people of urban America loved the new sounds.

Many traditionalists thought the disease of modernism so virulent and so widespread that only strong measures could save the country. The crusade to restore the old morality took many

111

forms. Citizens banded together in mobs and private associations, such as the Ku Klux Klan, to intimidate and punish those regarded as dangerous, while government lent its powerful helping hand. Trampling on the civil liberties of radicals and aliens, especially after the country entered the First World War, and during the Red Scare of 1919, the government restricted free speech and imprisoned dissenters. A new federal agency— the forerunner of the Federal Bureau of Investigation (FBI)— emerged in the struggle for internal security through repression. Radical aliens became subject to deportation in 1919 and mass roundups clamped thousands of unoffending people in jail.

The temptation to blame Europe as the source of all trouble finally triumphed over America's traditional hospitality to newcomers, its confidence in its capacity to absorb people from Europe's many cultures. Oriental immigration had already been cut off as unassimilable, and in 1921 the open doors that had welcomed the Old World's "tried, poor and helpless" shut firmly, allowing only a trickle to enter. Immigration restriction, however, could not and did not discipline those already here, the millions whose life-styles clashed with 100 percent WASP Americanism.

After over a century of campaigning, antiliquor forces, capitalizing on the patriotic and repressive mood of wartime America, finally succeeded in prohibiting the manufacture and sale of alcoholic beverages, and for over a decade the United States remained technically dry. Much of the prohibitionist leadership came from the Protestant churches which were simultaneously fighting a rearguard action against the inroads made by secularism and science at the expense of religious authority. The churches counterattacked with dramatic efforts to restore "the old-time religion" and to prevent the public schools from instructing youngsters in scientific explanations of the earth's formation.

But repression could not hold back the uncertain future. For good or for ill, America had become an urban, pluralistic society. Its people worshipped in different faiths, came from different parts of the world, and clung to many badges of cultural identity imported from the Old World. Americans still quaffed illegal booze, hotly pursuing the creature comforts devised by advanced technology. Yet repression was not a total failure. It gave those frightened by mass society the illusion that they could block change without fundamentally altering the directions of American development. And poisonous repression produced its own antidote. Under the threat of attack, Americans gained a clearer understanding of the meaning of individual liberty, the strengths of a pluralist society, and the liberating possibilities and worth of the new modes of life. The immigrants, the "wets," the civil libertarians, the modernist clergy, all resisted fear and hate and ignorance. Their lost or drawn battles of the 1920s would be fought again another day, and more successfully.

The Drive for Internal Security

During most of their history, Americans had maintained confidence in the durability of their way of life. Only rarely had hysteria gripped the country, bringing with it repression of unpopular elements, such as the Federalist drive against the Jeffersonian Republicans in the late 1790s, or Lincoln's suppression of militant opposition elements in the North during the Civil War. Three thousand miles of ocean secured the United States from foreign attack, and a tradition of settling differences among themselves peacefully seemed sufficient guarantee for the country's internal security.

In the twentieth century, however, many Americans lost their nerve. The appearance of radical revolutionary organizations, such as the anarchists, socialists, the Industrial Workers of the World, and after 1917 the communists, shook their belief in mutual trust. At the same time, America's involvement in the First World War dramatized the end of a century of isolation. For all the idealism with which Wilson had justified American participation, the overriding concern was fear of a German victory which would upset the world balance of power and endanger American interests. Postwar disillusionment, especially the failure to establish effective peacekeeping machinery in the League of Nations, betrayed Wilson's promise of a war to end all wars. None could foresee precisely how the Versailles settlement of 1919 sowed the seeds for the later rise of Adolph Hitler and the Second World War, but none could ignore the revolutionary crisis provoked by the war—especially not after the overthrow of the Czar in Russia and his replacement, first by a short-lived democratic regime, but then by communist dictatorship. The emergence of Red Russia encouraged revolutionaries elsewhere, raising their hopes that the Red Flag would someday fly elsewhere too. In this fearful atmosphere the American majority became prey to hysteria. John Lord O'Brian who worked in the Department of Justice during the First World War reported that people thought "a phantom ship sailed into our harbors with gold from the Bolsheviki with which to corrupt the country; . . . [German] submarine captains landed on our coast, went to the theater and spread influenza germs; a new species of pigeon, thought to be German, was shot in Michigan. . . ."

American reaction to foreign and domestic radicalism exceeded all sensible views of the challenge it posed. The repression visited upon dissenters originated in an irrational feeling of insecurity springing from gnawing doubts about the stability and justness of the social order. Frustrated by intractable problems of adjusting to mass society, threatened by fears they had in part concocted themselves, committed wholly in a World War they wished to avoid, Americans sought to impose conformity on the weak minority of nonconformists who made attractive scapegoats.

No group was more vulnerable than the Industrial Workers of the World founded in 1905. The "Wobblies," or I.W.W., inhabited the far left wing of organized American labor. Preaching revolution, not reform, as the only hope for working people, the Wobblies had strong following in the mining, lumber, and migratory labor camps in the West. Several dramatic strikes gained for them a reputation (not wholly deserved) for violence, but their revolutionary ideology, their attack on organized religion, and their use of the red flag frightened people. Never before had the downtrodden developed an organization as visible and as potentially dangerous as the Wobblies. Worst of all, they scoffed at the view that America was the Promised Land. "You ask me why the I.W.W. is not patriotic to the United States," explained one. "If you were a bum without a blanket . . . if your job never kept you long enough in a place to qualify you to vote; if you slept in a lousy, sour bunk-house and ate food just as rotten as they could give you and get away with; if deputy sheriffs shot your cooking cans full of holes and spilled your grub on the ground . . . if every person who represents law and order and the nation beat you up, railroaded you to jail, and the good Christian people cheered and told them to go to it, how in hell do you expect a man to be patriotic?"

Repudiated by the AFL and the Socialist Party, the I.W.W. was too radical to attract the American masses, but businessmen, especially in the West, wanted to take no chances. Under their prodding, the state and federal governments began systematically to harass the Wobblies, seeking to drive them out of existence. "Hanging is too good for them and they would be much better dead," suggested the *San Diego Tribune* as early as 1912. "Now I would execute these anarchists if I could, for they are absolutely useless in the human economy, and then I would deport them," suggested a congressman with a talent for over-kill, "so that the soil of our country might not be polluted by their presence even after the breath had gone out of their bodies." Since some Wobbly leaders were aliens, and Congress in 1903 for the first time had made radical beliefs grounds for deportation, the government used immigration laws to sanction mass roundups.

The repression of the war years did not end after the Armistice of November 1918. The postwar mania for internal security became an extension of the wartime spirit of intolerance, and the social dislocations accompanying demobilization intensified it. A fear of postwar mass unemployment set in as millions of soldiers returned home to look for jobs. Production levels held relatively firm, but the cost of living skyrocketed (increasing 20 percent between 1918 and 1920). This hurt Americans on salaries and fixed incomes, and contributed to the uneasiness which soon degenerated into hysteria.

Inflation produced a rash of strikes and stoppages which in 1919 involved four million workers. First the clothing workers, then the textile workers went out, demanding and winning

shorter hours and substantial pay boosts. Next, the AFL decided
to organize the virtually nonunionized steel industry. Half of
these men worked from 11 to 14 hours a day for poor pay, so
the union had little trouble signing up 100,000 recruits. But the
companies, led by U. S. Steel, fought back. Company president
Judge Elbert H. Gray would not negotiate, and the combination
of injunctions, firing of union organizers, and armed protection
for thousands of strike breakers, caused the AFL organizing
campaign to wither.

The company also spent heavily on propaganda to get
across its side of the argument, and to discredit the strikers as
"Bolsheviks." The coal fields witnessed labor unrest, too. The
United Mine Workers (UMW), now led by the aggressive John
L. Lewis, declared the wartime no-strike agreements dead. But
Washington sustained their validity until 1920 and imposed the
Lever Act to brand the strike illegal. Lewis, admitting that "we
cannot fight the government," ordered his men back to the
mines. Most of them continued to stay out, however, and as a
result won pay increases from an arbitration board.

Another strike, though it involved few men, held the public's attention and fed its fears. Boston policemen, earning inade-
quate salaries, obtained an AFL charter in 1919. The Police
Commissioner would not negotiate, and instead fired nineteen
of the union leaders. The policemen walked out in September.
Volunteer constables could not control the situation. When loot-
ing broke out the National Guard had to be called in. The striking
police officers were fired, and new men took their jobs. Governor Calvin Coolidge had done little to avert the crisis and strike,
but he gained national acclaim by rejecting Samuel Gompers's
protests about repression of labor rights. Said Coolidge: "There
is no right to strike against the public safety by anybody, anywhere, anytime." Most Americans agreed, and in that turbulent
year, 1919, conservative America doubtless would have denied
any right to strike.

Since Germany had been defeated in war, those concerned
with alien dangers concentrated on domestic radicals. Communist revolts in Germany and Hungary, and the formation of the
Communist Third International in 1919 stimulated such reac-

tions, as did the communists' prediction of speedy world take-over. In America, the Socialist party (founded back in 1901) split in 1919, the more radical wing forming the Communist party. All unrest and all violence were then blamed on the Reds or the Wobblies, or both. A general strike in Seattle early in the year had been crushed by use of police and vigilantes. A short time later, Seattle's mayor received a bomb in the mail, but it did not go off. Another such lethal package did explode in Washington, D.C., at a senator's home. That same day, a New York City postal clerk held up sixteen parcels for insufficient postage. All of them contained bombs, and they were addressed to John D. Rockefeller and Postmaster General Burleson among others. The absurdity of waging revolution "through the mails" (and failing to buy enough stamps in the bargain) suggested that the sender was a psychotic who happened to be a radical, but the public was in no mood for fine distinctions. All left-of-center politics became tainted with the charge of terrorism.

One of the prospective bomb victims was the Attorney General, A. Mitchell Palmer. Palmer, a Quaker, had a progressive record and had been appointed to the Cabinet because of supposed friendliness to labor. Though a supporter of women's suffrage, anti-child-labor laws, and the League of Nations, as Attorney General he set out to rid the country of radicals, thus becoming the prototype of the Wilsonian liberal gone sour. Although Congress refused to adopt a new, police-state sedition law sponsored by Palmer, he directed massive raids against radicals in late 1919. Hundreds of aliens, most with no criminal record, were deported, and several thousand U. S. citizens were held without charges, some for as long as a week, and then simply released. This was the police state in action, the worst peacetime violation of civil liberties since the Alien and Sedition Acts of 1798. Few Americans protested, however. Palmer became a temporary national hero with dreams of the presidency who esteemed the nickname, "The Fighting Quaker." But in 1919, Palmer was no joke.

Veterans' organizations such as the American Legion led the fight for 100 percent Americanism as did businessmen who hoped to weaken the labor movement by smearing it with the brush of radicalism. In the campaign against dissent the Bureau of Investigation, predecessor of the FBI, played a major role. Established originally by the Attorney General in 1919 to help curb interstate crime, in its early days the FBI concentrated on fighting organized vice rings. From its inception, the FBI tried to enlarge its jurisdiction and overcome traditional American hostility toward a secret police. Proclaiming itself the ears of the government against internal subversion, the bureau declared war against all disloyal and radical elements. Unable or unwilling to distinguish between the few radicals who were dangerous and the great majority employing peaceful means of protest, the FBI made indiscriminate arrests during the 1919 Red Scare. By the early 1920s, under the leadership of J. Edgar Hoover, it had secretly catalogued a half million Americans as dangerous. When Congress investigated the agency, it denied responsibility for searches and seizures which one U. S. senator described as "the lawless acts of a mob." And in the 1920s, as an arm of a corrupt Attorney General, the FBI spied on congressmen seeking to expose scandal in the executive branch.

During the height of the Red Scare, Charles Evans Hughes, the Republican presidential candidate in 1916, and future Chief Justice of the Supreme Court, tried to rally moderates: "Perhaps to an extent unparalleled in our history," he warned, "the essentials of liberty are being disregarded." Hughes spoke for the classes which maintained their poise, as did New York's Governor Al Smith, an Irish Catholic, who spoke for the ethnic masses so often victimized by the hysteria. In his message vetoing a batch of repressive laws, Smith recalled Benjamin Franklin's warning: "They that can give up essential liberty to obtain a little temporary safety deserve neither liberty nor safety."

Fortunately, the Red Scare subsided. The cooling off process began in New York, where the legislature had expelled five legally elected members simply because they were Socialists. This time there was protest, and Charles Evans Hughes led a group of "blue-ribbon" lawyers who defended the rights of the expelled assemblymen. The scare psychology began to look in-

creasingly ridiculous when supposed threats failed to material-
ize. Palmer then put all his hopes for radical unrest and personal
advancement on May Day, 1920. He called for extra police, and
standby orders to national guardsmen, but the revolutionary day
went by peacefully. Not even an explosion outside the Wall
Street office of J. P. Morgan & Co. which killed thirty-eight people
several months later could revive the panic atmosphere of 1919.
Palmer had been deflated, and in November, Americans voted
overwhelmingly for a man who promised relief from political
intensity and social unrest. Warren Harding observed: "Too
much has been said about Bolshevism in America."

The attacks on civil liberty led to efforts to protect the
victims through the courts with the help of the newly formed
American Civil Liberties Union. Founded originally by middle-
class progressives to defend the rights of conscientious objectors,
the ACLU became the country's principal libertarian organization. It fought government censorship and defended opponents
of the war and radicals caught in the net of the postwar Red
Scare. Increasingly, the ACLU came to the aid of labor unions
which became favorite victims of attacks on freedom of speech
and assembly in the 1920s.

At the same time, the United States Supreme Court became
a dramatic arena in which the judges had to determine whether
individual liberty could be protected in times of stress. The
Court upheld most state and federal prosecutions of radicals as
legitimate restrictions on liberty in the interest of maintaining
order. But to do so the antilibertarian justices (the "law and
order" advocates) had to develop a legal rationale that squared
repression with the American traditions of freedom and the
guarantees of the Bill of Rights. This gave libertarians an opportunity to force the courts to weigh carefully the liberty of the
individual against the state's need for security. The conflict produced a divided Supreme Court, although the majority usually
upheld the government. However two dissenters—Justices
Oliver Wendell Holmes and Louis D. Brandeis—argued elo-
quently for judicial protection of civil liberties, a view which the
Supreme Court eventually adopted a generation later, thus as-

suming for itself a new role as chief defender of weak and unpopular minorities.

In *Shenck* v. *the United States* (1919), Holmes had upheld the conviction of a socialist accused of obstructing the draft, but at the same time he defended freedom of thought and argued that "Persecution for the expression of opinions seems to me perfectly logical if you have no doubt of your premises and power. . . . But when men have realized that time has upset many fighting faiths, they may come to believe even more than they believe the very foundations of their own conduct that the ultimate good desired is better reached by free trade of ideas— that the best test of truth is the power of the thought to get itself accepted in the competition of the market. . . . That at any rate is the theory of our Constitution." That theory, he noted, is "an experiment, as all life is an experiment. . . . We should be eternally vigilant against attempts to check the expression of opinions that we loathe and believe to be fraught with death, unless they so imminently threaten immediate interference with the lawful and pressing purpose of the law that immediate check is required to save the country. . . ."

In a series of landmark decisions in the 1920s, the Supreme Court became the principal guarantor of individual liberty though it stumbled into this role reluctantly and haphazardly. The states posed the principal threat to civil liberty, especially after the war when federal wartime control lapsed. By 1920 thirty-five states had adopted legislation which restricted the free speech of radicals. Civil libertarians, therefore, searched for a constitutional basis that would enable the federal judiciary to restrain the states. That occurred in 1923 when the Court struck down an Oregon law, backed by the Ku Klux Klan, that required Catholics and others who preferred to send their children to church schools to enroll them in the public school. This decision opened the way for further extension of the Fourteenth Amendment to protect citizens against state laws that limited freedom of speech and the press, and eventually to other provisions of the Bill of Rights *fundamental* to individual liberty. In 1927 Justice Brandeis, in a dissenting opinion, added his ringing voice to Holmes's earlier reasoned defense of freedom:

Those who won our independence believed that the final end of the state was to make men free to develop their faculties. They believed liberty to be the secret of happiness and courage to be the secret of liberty. . . . They recognized the risks to which all human institutions are subject. But they knew that order cannot be secured merely through fear of punishment for its infraction; that it is hazardous to discourage thought, hope, and imagination; that fear breeds repression; that repression breeds hate; that hate menaces stable government. . . . Recognizing the occasional tyrannies of governing majorities, they amended the Constitution so that free speech and assembly should be guaranteed.

Fortunately for the liberties of Americans, the quest for national security through repression had ebbed by the mid-twenties, as Americans regained confidence amid unprecedented prosperity. Radicalism, of the socialist, communist, or Wobbly varieties, was weak; organized labor declined in strength; and wartime nationalism became a distant memory. In retrospect, the decision to get involved in Europe's woes in 1917 came under increasing attack from conservative and progressive opinion. But the hysteria did not wane until Congress ended unrestricted immigration, which champions of 100 percent Americanism had long insisted was the main source of subversive ideas and radical supporters.

The Heyday of Racism

Bigotry and racism flourished in postwar America as never before. Racist ideology became respectable and widespread. Those Americans who crowned the Nordic "race" as the superior race relegated millions of Americans to a condition of hereditary inferiority, especially the newcomers from southern and eastern Europe, as well as the older proscribed and oppressed groups, Negroes and Indians. Hatred of Jews and Catholics reached a high point when millions of Americans—North and South—flocked to join a revived Ku Klux Klan. The Klan promised to suppress by force if necessary those who were turning America into an urban, secular, and pluralistic society. Xenophobia did begin to subside by the mid-1920s, but not before it had intimidated its intended victims, and debased those who had sought to conquer fears by organizing to hate.

By the 1920s, Congress finally gave in to the exclusionist pressure groups that had campaigned against foreigners for two generations. The imposition of a literacy test for immigrants in 1917 had not prevented the arrival of nearly a million foreigners in 1920, and millions seemed poised to abandon war-weary Europe in search of the American Dream. "America must be kept American," opined President Calvin Coolidge on signing the immigration bill of 1924, the National Origins Act, and he meant a very particular type of American. The new measure ended unrestricted immigration from Europe and established a quota system for the Eastern Hemisphere based on an ethnic group's proportion in the 1890 census, thus discriminating against the "new" in favor of the "old" immigration from Northern Europe. It also limited immigration to no more than 150,000 persons per year.

This historic reversal of a policy that had welcomed men from all parts of Europe reflected a loss of faith in older ideals. Once the country had been confident of America's ability to assimilate Irish, German, Russian, or Italian peasants, and countless other strangers. The 1920s saw that commitment shelved. The First World War had increased doubts about the loyalty of the hyphenated Americans, and about the effectiveness of the "melting pot." The newcomers herded together in urban ghettoes, formed ethnic churches and benevolent societies, they voted for friendly politicians, and they maintained many Old World customs—all understandable attempts to cushion the massive disruption in their lives caused by emigration to America.

The native-born mistook the immigrants' tendency to conserve their past and its traditions for hostility to American ways, though none had a more naïve faith in the promises of their adopted country than the newcomers. Immigrant adaptation and success in America, limited though it was, seemed threatening to the native-born. As the attacks mounted in the early 1920s, the immigrants found themselves too weak, too politically isolated, and too divided to influence public policy. A few of their spokesmen poured scorn on the racists. One such spokesmen was Fiorello La Guardia, Republican congressman from a polyglot district in New York City. He, himself, was a second-generation hyphenated American—his father was Italian, his mother Jewish, and he an Episcopalian. La Guardia confessed impishly: "I have no family tree. The only member of my family who has is my dog Yank. He is the son of Doughboy, who was the son of Siegfried, who was the son of Tannhaueser, who was the son of Wotan. A distinguished family tree, to be sure, but after all, he's only a son of a bitch."

The postwar Red Scare helped fuel the anti-immigrant nativist impulse. Most aliens were actually conservative or apolitical, but a handful of revolutionaries from Eastern Europe made plausible the nativist identification of all "new" immigrants with subversion. Furthermore, the postwar disillusionment with the ability of progressive reform to deal with social maladjustment left people open to irrational appeals. They blamed all problems on the "un-Americans." Middle-class progressives regarded foreigners ambivalently, recognizing, as did businessmen, the economic advantages of unrestricted immigrant labor; but many still felt that the immigrants undercut wages, supported corrupt political machines, and preferred to live in squalor. A typical progressive, a native-born Protestant, mingled a desire to help the downtrodden with a paternalistic distrust of those in need of benevolence.

On the whole, however, progressives resolved their ambivalence in favor of the alien. The thrust of the progressive impulse had been a conviction that rational social control would maximize equality of opportunity and restore cohesiveness and stability. "I now have one Catholic in my Cabinet," boasted Theodore Roosevelt back in 1908, "and I now have a Jew in the Cabinet; and part of my object in each appointment was to implant in the minds of our fellow Americans of Catholic or of Jewish faith, or of foreign ancestry or birth, the knowledge that they have in this country just the same rights and opportunities as everyone else. . . ." But the collapse of progressivism after the First World War convinced many Americans that only a coercive "100 percent Americanism" could assure stability at home. Instead of responding to the conditions that provoked thousands of steel workers to strike in 1919, they acquiesced as the government and the steel mill owners crushed the strike. That thousands of strikers were foreign born, and that they had a Communist leader, provided final proof that the country must act to stem the influx of un-American forces.

Under these pressures, businessmen, earlier opponents of immigration restriction, gave way before a coalition of racists who blamed the newcomers for their own relative decline in power and status, the American Federation of Labor which blamed immigrants for undercutting wages, and some ex-progressives who argued that immigrants, not the conditions they encountered, produced squalor and corruption in urban America.

But bigotry did more than provide an outlet for expressing fears. Despite twisted efforts to justify racism scientifically, the insistence that ethnic groups and races differed in basic intelligence and morality remained at bottom irrational, catering to deeply felt needs of people "isolated from each other in strange places" who "could no longer recognize the brotherly gesture." The strain of living in a mobile society, a society in which neither tradition, the family, nor the church could adequately cushion an individual's struggle for success and self-esteem, led some to seek a racially defined nationalism. "It was an innermost necessity of their being," a historian has explained, "that they should come to recognize their brothers. If they could exclude or set apart the strangers, the outsiders, then they might somehow come to know each other." Yet long before the new immigrants from Europe, and in sharper ways, American Indians and blacks had suffered the consequences of racism.

The Indians

In 1787 Congress pledged "utmost good faith" toward the Indians, and promised that "their lands and property would never be taken without consent." But in the century that followed, Americans repeatedly warred against the Indians whose effective resistance collapsed by 1880. First, Indians east of the Mississippi had been removed to the "Permanent Indian Reservation" in the West. But American settlers soon demanded those lands, once considered worthless. Then the Indians were herded into fixed reservations to free more land for white settlement. As white pressure mounted again, new treaties reduced the size of reservations, leaving the Indians with the poorest lands.

In the 1880s the reservation system itself came under attack. Whites who coveted the Indians' remaining lands wanted the reservations broken up. Eastern humanitarians and reformers expressed shock at the wretched living conditions on the reservations, arguing that Indians had no future as long as they lived in primitive, tribal societies. The reformers wanted to transform the Indians into farmers so that they could be assimilated into the national mainstream. The Dawes Act (1887) entitled each Indian head of household to 160 acres; the remaining undivided lands were to be sold and the proceeds used for Indian education.

The Dawes Act failed. White speculators easily cheated Indians out of their lands, and in the half century after its passage Indians lost 86 million of their 138 million acres. The more perceptive tribal leaders fought against the breakup of the reservations. The assimilationist policy reflected Americans' failure to appreciate the vitality of Indian culture or to foresee the devastating cultural shock Indians would experience when torn from their ancestral social organization. Boarding schools separated Indian children from their tribes and sought to turn them into aliens among their own people when they returned. Bureaucrats sent from Washington ordered Indian men to cut their long hair, ignorant or scornful of the importance Indians placed on preserving their native life-styles. Left with worthless lands, without capital or skills, Indians sank into pauperism. As in the past, disease took a frightful toll. Not until 1910 did the Indian population, which had declined from between one and two million to a little over 100,000 after three centuries of contact with whites, begin to increase.

Despite recurrent efforts by white philanthropists and missionaries to aid the Indian, most Americans remained indifferent. "I suppose I should be ashamed to say that I take the western view of the Indian," admitted President Theodore Roosevelt. "I don't go so far as to think that the only good Indians are the dead Indians, but I believe nine out of every ten are, and I shouldn't inquire too closely into the case of the tenth."

The Black Man in the Age of Segregation

In the late nineteenth and early twentieth century, Americans also thought they had achieved a final solution in black-white relations. The end of Reconstuction and the withdrawal of federal troops from the South in 1877 left the blacks at the mercy of their white brothers. Without resources, the ex-slaves became tenant farmers or sharecroppers hopelessly tied to the soil by debt. Black political power withered in the face of terror and campaigns for Negro disfranchisement. During Radical Reconstruction, Negroes had gained some social equality, at least in public transportation and in such public places as theaters and restaurants. But the turn-of-the-century drive for segregation of the races proved irresistible. Public schools had always been segregated, and new "Jim Crow" segregation legislation passed in the 1880s and 1890s by nearly all-white legislatures, formalized discriminatory practices that earlier had been extralegal and inconsistently applied. The Supreme Court permitted segregation by invalidating most of the postwar Civil Rights Acts and interpreting the Fourteenth Amendment narrowly. Then in *Plessy* v. *Ferguson* (1896), the Court held that railroads could segregate passengers racially so long as they provided "separate but equal" facilities. The Court later extended this principle to other public facilities, including schools. The new doctrine was a subterfuge, for everyone knew that facilities for Negroes were not equal. But northerners, convinced of black inferiority, and eager to bind the wounds of the Civil War, had long before abandoned the rights of black people.

Assured of a free hand, white southerners systematically robbed black people of their remaining rights in the two decades after 1890. Jim Crow legislation subjected Negroes to constant, everyday humiliation. Hotels, restaurants, and theaters refused to receive them, railroads relegated them to filthy "smoking cars," and they had to ride in the rear of streetcars. Shopkeepers served them last and denied them the courtesy titles of Mr. and Mrs. Through a variety of devices—poll taxes, discriminatory literacy tests, and the all-white primary election—blacks also lost the vote. Despite the effectiveness of legal pressures in condemning Negroes to second-class citizenship, southerners also employed terror to keep Negroes in line. Lynch mobs became a part of the southern way of life. Lynchings averaged a hundred a year in the 1880s and 1890s, and then tapered off; yet between 1918 and 1927, 416 blacks died at the hands of lynch mobs. They included a pregnant black woman who, in May 1918, was strung up by the ankles, soaked in gasoline, and burned alive as the fetus of her unborn child was cut out and smashed. A fusillade of shots then riddled her body.

The lynch mobs had revealed graphically racism's effects: fearful and guilt-ridden after three centuries of exploiting blacks and infected with the recurrent need to assert their supremacy, whites resorted to barbarism. They justified lynching as necessary to "protect the honor" of white women, though less than a quarter of the lynch victims were accused of rape. "Whenever the Constitution comes between me and the virtue of the white women of South Carolina," bellowed a senator from that state, "then I say 'to hell with the constitution'. . . ." With such blanket support from the leaders of southern society, it is not surprising that the mass of whites periodically lost control.

By the twentieth century, white southerners had perfected a system of white supremacy which kept blacks poor and subservient. The principal force behind this drive for racial domination was the need to find alternative means to slavery for controlling the blacks. But the timing and intensification of the trend toward a complete system of Jim Crow reflected increasing tensions within white society as well. As long as white southerners had to defend themselves against a hostile North, they repressed their own differences, forming a united, Democratic front. But economic distress in the late 1880s and in the 1890s weakened white solidarity. Poor white farmers who found conservative white leadership unresponsive to their needs either became Populists or they backed Democratic, agrarian politicians. From time to time, poor whites cooperated with blacks to work for common economic goals, but such cooperation was short-lived, opportunistic and fragile. Conservative

Democrats bought black votes to turn back the challengers. This corruption enraged the agrarians, who demanded disfranchisement of blacks. The frustration and ultimate defeat of Populism in the late 1890s left agrarian politicians without effective issues.

Racist demagoguery filled the void. Mississippian James K. Vardaman, typical of the new breed, campaigned for governor in 1900 in a lumber wagon drawn by eight oxen, a visible symbol of his identity with the poor whites. "The Negro," he charged, was a "lazy, lying, lustful animal which no conceivable amount of training can transform into a tolerable citizen." "We should be justified," he argued, "in slaughtering every Ethiop on earth to preserve unsullied the honor of one Caucasian home."

Northerners were no strangers to negrophobia. In the early twentieth century, improved farming methods in the South reduced the planters' need for labor at the same time that Negroes were finding alternative employment in the North, especially after the First World War shut off European sources of cheap labor. In 1910, only 10 percent of American blacks lived outside of the South; by 1920, the figure rose to 20 percent.

As the number of Negroes in the urban, industrial centers grew rapidly, they competed with whites for jobs; and the participation of black soldiers in the First World War (fighting in segregated units, however) further raised Negro hopes for integration. Racial tensions mounted to an unprecedented level and erupted into race riots in Chicago, Philadelphia, Washington, and other cities between 1917 and 1919. Seventy blacks died at the hands of lynch mobs in the latter year, some of them uniformed war veterans. In Chicago, two weeks of rioting left the chief Negro district a shambles.

In the face of overwhelming white hostility, northern and southern blacks found both major political parties indifferent at best, hostile at worst. The Republicans had once courted the northern Negro vote, but the party realignment of 1896 gave the GOP such a commanding majority in the Northeast and Midwest that it could ignore the black vote which earlier had possessed some strategic value. Theodore Roosevelt invited Booker T. Washington, the most prominent Negro leader of the day, to the White House in 1902, but this token gesture provoked so

much criticism that he regretted making it. President Taft
ignored blacks and cultivated white southern Republicans, and
Woodrow Wilson, a southerner by birth, and heavily indebted to
that region for his election, resegregated the federal civil
service.

In view of these realities, and the absence of anything resembling "Black Power," it is not surprising that Booker T.
Washington adopted an accommodationist philosophy. An ex-
slave, Washington became head of the Tuskegee Institute, a
vocational training school in Alabama, from which he urged
blacks to postpone their quest for political and social equality.
They should instead place their hopes on self-help by learning
skills that would uplift black people economically. The Negro, he
reassured the country, was "fast learning the lesson that he cannot afford to act in a manner that will alienate his southern white
neighbors." At the Atlanta Exposition in 1895, Washington
won national acclaim for his philosophy. "No race can prosper,"
he proclaimed, "till it learns that there is as much dignity in till-
ing a field as in writing a poem. It is at the bottom of life we
must begin." He exhorted whites to help Negroes help themselves economically by "casting down your bucket among my
people . . . who will buy your surplus land, make blossom the
waste places in your fields, and run your factories." Blacks,
Washington promised, would repay white benevolence tenfold:
"You and your [white] families will be surrounded by the most
patient, faithful, law-abiding and unresentful people that the
world has seen."

White politicians and philanthropists responded enthusiasti-
cally. Washington acquired money and power with which he
dominated the Negro community. He tirelessly preached his
message of self-improvement. "It has been interesting to note,"
he boasted, "the effect that the use of the toothbrush has had in
bringing about a higher degree of civilization among the students [at Tuskegee]." And despite overwhelming evidence to
the contrary, Washington reassured blacks: "Every persecuted
individual and race should get much consolation out of the great
human law, which is universal and eternal, that merit, no matter
under what skin found, is in the long run recognized and
rewarded."

Though Washington publicly preached passive accomodation to white supremacy, privately he worked to oppose further erosion of the political and social rights of black people—but with little success, for his power came by virtue of his recognition by the white community. Operating from a position of black powerlessness, Washington thought his proposals offered the best hope under the circumstances. A small but growing black middle class, making money in businesses that served the black community—insurance companies and banks, shops, and mortuaries—agreed with him.

Eventually, however, some Negroes rose to challenge Washington's leadership. Led by W. E. B. Du Bois, a northern-born sociologist and historian trained at Harvard, they argued that accommodation was doomed. "Is it possible and probable," Du Bois asked, "that nine million men can make effective progress in economic lines if they are deprived of political rights, made a servile caste, and allowed only the most meager chance for developing their exceptional men?" At a time when industry, not agriculture, was the economic wave of future, Washington encouraged blacks to become better farmers. At a time when Negroes needed above all to believe in themselves, Washington reinforced their self-doubts. "Manly self-respect," Du Bois insisted, "is worth more than lands and houses, and . . . a people who voluntarily surrender such respect, or cease striving for it, are not civilizing."

A brilliant, highly educated man, Du Bois gave voice to deep anguish. "One ever feels his twoness," he noted, "an American, a Negro; two souls, two thoughts, two unreconciled strivings; two warring ideals in one dark body, whose dogged strength alone keeps it from being torn asunder." The black man, he explained, did not want "to Africanize America, for America has too much to teach the world and Africa." Nor did he wish to "bleach his Negro soul in a flood of white Americanism, for he knows that Negro blood has a message for the world. He simply wants to make it possible for a man to be both a Negro and an American, without being cursed and spit upon by his fellows. . . ." Above all, Du Bois preached that Black is Beautiful: "the unknown treasures of their inner life, the strange rendings of nature they have seen, may give the world new points of view and make their loving, living, and doing precious to all human hearts."

In 1908 a small band of whites and blacks, including Du Bois, founded the National Association for the Advancement of Colored People (NAACP) to fight for political and social equality. Adopting a strategy of protest and resistance, in 1915 they won their first legal victory when the Supreme Court declared unconstitutional an Oklahoma law devised to disfranchise Negroes.

The new strategy of protest and the assertion of Negro pride found a receptive audience among the small, but growing, black middle class in the northern cities. Thereafter the NAACP continued to work through the courts to protect the constitutional rights of blacks, and it also campaigned against lynching. In the 1920s the House of Representatives passed a federal antilynching law, but southern senators talked it to death, denouncing the measure as an invasion of states rights. The South, they claimed, could deal with lynching perfectly well without outside interference.

The northward migration of blacks from the South was creating black ghettoes in the North. None could rival New York City's Harlem in importance or vitality. In the 1920s, it became a center for black artists, who found mutual support among one another and produced poems, novels, sculpture, and music expressing racial pride. For the first time, a cultural and intellectual black elite attracted white attention and admiration, helping to break down racist stereotypes. But more important, the Harlem Renaissance gave black intellectuals pride in themselves by restoring confidence in the black man's creative capacities, an indispensable precondition for Negro advancement. Calling themselves "The New Negro," they proclaimed that "the day of 'aunties', and 'uncles', and 'mammies' was gone." They were optimistic about the Negro's future in America and thought integration a realistic though distant goal. But they lacked a concrete strategy or an efficient organization for achieving that goal, and neither the NAACP nor the Negro intellectuals were able to sink deep roots among the Negro masses.

Marcus Garvey, founder of the Universal Negro Improvement Association, had both strategy and organization. A West Indian, Garvey migrated to Harlem during the First World War when the Negro capital was growing rapidly, as blacks poured in from the South. They nourished new hopes inspired by economic opportunity and the chance to escape the southern caste system. When wartime prosperity gave way to unemployment, Negroes were the worst hit, and at the same time antiblack rioting erupted in many northern cities. Garvey offered blacks new hope and built the largest Negro organization the country had ever seen. He preached black nationalism, instilling pride in race and demanding racial solidarity. "Black men, you were once great," this magnetic orator intoned, "you shall be great again." Garvey insisted that blacks could advance only by rejecting integration into white society—an impossible goal—and building instead a powerful black community. He organized black-owned businesses, including the ill-fated Black Star Steamship Line, which sold thousands of shares of stock to Negroes unaware of Garvey's incompetence as a businessman.

Given to grandiose visions and racism, Garvey placed his greatest hopes in the liberation of Africa from western colonialism and its transformation into a Black Empire with Garvey as its leader. The Garveyites attempted to promote migration of blacks from America to Africa, where they would play a leading role in the struggle, but with no more success than in their business ventures.

None of Garvey's schemes materialized. Convicted of using the mails fraudulently, he went to jail in 1925 and the movement collapsed. Despised by most Negro leaders as a racist and a charlatan, this "Black Moses" held the affection of the Negro masses. Garvey did something new: he made the poor black "feel like somebody among white people who have said they were nobody," as a Negro sociologist explained. But such feelings were short-lived, for in the end Garvey merely sold escapism, and his ragtag program offered no realistic strategy in the struggle for racial justice.

The philosophy of protest enunciated by Du Bois and institutionalized by the NAACP, and the surge of black pride in the Harlem Renaissance and in Garvey's nationalism laid the foundations for a revolution in race relations a generation later. But until white attitudes toward all ethnic, religious, and racial minorities changed significantly, blacks could not progress. In the 1920s, however, hatred of Jews and Catholics, blacks and Indians, Irish and Italians remained powerful rooted in the tensions generated by the shift to mass society. The triumph of Prohibition and the attack on science by religious fundamentalism further demonstrated that Americans were at war with themselves.

Religious Crisis in Modern America

The Protestant churches entered the second half of the nineteenth century confidently. Despite the formal separation of church and state, Protestantism still helped to define American culture, and most people considered themselves Protestant, whether affiliated with a church or not. The denominations had met the challenge of national expansion between 1820 and 1860 with a prodigious evangelical and reformist effort. The churches followed settlers as they moved west and revivals rekindled enthusiasm when it lagged in the eastern cities as well as in rural communities. Finally, the Civil War provided an unanticipated occasion for transcendence by sacrificing self-interest in a noble cause. The churches, North and South, claimed divine blessing for their respective sides: "As He died to make men holy/ Let us die to make men free," sang the Union armies in "The Battle Hymn of the Republic." Across the battle line, southerners never doubted that God was on *their* side.

In the seven decades after Appomattox, however, the church in general, and the Protestant denominations in particular, faced serious challenges to their moral authority and institutional power. The growing percentage of Catholics and Jews in the cities undercut the Protestants' near-monopoly. The mounting prestige of science and the spread of secularism, both nourished in an increasingly urban society, weakened the hold of religion over minds and emotions. The churches attempted to meet these challenges by modernizing theology, by espousing a social gospel, by adapting revivalist techniques to new conditions, and by legislating Christian morality through politics. They also made frantic and ultimately unavailing efforts to impose the old-time religion (with its reliance on the supernatural) on a people who more than ever viewed the world through the eyes of science and acted on the assumption that God's only kingdom was here on earth.

Darwin's theory of evolution popularized naturalistic explanations of phenomena that traditionally had been the province of the churches. Christians read in the Bible that God created the world in five days, and on the sixth he created man. Darwinism, however, maintained that evolution produced all forms of life, man included, in a long process during which organisms adapted to environmental demands. Species which successfully adapted survived; those that did not, like the dinosaur, died out. If man, like other animals, resulted from evolutionary chance, could people still consider him the final and crowning touch of a Divine Creator? Scientists dismissed the literal truth of the Bible, and after generations of biblical scholarship which had critically subjected the scriptures to the test of internal consistency, skepticism could no longer be brushed aside. If people could no longer trust in the authority of the Bible or rely on supernatural accounts of creation, they might then reject all of religion.

The churches responded to this threat in two ways. Those denominations with their roots deepest in the South and in the countryside among blacks, poor whites, and the less educated, among whom science and secularism had made little impression, rejected Darwinism and all Bible criticism as blasphemous. "Give me that old-time religion," they sang exuberantly, "that's good enough for me." But the more middle-class denominations, such as the Presbyterians, Episcopalians, and Congregationalists, with a tradition of a well-educated ministry serving constituencies deeply attracted by science and secularism, tried to reconcile science with religion. Evolution, after all, gave scientific approval to rugged individualism, the dominant social philosophy of the Gilded Age. Evolution, John Fiske had explained in the 1880s, was simply "God's way of doing things." Henry Ward Beecher, the leading minister in post-Civil War America,

agreed: "Science is but the deciphering of God's thought as revealed in the structure of this world; it is merely a translation
of God's primitive revelation." Accepting both evolution and
biblical criticism, many ministers attempted to find a rational
basis for Christian belief, since they saw little prospect of maintaining religiosity by appealing to blind faith.

Some went further and attempted to make the churches
more relevant to human needs through the social gospel. By
ministering to the temporal condition of the oppressed, social gospelers offered Christians the means of expressing their faith in
daily life, and a tangible way of spreading Christ's message. In
this way some thought Protestants could resist the secular trend
that divorced man from God, and could win back to the
churches thousands of backsliders among the urban working
classes.

At first the modernist response appeared successful, but
ultimately it weakened the authority of religion. Concessions to
science to shore up religion endowed science with additional
respectability and prestige. For a while the conflict between the
scientific, secular world view and supernatural religion subsided. The modernist churches were complacently confident that
the latest threat had been mastered when, in fact, religion suffered a continued, though often imperceptible, erosion in
authority—especially among the educated. The modernist
churches, however, were caught in a hopeless dilemma. They
had become prisoners of their culture, servants of their congre-
gations, and they could not resist science without risking shattering confrontations.

Catholics and Jews, no less than Protestants, had to meet
the challenge of modern science. The rise of the city, however,
posed a special challenge for Protestant denominations. As millions of Protestants moved from farms to the cities in the late
nineteenth century, they often left their fathers' religion far behind. In a rural society, Sunday churchgoing started a day in
town, people mingled and visited with neighbors, and thus found
escape from the routine and isolation of farm life. But in the
bustling cities, neighbors were nearby; the ball park, the Sunday
newspaper, the theater (and later the movies), and the saloon

competed with churchgoing. In addition, the cities also housed many Catholic and Jewish immigrants, whose tendency to settle among their own kind facilitated the transfer of Catholic and Jewish worship to the New World. Protestantism thus faced for the first time a serious challenge to its near-monopoly. To reclaim Catholic and Jewish urban immigrants from heresy and native-born backsliders from apathy became one of the principal tasks of post-Civil War Protestantism, a task made all the more difficult by the scientific challenge to faith. The cities were the mainspring of modern society, and to lose them to the enemies of the Protestant God was unthinkable.

The Young Men's Christian Association (YMCA), founded before the Civil War, became a vital part of the crusade for the cities. The Y offered rural folk coming to the big city a temporary home suffused with a Protestant atmosphere, and it entered deeply into the lives of the cities by providing scarce recreational and charitable services. In many towns and cities, the Y was a tangible reminder that God had not forsaken the urban dweller. Its weakness, however, lay in the fact that people could use its services without joining a neighborhood church or abandoning secular attitudes.

The Y concentrated on winning back young people, and the same strategy lay behind the International Sunday School Union. Applying the technique of large-scale organization to the problem of religious education, the Sunday school movement proved the most effective means the churches devised to maintain their grip. So successful was the Sunday School Union in training teachers and providing educational materials, that Bible classes were extended to adults as well.

In addition, the Protestant churches established missions to the immigrants, but these met with little success—for the foreign-born saw them as threats to their desire to re-create, in the urban ghettoes and as best they could, the communal life of the Old Country. They preferred to cling to the faith of their fathers and establish a structure of their own associations including churches they controlled.

Protestants also poured new energy and resources into revivalism, adapting it to urban conditions. The leading late nineteenth-century revivalist was Dwight L. Moody, a short, rotund former shoe salesman who first became active in the Chicago YMCA and later developed into a lay preacher of worldwide reputation. Moody succeeded in urban revivalism because he skillfully combined business methods of organization with sentimentality. Moody carefully planned his big-city revivals. He insisted on obtaining broad interdenominational cooperation in advance. This enabled him to raise large amounts of money, especially from businessmen who hoped that a supersalesman pushing the soothing consolation of life after death might curb lower class unrest.

Moody had little patience with the notion that all men were brothers: "Show me a man that will lie and steal and get drunk and ruin a woman," he once asked, "do you tell me that he is my brother?" With large financial resources and a mastery of publicity, Moody built immense tabernacles in the large cities. As a layman, Moody had a knack for speaking simply. He avoided theological complexity for simple appeals to the heart. "The great truth we want to remember," he preached, "is that God loves the sinner. He hates sin, yea, with a perfect hatred; but he loves the sinner. God is love." Moody also had a keen sense of showmanship. His warm and friendly revivals had a carnival atmosphere, and he advertised them fittingly on the amusement pages of local newspapers. Huge, massed choirs sang sentimental hymns, and when Moody wept, the crowd wept with him. "Ah, it is that tender weeping power in dear Mr. Moody," reported a minister, "that is so overwhelming." The thousands who flocked to hear Moody seemed to prove the effectiveness of revivalism. Yet however much Moody succeeded in a city, the local minister soon felt the need again for his services. The saved had become sinners again.

Yet faith in the effectiveness of revivalism persisted among the evangelical, antimodernist denominations. In each generation since Moody, another revivalist has risen to walk in his steps and adapt slightly the methods of the master. In the early twentieth century, the Reverend Billy Sunday established his primacy. Sunday endeared himself to big-city ministers, whose churches were losing worshippers and running at a deficit, because they thought, "He can deliver the goods." He perfected the bureaucratic organization of the urban revival, collecting money and putting together the Sunday Party, a corps of experts in every phase of revivalism. When critics noted that Sunday had become a millionaire, the revivalist replied that "it cost him only $2 for every soul he 'saved' . . . less proportionate than other living evangelists."

Sunday's appeal was even simpler and more vulgar than Moody's. "What I want and preach," he said, "is the fact that a man can be converted without any fuss." Sunday adapted his message to the guilt-ridden consciences of people who feared secularism as they embraced it. "Let me tell you," he reassured them, "the manliest man is the man who will acknowledge Jesus Christ," who, according to Sunday, was "the greatest scrapper that ever lived." Turning to the women, Sunday promised: "Ladies, do you want to look pretty? If some of you women would spend less on dope and cold cream and get down on your knees and pray, God would make you prettier." But he warned youth: "A young man would not come to see a girl of mine in the parlor unless I had a hole cut in the ceiling with a Gatling gun trained through it."

Sunday also wrapped himself in the flag, preached racism, and told cheering crowds in the 1920s, "America is not a country for a dissenter to live in." The leading dissenter of the day, the Socialist Eugene V. Debs, regarded the evangelist as "a ranting mountebank, who, in the pay of the plutocracy, prostitutes religion to perpetuate hell on earth." But Sunday made no concessions to Darwin, modernist Christianity, or to the social gospels. "The fatherhood of God and the brotherhood of Man," he sneered, "is the worst rot that ever was dug out of hell and every minister who preaches it is a liar."

In the 1920s, the conflict between modernist Christianity and conservative fundamentalist Christianity exploded, revealing the depth of the American Protestants' division. Outwardly the churches in the 1920s remained prosperous, with an upward growth trend. The percentage of the population with a church affiliation rose from about one-third in 1890 to about one-half by 1930. But these raw statistics can deceive. As the number of church members grew, the meaning of religious affiliation changed. "Even if going to church doesn't give us anything else," explained a midwesterner in the 1920s, with charming logic, "it at least gives us the habit of going to church." People went because "it was the right thing to do," a sign of middle class respectability, and all the while religiosity declined. "I guess I usually get something from church when I go," someone admitted, "but in summer, we mostly go out in the car Sundays." Ministers sensed the change. "My people seem to sit through the sermon in a kind of dazed, comatose state," observed one, unhappily. "They don't seem to be wrestling with my thought."

Religious affiliation became an increasingly ritualistic act to many, devoid of piety or intellectual commitment, and the decline in belief infected the ministry itself. A comparison of the theological beliefs of Protestant seminary students with those of the older generation of ministers in the 1920s revealed that a majority of the younger generation did not believe in the literal truth of the Bible, the virgin birth of Christ, a final judgment, or the actual existence of heaven and hell. All this confirmed the claim of the fundamentalists—those who clung to orthodox, supernatural versions of Protestantism—that modernism had undermined the foundations of Christian belief. "The greatest menace to the Christian Church today," declared a leading fundamentalist theologian, "comes not from the enemies outside, but from the enemies within: it comes from the presence within the church of a type of faith and practice that is anti-Christian to the core." The fundamentalists, who launched a campaign to regain control of the institutional structure of American Protestantism, enjoyed a mass popularity, especially among country folk or those who had recently migrated to the cities. They reached millions struggling with the problems of adjusting to mass society, dependent on but fearful of science, frightened yet fascinated by the strangeness of city ways. Everything that people thought wrong with America—the new sexual mores, the evils of city life, drunkenness, political radicalism, or the assertion of women's rights—could be and was blamed on the loss of faith in old-time religion.

Not all, but most fundamentalists were socially conservative, and all believed that morality stemmed from belief in an omnipotent, miracle-working God, and on a literal reliance on the Bible. Above all, fundamentalists felt that any attempt to reconcile religious faith with scientific principles meant the end of faith. Fundamentalists protested against secularism and the reason and science on which it rested. They made their last stand in the 1920s because by then the new trend to the life-styles of secularized mass society had become unmistakably clear. Later, the fundamentalist crusade appeared a pathetic and anachronistic attempt to reverse the tide of history, and never more so than at the most famous trial of the decade in Dayton, Tennessee.

In the 1920s, fundamentalist pressures led several states to outlaw the teaching of Darwinian evolution in the public schools. Tennessee passed such a law in 1925; two years before six professors at the University of Tennessee were fired for teaching scientific evolution. John Scopes, a high school biology teacher in Dayton, decided to test the law. There then unfolded the dramatic "Monkey Trial," pitting William Jennings Bryan, the nation's leading fundamentalist layman, against Clarence Darrow, an agnostic Chicago lawyer who had made a career of championing unpopular causes. Bryan, three-time Democratic candidate for president, and former Secretary of State, who as champion of rural Protestantism in the South and West had spent a lifetime battling for social justice, believed that "some devitalizing force" was causing Americans "to forsake their spirituality for crass materialism." Scopes, the defendant, became almost forgotten in the battle between Darrow and Bryan, the one championing faith in science and reason, and the other in God and divine revelation.

The drama in the courtroom divided the country, especially after Bryan took the stand, confident he could defend the infallibility of the Bible against Darrow's famed skepticism. Bryan proudly professed belief in the literal truth of the Bible. The world went back to October 23, 4004 B.C.; the deluge came in 2438 B.C. He insisted that God created the sun on the fourth day, and that there had been evenings and mornings without sun. Women suffered at childbirth because Eve ate the forbidden apple. God, however, punished the serpent which tempted her by forever condemning it to crawl on its belly. "How do you suppose the serpent got along before that?" asked Darrow sardonically. Bryan rejected the theory of evolution because it lacked biblical support, and in his view it was only a scientific guess. "Apparently," wrote a scientist, "Mr. Bryan demands to see a monkey or an ass transformed into a man, though he must be familiar enough with the reverse process."

Though the big city press and the urban upper middle classes chuckled over Bryan's ignorance of science and his child-like faith in the Bible, he won the case and the plaudits of millions of fundamentalists. Scopes had to pay a fine. Prophetically, however, Darrow won the admiration of the youngsters of Dayton High School. They gave a dance in his honor, for, as one of Darrow's associates explained: "They seemed to recognize that this was their battle . . . it represented the issues between the eagerness of youth and the fear of age. Any pleasure unconnected with the church had been condemned by their elders. Smoking, dancing, free association between girls and boys, games and movies on Sunday had been their issues at home. Here were champions indeed." And a few days after the trial's end, Bryan collapsed and died suddenly—from overeating, his detractors claimed maliciously.

The attempt to legislate the theory of evolution out of existence did not succeed, but the fundamentalist impulse has persisted because there remain dwindling numbers of Americans who still have not made their peace with the modern world. (In 1969, the California State Board of Education ruled that Darwinian evolution should be taught as one of several theories of evolution.)

Prohibition: "The Noble Experiment"

Despite these deep divisions within Protestantism, most churches joined in supporting a new crusade against liquor early in the twentieth century. Almost a century after the launching of the first campaign for temperance, total prohibition triumphed. As in the past, the churches, particularly the fundamentalist ones, formed the vanguard. Liquor, the clergy argued, doomed millions of souls and signalled the spread of secularism and materialism. Social gospelers and other progressive reformers agreed, though for different reasons. Crusaders for social justice denounced liquor as a cause of poverty and urban disorder. The liquor interests, they argued, were a powerful "trust," growing rich by exploiting the poor and corrupting the politicians. Doctors and scientists added their voices. Little had been known about the precise effects of alcohol before 1860, but now scientific research concluded that alcohol, even in moderate amounts, harmed the body. Businessmen also joined the crusade; liquor, they thought, made workers less efficient and more prone to industrial accidents.

These arguments took on greater force as the cities, with their polygot inhabitants from a dozen parts of Europe, appeared to threaten the dominance of native-stock Protestants of British extraction. By 1919, Roman Catholics, for instance, outnumbered other church members in fifteen states. The newcomers often drank heavily, and opposed temperance and prohibition movements. The consumption of alcohol reached an all-time high during the peak years of prewar immigration—further evidence that something had to be done. The insecure old-stock elements attempted to assert their superiority by imposing their standards on the newcomers. Prohibition thus became a means of banning an objectionable "un-American" habit, and coercing aliens into assimilation, another part of the campaign for 100 percent Americanism.

The Nineteenth Amendment to the Constitution, ratified in 1919, outlawed the manufacture and sale of intoxicating liquor. Its adoption resulted from skillful political pressure applied by the Women's Christian Temperance Union and the Anti-Saloon League. Founded in 1893, the League organized the "dry" Americans, and by 1915 it had a professional staff of 1500, with 50,000 field workers, many of them supplied by the churches. With the adoption of Prohibition, Billy Sunday predicted, "Hell will be forever for rent." William Jennings Bryan went further: "The reign of tears is over. The slums will soon be only a memory. We will turn our prisons into factories and our jails into storehouses and corncribs. Men will walk upright now, women will smile, and the children will laugh."

For fourteen years, the United States remained legally dry. In fact, however, the production and consumption of alcohol did not stop; it simply went underground. And in the end Prohibition turned into a nightmare. From the outset, millions refused to comply, including President Warren G. Harding, though he campaigned as a staunch dry. The Yale University Club laid in a 14 year supply of liquor, and those with less foresight and cash bought illegal booze from bootleggers. Two thousand badly paid prohibition agents had the impossible task of preventing drinking in a nation of 100 million people.

Production moved from the factory into the home. Eventually it became the special province of the underworld. Prohibition did not create organized crime—criminal syndicates already flourished in the big cities—but now gangsters, imitating Big Business, perceived the advantages of limiting competition, consolidating resources, and enlarging their take. Prohibition shifted an estimated $2 billion annually from the liquor manufacturers to the bootleggers and gave organized crime enormous sums of money for intimidating other businessmen. Big-time crime, like big business, was the achievement of powerful men such as Al Capone, the kingpin of the Chicago underworld. Unlike John D. Rockefeller, who bought out his competitors or drove them into bankruptcy, Capone cut them down with the Thompson submachinegun, or dropped them, weighted with chains, in Lake Michigan. At their height, the Chicago gang wars of the 1920s produced 400 murders in one year.

Enforcement proved impossible because the government could only devote a fraction of the resources necessary. President Herbert Hoover estimated that it would take a quarter of a million men to make America dry, but taxpayers would not pay that price, and prohibitionists feared that stringent enforcement would arouse so much opposition that it might result in repeal. In many parts of the country, juries refused to convict offenders, and enforcement agents were hated. They did manage, however, to kill several hundred people during the decade, causing Jane Addams to insist that "what the prohibition situation needs first of all is disarmament." The drys, however, had no patience for such "gush stuff about murders by men who make mistakes once in a while." There were other kinds of mistakes, even more common. In October, 1928, wood alcohol killed 25 New York guzzlers.

Prohibition did not stop all Americans from drinking, but it did dry up large parts of America, those inclined to be dry anyway. In 1932, 61,000 Americans were convicted of violating the Nineteenth Amendment and 45,000 got jail sentences; millions of gallons of booze were destroyed together with thousands of stills. But if small-town and rural America was drier than ever, urban America was as wet as ever. New York City for instance had 32,000 speakeasies in the 1920s, evidencing the widespread erosion of respect for law among the law-abiding, especially among Americans of immigrant stock. As for millions of native-born Protestants who accepted modernity, Prohibition was a reminder that an older, rural America still held power. Will Rogers, the country's leading satirical humorist, with a keen nose for hypocrisy, got to the heart of the matter: "If you think this country isn't dry, just watch 'em vote; if you think this country ain't wet, just watch 'em drink. You see, when they vote, it's counted, but when they drink, it ain't." Above all, Prohibition, like fundamentalism, represented a desperate effort to resist changes that were turning America into a pluralistic and secular society, in which no single culture ruled. In 1933, with the repeal of Prohibition, those who feared "the demon rum" because they doubted their own ability to resist it would now have to rely entirely on self-control.

The Wages of Fear

Fear of science and cities, fear of people different from the native-born Protestant majority (with radicals, Negroes, Catholics, and Jews the objects of particular scorn), fear that Americans, more than ever, were abandoning religious faith for worldly satisfactions, all these phantoms haunted America in the 1920s. The country luxuriated in the dizzying prosperity created by industrial technology, but though almost everybody wanted a new car and a radio and looked forward to visits to the movie palace or to the big city, many felt a sense of loss and betrayal.

Amid all the rapid change and after the disillusion of the First World War, people seemed isolated from one another and unable to find a larger meaning for their lives. On an unprecedented scale, the middle classes joined clubs: country clubs, social service clubs, business and professional clubs. One midwestern city, for instance, sported 458 clubs in the 1920s. With the church, the neighborhood, and the family no longer as important as before, the club filled a real need for fellowship. Club membership, people explained, "makes you realize the other fellow hasn't got horns on and ain't out to get you."

A more sinister response to the need for a sense of community and to the pervasive fears in postwar America among native-born, lower middle classes was a revived Ku Klux Klan. The Klan in the 1920s recruited between four and six million members, primarily in the WASP midsection of the country, North as well as South. It was not simply a rural phenomenon, but infested the cities, which were full of the most "threatened" people, the recent migrants from the countryside. "We want the country ruled by the sort of people who settled it," declared an Ohio Klan leader. "This is *our* country and we alone are responsible for its future." Above all, the Klan catered to a paranoid sense of deprivation which created a psychological state of siege. "Every criminal, every gambler, every thug, every libertine," claimed a Klan handbill, "every girl runner, every home wrecker, every wife beater, every dope peddler, every moonshiner, every crooked politician, every pagan Papist priest, every shyster lawyer . . . every white slaver, every black spider—is fighting the Klan." The Klan psychosis combined political animus against blacks, Jews and Catholics with morbid sexual fears.

With its complicated ritual, its secrecy, and white robes and hoods, its burning crosses, its willingness to use violence, and its sense of solidarity, the Klan had undoubted appeal. It posed as a vigilante organization with the guts to fight evils ignored or underestimated by established institutions such as government. For a short time, the "Invisible Empire" became a powerful political force in several states. But by the mid-1920s the Klan suffered a decline. The top leaders fought among themselves for the profits, scandal tarnished their image (the Indiana Klan leader was convicted of murder), and respectable upper-class businessmen and politicians who had first encouraged the

Klan pulled out. Most of all, the social anxieties that made millions of Americans susceptible to the Klan's appeal had begun to subside.

Not before, however, The Commonwealth of Massachusetts executed Nicola Sacco and Bartolomeo Vanzetti, two Italian anarchists convicted of murder in an armed robbery, and aroused liberal consciences throughout the Western World. Many doubted their guilt, and many more doubted that they had received a fair trial. The case made people wonder whether American justice had framed and executed two men because they were foreigners and radicals. "If it had not been for this thing," said the uneducated but eloquent Vanzetti in the courtroom after sentencing, "I might have to live out my life talking at street corners to scorning men. I have died, unmarked, unknown, a failure. Now we are not a failure. This is our career and our triumph. Never in our full life could we hope to do such work for tolerance, for justice, for man's understanding of man as now we do by accident. Our words—our lives—our pains—nothing! The last moment belongs to us—that agony is our triumph."

Whether Sacco and Vanzetti were guilty as charged remains uncertain. Yet one thing is clear: those who cheered their execution thought it a blow against dangerous foreigners and radicalism; and those who believed the Italian anarchists had been victimized found fresh proof that Americans had lost their nerve. Inevitably, the tensions of mass society which resulted in attacks on civil liberties, the rise of fundamentalism and the Klan, and the triumph of Prohibition also shaped American politics in the 1920s.

Document: Clarence Darrow, Dissenter
Darrow on Prohibition
Darrow on Immigration

Born in 1857, Clarence S. Darrow was the son of a small-town furniture maker and undertaker who was also the village atheist. Absorbing his father's skepticism, Darrow went on to become the most famous trial lawyer of his generation, "the at-torney for the damned." With extraordinary psychological un-derstanding of human beings, uncanny ability to persuade juries, and deep compassion for society's forgotten and despised, he defended radicals, working people, labor leaders, blacks, the criminally insane, rich and poor.

Like so many Americans of his generation, Darrow's con-version to reform was partly the product of exposure to social injustice, in his case to the grim realities of industrial Chicago in the late nineteenth century. In 1893 he resigned as corporate counsel for the Northwestern Railroad to defend the future Socialist leader, Eugene V. Debs, indicted for leading a strike by the American Railway Union against the Pullman Company. From that time, Darrow participated in the struggle for social justice for the working classes, for a more humane system of criminal law, and for a society which recognized man's fraility and fallibility, and made tolerance, compassion, and openmind-edness its guidelines.

As a champion of organized labor, at a time when work-ers forming unions were met by violent opposition from employ-ers and stern resistance in the courts, Darrow boldly proclaimed that "nine-tenths of the laws are made nowadays by the judges and that they are made in the interests of the rich and powerful and to destroy the poor. . . . Justice is like sugar or salt. . . . The amount you get is regulated by the amount of money you have." Accused of bribing a juror while defending the McNammara brothers, two labor leaders charged with dynamiting the Los Angeles Times *building, he addressed the jury in his own de-fense. "What am I on trial for?" he asked. "I am not on trial for having sought to bribe a man. . . . I am on trial because I have been a lover of the poor, a friend of the oppressed, because I have stood by labor for all these years, and have brought down upon my head the wrath of the criminal interest in this coun-try. . . ."*

Though Darrow won many of his great cases—he lost only one client to capital punishment—his was the voice of dissent, powerful but not persuasive to large numbers of Americans in his generation who sided with capital against labor, with funda-mentalism against science, with Puritanism against the New

Morality. But Darrow was prophetic. In the 1920s, for instance, he strongly opposed racist immigration policy and Prohibition. In the excerpts reprinted below from debates in which he participated on these topics, Darrow championed social tolerance and cultural pluralism, which gained increasing acceptance in the generation after he died in 1938. "Clarence," explained one of his friends, "opened up people's minds and made them more ready to see the difficulties faced by the underdogs of society." He was, wrote another, the "Defender of the defenseless," the "undisputed king of human kindliness."

Clarence Darrow on Prohibition, 1924

I will say this: that it has been a long time since I have participated in a debate where I have had an opponent who has stated the position as fairly and as clearly as Dr. Holmes. And I shall agree with a good deal he said—but not all of it.

I could present miles and miles of statistics to show that everybody was richer and happier and behaved better when they had a chance to drink. Those statistics wouldn't be worth a continental—m-m—continental. He can produce just as many to show that they are happier and better and richer if they don't drink. He is quite right in saying statistics are of no value.

And then, I don't care a continental which way a man gets rich. I am not interested in getting rich—any longer.

This question is not a question of statistics. I have been in statistic factories. I know how they are made. It is, as Dr. Holmes stated, a pure question of the philosophy of government. And I am very glad indeed to have this question presented by the able man that I know Dr. Holmes to be. I have never yet found a debater or prohibition speaker who would do it. They talk about little Johnny's father, who wouldn't come home and take care of his sick mother; and they tell you how many prisoners are in jail, who all got there by drinking, and they tell you all these things from which you can draw no conclusion whatever.

This is a question of the philosophy of government. I will go slightly further than he goes. I know how accurately he described government. A great many people in this world, unless they act with a certain kind of organization, are apt to bump into each other. And if there is too much organization, why, they can't move at all. And it is better to have some bumps than no movement, and you have got to take it all together. How tight you are going to tie a people and how much you are going to let them bump is a question of practice and theory. If Dr. Holmes knows of any way in the world to draw the line that will include all cases, why, he would contribute something to me, if not to the rest, if he would tell what that way is.

I know that there isn't any—that is, I know up to this time. It is a question of infinite trial, of infinite mistake, of infinite going in and coming out. It depends upon the people. It depends on where they live. It depends on the kind of people they are. It depends upon ten thousand things as to how close the organization should be knit together. You may knit it so close that they will all suffocate. You may leave them so far apart that they can't move without bumping, and there you are.

Now, where is the line? I don't know. Does Dr. Holmes know?

I am one of those, I will admit in starting, whom he has more or less defined as doubtful and suspicious of authority. I don't like it. I think the less we have, the better. He describes that as bordering on the philosophical anarchist view. I would speak for that as against the extreme socialist view, which says that everything on earth should be regulated or controlled. Society is always moving between those two views. And as a practical matter, neither one is correct. Society will never submit to an organization, in my opinion, where there is no authority of any sort by one man or another or by collective organization over others; and it will never, for long, submit to what is still more intolerable, the complete enslavement of the unit by the mass.

Now, you can't find where the line is—and I can't find where. I am here to say that prohibition is 'way over the line in reason, in logic, in human experience. There are other things that are clear beyond the line. They have been wiped out gradually. Then the people got a brainstorm—and they have come back again.

If there were any line that could be drawn, people haven't

got the intelligence and tolerance to draw it. They are like a flock of sheep. All go one way at one time and another way at another time.

One mistake that we make is assuming that human beings are reasoning animals. Human beings do not reason. They act from the strictest personal motives and are influenced by the mob, first of all, and sometimes they go one way and sometimes they go another. That is one of the main reasons why I am so suspicious of authority. And I think that to preserve any liberty whatever to the individual, we must watch carefully to prevent the encroachments of what we call the state or organized society.

Now, let me refer specifically to some of my friend's remarks. He says that he doesn't object to a man drinking if he goes off alone. Well, that is the way I do it generally. But he objects to society drinking. Well, society doesn't drink—only individual men and women drink.

I object to a man being drunk if he gets in the way of anybody else. I don't mind his being drunk alone. But if I want to take a drink and do not get drunk where I interfere with anybody else, should society then tell me that I can't drink? Or, if Brother Holmes—no, I will not use him; I will take the chairman —if he hasn't got any more sense than to get drunk, is that any reason why I, who do not get drunk, shall not have anything to drink? Now—is it?

He says that, of course, to forbid us smoking would be sumptuary legislation and nobody would stand for it. Wouldn't they? There is a big movement in this country today to pass legislation against smoking—and every man and woman in it is a prohibitionist.

Now, I don't believe in encouraging prohibitionists. There isn't anything that they would stop at. They would pass a law to make you go to church—as they have done. They did that in New England, and they picked out the church. They would send you to jail if you didn't go to it. And then they passed a law against your sleeping in church—and that took all the pleasure out of religion.

I say that nobody in their right senses would trust their individual liberty to the people who believe in that sort of legislation.

My friend says he believes in liberty—liberty of speech, liberty of the press. I can talk about beer, but I can't drink it. What is the use of talking about it? All that makes it worse when I can't drink it. Right now in this discussion I get thirsty just talking about it.

Can you have any liberty without liberty of action? Liberty of thinking and liberty of talking—well, everybody doesn't like to talk as well as my friend and I do.

Of course, I know perfectly well that a man isn't absolutely free. In fact, I don't know that he is free at all. He imagines he is, and that is something. I know that everybody gets tied up in all sorts of ways.

He says that in matrimony a man sacrifices fifty per cent of his freedom. I think he has got the percentage rather low. Somewhere around one hundred would be better. But if a man does it—why, he does it. I would object to the state forcing it on us—forcing us either to get in or stay in.

If a man goes on a steamboat, he sacrifices some liberty, if it is out on the ocean; but that is different from putting him on it. Men may voluntarily accept certain conditions, but that isn't the state's affair, and the state should not have anything to do with putting you there or making you stay.

Now, let's see whether we can get any kind of basis here on this question—and it isn't easy when one meets the issue fairly and openly, as my friend does. Shall we support a theory of government where the majority, by a vote, may make anything criminal if they do not believe in it?

Now, they can do it. I never talk about the "rights" of anybody. There is no such thing as "rights," anyhow. It is a question of whether you can put it over. In any legal sense or any practical sense, whatever is, is "a right." If you can put it over, all right!

I don't believe in the Eighteenth Amendment, but it is here. And I wouldn't believe in it if I knew that the people in this country could get richer under it; I still don't believe in it. Of course, they would get richer without coffee, in which he seems to believe, and he probably drinks it. Everybody believes in what they want and they are not interested in what the other fellow wants, unless they want it, too.

I am not interested in making the people richer or even healthier. I don't know about making people better. Maybe, if I made them better—what I think is better—they would be worse. I am rather interested in letting the individual do his own thinking, if any, but he would have more fun while he was doing it.

Now, let me admit for the sake of argument. He has told you what area was dry in the United States—a great area, but not much besides area. All the desert—that is dry. All the South —that is dry, as far as the Negroes are concerned. Railroad employees are dry. That doesn't mean the presidents, mind, or the general managers or any of the officers. Oh, no, I know them myself. It doesn't mean them. The prairies are dry and the farmers—I never count them either.

But the vast centers of population, where all the feeling for liberty that still persists in this country is kept alive, the great centers of tolerance and independence and thought and culture, the cities—all of them were wet before prohibition, and since.

It isn't a question simply whether prohibition would be good if there ever was any such thing. Of course, we don't know whether it would be good or not, yet. I never knew anybody with money who couldn't get a drink. Do any of you? I would agree to find places here, although I am a stranger. I wouldn't have to look far. They would come to me. I never knew anybody in this land of ours, under the Amendment and under the Volstead Act, to go thirsty.

Of course, it has raised the price. It hasn't placed it within the reach of all. It has substituted whiskey for beer to many people—which I think is a poor substitution. It has made people drink gin and whiskey where they once chose wine—which is a poor substitution. It has done all of those things. And I imagine there is no system of prohibition under which it will not always do those things, and that is practically the only thing it will do.

Now, suppose we admit, for the sake of the argument, that sixty per cent of the people of this country would vote dry. If sixty per cent of the people do not believe in something that the other forty per cent believe in, should they send the forty per cent to jail for what they do?

Now, there is your question. What proportion of a population should believe that certain acts are criminal before passing a criminal statute? If forty per cent of the people of this country believe that a thing is innocent, do you think that the sixty per cent who do not believe it would send that forty per cent to jail if they were tolerant people?

I assume that sixty per cent of the people in this country believe in either the Protestant or Catholic religion, or think they do, and believe that it is very necessary to man's welfare on earth and absolutely necessary to his welfare in the hereafter. Are they justified in passing a criminal statute and sending heretics to jail?

They have done it, and they may do it again, because intolerance is just as strong in the world today as it ever was. And when we permit it to have its way, nobody knows who will be the victims. Intolerance is ever vital and living. They not only have sent them to jail for heresy, but they have burned them at the stake for it. They broke them on the rack. They visited every means of torture upon them, simply because of a difference in religious opinion.

I suppose my friend will say those were sumptuary laws. What is a sumptuary law? A law regulating your personal habits or your personal conduct. He says it would be a sumptuary law if you passed a law against drinking coffee. Then why not if you passed one against drinking beer? It is a sumptuary law if it is against drinking coffee, but it is not a sumptuary law if it is against drinking beer. Why didn't he tell us why that was? Nobody could tell us which of the two is better or worse for the constitution. And if it is worse, what of it? I might take a little chance on my constitution for something I wanted to do. What is the use of taking such good care of your constitution, anyhow?

What is a sumptuary law? Here is the state of New York, that forbids the playing of professional baseball on Sunday. They may have changed it lately, I don't know. They are getting wickeder and wickeder, every day in every way. But Pennsylvania is so good that they can't do it yet. They would forbid you going out in your automobile (if the law were strictly construed) on Sunday.

He says that liquor is in the way of automobiles. Well, then, let's get rid of the automobiles. Now, he might prefer having an automobile. Well—I have no automobile, so I would rather have beer.

It all resolves itself into a question of either you getting your ideas over or the other fellow getting his ideas over. And that seems to be the common idea of government. Instead of tolerating each other's frailties and getting along as best we can with each other's peculiarities, we say that if it is right for me it is right that you should do the same thing, because I know what is right and you don't know what is right.

Now, if it is a sumptuary law to forbid the one thing, why it is a sumptuary law to forbid the other thing. Some fellow might forbid eating johnnycake. Well, it wouldn't hurt me, but I would hate to have them tackle pie. Yet pie, I know, isn't nearly as healthy as johnnycake. Perhaps that is the reason I like it better. Really, I never did like anything that was healthy or anybody that was healthy. It is—well, kind of too healthy—there is not enough excitement about it.

Is this glorious state of ours—and all the wisdom isn't in Congress, although I sometimes think that all the ignorance is— to appraise a human being, measure him up and figure out his appetites and his tastes and his capacity, and then just determine what sort of food and what diet will keep him alive the longest? We would have a fine time, wouldn't we?

Now, if we put this question to the members of the Women's Christian Temperance Union, I know I would be out my beer. But I know that all of them would stick to coffee and tea —every last one of them—and it wouldn't change their minds a bit if we told them it was killing them by inches; they would keep it because they like it.

And, after all, that is mostly why we eat and drink. Is anybody going to change this human race so that it will be rational according to what will produce the most muscle and the most fat and the least brains?

Take out of this world the men who have drunk, down through the past, and you would take away all the poetry and literature and practically all the works of genius that the world has produced. What kind of a poem do you suppose you would get out of a glass of ice-water?

Why, there is nothing to it. Who is the fellow that is going to measure up the human being and tell him what he needs—what will make him stout like a horse, or make him live long like an elephant—and then pass laws to see that he conforms?

Do not the desires and the emotions and the feelings of the human beings count? Why, by the time the state, moved by the reformers, makes every man over in its own likeness, what do you suppose he will look like?

That is what they have always done. Haven't we had enough experience in the past? Let anybody look at the long trail through which the world has wended its way, and then say whether the fight for liberty is worth while, whether we should meekly surrender because, forsooth, somebody tells us we can live longer and we can drive an automobile better if we don't have a drink.

What have we done in New England, for instance? We have had laws against witchcraft, and old women have been put to death for being witches. Of course, if they had put young women to death, there would be some sense in it.

It was made a criminal offense to go to a theater. It was a criminal offense to dance—although, of course, everybody was going to have the privilege of dancing in the hereafter if they were bad, much to the pleasure of the Puritans. It was a criminal offense to go anywhere on Sunday, except to church. And it was a criminal offense not to go there, else they wouldn't have gone.

The prohibitionist is the lineal descendant of the Puritan. I didn't know it before, but even my friend here says that he came from Massachusetts. But he believes somewhat in freedom. He believes in the liberty of speech and of the press. Well, there are some people that like to do something besides talking and writing. That doesn't cover the whole range of liberty. Almost every sort of conduct has been hedged around in this world by fanatics.

Now, I will tell you what is back of it all. It may take some time for it to get into some of your heads, but I will tell you. It is this old heaven-and-hell idea that God, somehow, levels things up, and if you are happy in this world you are going to be tortured in the next. They all believe in futures. They are going to be happy somewhere else. There is a large percentage of the population of this country and the world that have got it into their heads that happiness is sinful. They must not go to the theater, they must not drink, they must not do anything they want to do, but just something they don't want to do. Now, that is the basis of it all.

Let's see about this question of liquor. It has always been on the earth and always been used—many times to excess, of course. Food has also been on the earth and also used, generally to excess. I never saw anybody that didn't eat too much, if he could afford it. And if you go down to the graveyard and look them over and learn their history, I will guarantee you will find that there are ten funerals pulled off where the corpses would have lived longer if they hadn't had so much to eat, to every one that would have lived longer if it hadn't drank so much.

Suppose the question of eating certain kinds of food or drinking certain kinds of liquid were put up to the community, and forty per cent of the people thought it was right. Who are the other sixty per cent who would have the audacity to send those forty per cent to jail for doing something the sixty didn't believe in?

On how many questions do two people think alike? They can go only a certain way, when they branch off and leave each other. Men ought to hesitate a long time before they vote that a certain thing is a crime—and prohibition means crime.

I have been raised, we'll assume, to drink beer. Nature ferments the cider and the grape-juice, and the world has always used it—the good and the bad alike—in churches, also. They have used it on all occasions. They have used it for the festivity of the wedding and the sorrow of the burial, for all time. And probably three-fourths of the people of the earth believe they should have a perfect right to use it—and at least forty per cent of the people of the United States.

If the doctrine should prevail that when sixty per cent of the people of a country believe that certain conduct should be a criminal offense and for that conduct they must send the forty per cent to jail, then liberty is dead and freedom is gone. They will first destroy the forty per cent, and then turn and destroy each other.

In this world of ours we cannot live with our neighbors without a broad tolerance. We must tolerate their religion, their social life, their customs, their appetites of eating and drinking, and we should be very slow, indeed, when we make criminal conduct of what is believed by vast numbers of men and women to be honest and fair and right.

This prohibition law has filled our jails with people who are not criminals, who have no conception or feeling that they are doing wrong. It has turned our federal courts into police courts, where important business is put aside for cases of drunkenness and disorderly conduct. It has made spies and detectives, snooping around doors and windows. It has made informers of thousands of us. It has made grafters and boodlers of men who otherwise would be honest. It is hateful, it is distasteful, it is an abomination, and we ought to get rid of it, and we will if we have the courage and the sense. . . .

Let me just see how logical my friend is. He said that if he lived in a flat and some family got to playing the piano and dancing and having a good time until three or four o'clock in the morning so that he couldn't sleep, wouldn't he be justified in having them arrested for breaking the peace? Yes. But that isn't what he would do. He would get a constitutional amendment passed to destroy every piano in the United States.

Now, he says that he wouldn't bother people who drink coffee, although he doesn't drink it himself. Well, that is good of him. I wish he wouldn't bother about the people who drink beer. But he says the trouble comes when a thing slops over into the community. None of mine ever did. He says, "If you do it alone, all right." Let's see about that. I never got drunk in my life. I never drank much—before. And I don't believe I ever disturbed any neighbors on that account—and I don't believe there is one in a thousand who ever drank, that did. Now, I don't object to his bothering the one in a thousand. Arrest him, send him to jail. With me it doesn't slop over, and yet you are going to take care of that fool fellow who gets drunk and disturbs the peace, by not giving me any beer.

Who did put over this fool prohibition business? Was it the

killjoys? I came from the country, and up to the time I was ten years old, I used to be dragged to church on Thursday nights to listen to a prohibition meeting, and I will bet I signed the pledge a thousand times. There wasn't anything to drink within fifty miles of me, but I signed the pledge, and everybody else did. That was all we had to do in the country. The meetings were always held in churches, Presbyterian, Baptist or Methodist, as a rule. I am not crazy about them—I might just as well admit it. I don't mind their going to heaven in their own way, but I want them to let me go to hell my own way, in peace. God will take care of me after I get there. These are the backbone of the pro-hibition movement of America today, and they always have been.

Is there any question about all this? Let's see. You have heard of the Anti-Saloon League, haven't you? They have been holding meetings in this country, in the churches, for years. They have an organization, and whenever a congressman would rise with a little bit of intelligence, they would pick him off. Of course, that ought to be a good reason for picking off a congress-man. But if a man were "dry," even though he might be a thief, a crook, or the worst enemy the world ever had, every blooming fool fellow who belonged to that League would vote for him. If he were a statesman, a philosopher, a historian, a wise man, but took a drink, he would have to go. So they loaded up the Congress of the United States with nincompoops, with brainless people who would take their commands and sell their souls for votes—and they voted this country dry while these congressmen had liquor salted away in their cellars. A set of hypocrites and vote-mongers who voted this country dry while they had liquor in their cellars, and they have had it there ever since. There is no question about it; not the slightest.

Science? Did anybody ever do anything from science? No. Science never affected the opinions of men. We have had science, plenty of it, for fifty, sixty or a hundred years, but Billy Bryan and Billy Sunday still draw crowds. Nobody cares about science—never did, unless they are going to make some chemi-cal compound.

How did they get this law through? Everybody knows how they got it through. Under false pretenses. They got it through by, first, a system of regulations which might have been all right in wartime, to save food and save labor, and so they cut down on the liquor supply. For quite a while I didn't have any sugar, either. Why didn't you prohibit that? Also butter, and a whole lot of other things.

They fixed up that law in wartime, when everybody but the prohibitionists were fighting—and they were policing the camps to see that the soldiers didn't get a drink, because they said they couldn't fight if they had something to drink. Didn't the Germans fight? Didn't the French fight? And even our fellows, when they got over there, where things were free, and they were in a land of some kind of liberty, and had something to drink.

And so the things which came purely as a war measure, they foisted on the country in time of peace, and these trafficking, miserable politicians voted for it, scarcely one of them believing in it. And they never did submit it to the people. They passed it through state legislatures, under the threats of this League that held the whip above their backs, and is doing it today, until nobody dares speak. That is how it came here.

What I say is this: No man who has in him the spirit of tolerance, or any regard for the opinions of others, would pass a criminal statute which would make criminals of forty per cent of the people of the United States. He would hesitate and doubt whether he was right. He might elect a president, he might elect an official, but when it comes to sending a man to prison for an opinion or a habit or a custom or a practice, no man who has any regard for the rights of other men would do it when forty per cent were one way and sixty per cent the other way. If such were the case, what would become of most of us on some things? I know that more than sixty per cent of the people of this country would be against my religion. If we didn't keep the other fellows so busy fighting amongst themselves, it might be dangerous for us. You might land in the midst of the forty per cent at any time.

What would my friend do if they should pass a law in the United States that he couldn't enjoy the religious privileges which he enjoys today? And there has been many a time in the history of the world when he would have been burned at the stake for it if he had held out that long, and I think he is one of the kind who would. What would he think if the religious fanatics of this country should say that he couldn't preach freedom of thought, freedom of religion, obedience to conscience? It would be easy to get sixty per cent to say that, if they ever got their minds on it. And they don't ever need minds—they need votes, that's all. Do you suppose he would obey it? I don't believe he would. Do you suppose he would think it was right because a bare majority said so?

And yet all that he has said, in every position he has taken upon this question, is encouraging the bigotry that has made this world run red with blood. I don't care what a man believes, and I am not interested in his habits. He seems to be tricked more than anybody else by those two words, "white slavery." I wonder where he got them? Must have been at church. Of all the fool things ever put over in the United States that foolish talk was the worst. It never amounted to anything. Never was anything—just simply catchwords.

Social organization—control of men—regulating their diets and regulating their habits. For what? You are getting pretty close to the danger line when you begin it. And who are the ones that would do it? Have they the knowledge, the information— have they the scientific training to do it? Have they the wide tolerance, the spirit of "live and let live," which ought to prevail with any and all before they undertake the regulation of their fellow-man?

Now, my friend has tried to be fair about his statements, and I want to be fair about mine. I know that all the human ills cannot be cured, cannot be regulated, etc. Some fellow will get drunk and run an automobile, and somebody will get killed. Well —he would have died anyhow, sooner or later. My experience is that a very large majority of the human race die some time, and in some way. And I do not believe in picking out this thing or that thing or the other thing, which may have caused some particular death, and destroying it in a moment of anger or a moment of fear, regardless of what consequences will follow from it.

Now, suppose you were in trouble and wanted a real, human-being friend, and you knew that here was a prohibition-ist and over here was a fellow who drank. Which side would you take a chance on? Haven't the prohibitionists been the joy-killers since the very beginning of time? I cannot understand how my friend here, with his broad views and his intelligence, came to be one of them, except that he came down through the preacher line, and some of it lingers. For you know, "You may break, you may shatter the vase if you will, but the preacher psychology sticks around still."

Am I right in saying that they are the joy-killers, who look with envy upon people who have a good time? The people who would forbid you to drink, would forbid you to dance, would forbid you to go to the theater. I will guarantee that half of the prohibitionists in this country would close the theaters on Sunday —no, nine-tenths of them would, and most of them would close them every day. They would forbid dancing. It is a question of joy.

Now, I don't mean to say that books were written and pictures were painted because of alcohol. But it takes a certain kind of nervous system, a certain kind of imagination, a certain kind of temperament to write a book or paint a picture—a book that anybody will read or a picture that anybody will look at—and that same kind of a nervous system has always craved some liquor, and always will.

If you could gradually kill off anybody who ever drank, or wanted to, and leave the world to prohibitionists—my God, would any of us want to live in it?

Clarence Darrow on the Immigration Law, 1929

I am glad my friend wants to meet this question squarely. Facing things squarely is what I believe in doing, and he does also.

The law as it stands today, passed in 1924, provides that 150,000 immigrants may come to the United States annually, and that the number should be fixed for each country according to the number of citizens of that country who had emigrated to the United States, but that it should be the number of citizens who had emigrated previous to 1890—thirty-five years before the law was passed. Instead of using 1924 as the basis of immigration quotas, they dated it back thirty-five years. Why? So they could get Nordics from England and Scotland, and Norway, and Sweden, and exclude the people from Italy, France, and the Balkan states, and Russian Jews.

The problem is clear. Our friend does not dodge it. To him and to some other people here who claim to be old stock, the northern European Nordics are the salt of the earth. I am a foreigner; my people didn't get here until about 1710. They got here, and now I am asked to close the doors to the people who come over on a later ship. I am not for it, for several reasons.

Our friend talks about the rights of countries to do things. Countries have rights only when they have power to enforce them. I don't agree with him because I have imagination; that is all. I can imagine myself being an Italian and wanting a better chance, or being a Russian Jew and wanting a better chance, or being an Austrian and wanting a better chance. It is hard for me to forget that there are other people on earth besides the stock I came from.

He speaks of the people in the United States now as if they owned this country. Why, the first of them came over on the Mayflower. They couldn't stay at home without going to jail for debt. They were selfish, superstitious, and bigoted in the extreme. They came over here to get a chance. The real American was the Indian, and they solved that problem by killing him. The land was occupied, but they took it, and then our Puritan fathers proceeded to pass the most outrageous laws that any country ever knew anything about.

What are our institutions, anyway? He spoke of trial by jury. There is a very strong, active element in the United States now who are trying to destroy trial by jury, and every last one of them is a Nordic, and they are rich. I know of some of these Nordics who have taken the best mines and the best buildings, and the land of America, and they want to keep every last one of the rest of us out. My ancestors came here to get a better chance, and I don't believe in closing the doors on the people who would like to come for the same reason now.

We are told that the laboring man is against immigration. I don't know what he is for and against this year, and he doesn't know what he is for and against next year. I have always been for the poor man, but I am not for injustice as I see it either for the rich man or the poor man. Who are these working men? Most of them haven't been here as long as I have. I have been here so long that I don't need to work. Is it justice to allow these late comers to close the doors and allow nobody else to come? If there is anything like justice, and the rules are not strict, I don't want to believe that stuff. And I am not going to, because even if I haven't found any clear idea of justice I have a clear idea of imagination, of common barnyard sympathy, and it tells me that the people of the world must be treated somewhat alike.

We are told that we must not have the Sicilians here because they are people who rob the rich; well, I should worry. Where do you suppose these rich people get all the money they are getting robbed of? The reason for this is that a few of them think they own America and they want to reduce the people to slavery, and they are doing it almighty fast. They are doing it while they talk of elections and fake prosperity. It is only people who have had prosperity who are prosperous. They own all the mines, all the coal, all the lumber, and everything else that is worth owning. They will soon own all the stores, and the little corner storekeeper can go and tramp the streets, and I wouldn't care much, for they have always been fooled by the very people who are now trying to get their property away from them.

They are combining one thing with another, until they will soon have it all. If the people from southern Europe can help us equalize it, I am for them. But I have no feeling of the divine right of property; not a particle. These things are arranged in this world in a particular way partly because it happened so and partly because they who are on top are the strongest.

Are these descendants of the Mayflower such wonderful people? I don't know. They used to hang old women in New England for being witches, and everybody knows that an old woman couldn't be a witch. These Mayflower descendants are the most devoid of human sympathy of any people on the earth today. What do they care about people? They like to work; that is all.

And do you talk about labor unions being interested in this question? Well, I expect you can fool all the working people as you can the farmers. I think I read in your book, Mr. Stoddard, that the machine power of the United States is equal to the labor of three billion people. Well, at least that statement was correct.

A lot of others may have been. We have three billion man-power in the nation, and the working man is afraid to have one hundred and fifty thousand people come into this country in a year. When we learn to take care of the production of these machines, we can take care of the whole world if we want to.

And there is another point. This country isn't a quarter settled, nor a tenth. If it were, and we had the proper social order, would we be poorer than we are now? Three men at work will probably produce more than three times as much as one can now; probably six times as much. Then with proper systems of distribution we shall be so rich that we will die of fat. We can produce now infinitely more than we can consume because the poor people haven't a chance to buy anything. To me, this whole idea is narrow, selfish, unimaginative, and cruel; somehow I can't believe it is a good thing. I think it would be a good thing for the United States to get a little idealism into her.

My friend is entirely wrong when he says that this act was brought about by a bright light which dawned in 1920 and grew until in 1924 it resulted in the most unjust law that America ever passed—and that is going some. Do you suppose it was passed because there was any need on the part of the working man? Did it grow out of any idea of political expediency? No; it came from the mistaken idea of patriotism. This kind of patriotism is a heritage from the war; it was handed down by the army, the navy, and now it is being dispensed throughout Rotary Clubs, the Eagles, and other clubs that are shouting themselves hoarse about patriotism; they know nothing about it.

The whole movement is narrow, stupid, mean, contemptible. I can, I believe, point out a few broad principles that should affect human beings. We have wandered from the ideas of the past; we used to encourage people to come here. The only habit or custom they have that is different from ours is that they take a drink of wine in the open, whereas we have to hide to drink ours. I have traveled quite extensively abroad and some in America, though I prefer to travel in Europe because of the present drought in America. Of course, Canada will do.

Are our political institutions any different than theirs? Before the war the king of Italy had no power; Italy was governed completely as England is governed by Parliament. Today she has a usurper who is an absolute tyrant, but the Italians don't like him any more than we do, and some day he will forget to put on his steel shirt, and it will be the last of him.

And was there any difference between the Italian government and the British government before the war? They sent their boys and had them killed for democracy, just as we did. And now that the war is over we say, "You can't come and associate with us descendants of the old Puritan fathers who hanged old women as witches."

When was it that that load of Pilgrims came over? That was about 1620, I believe. And they landed on Plymouth Rock; that was a tough day. What is there about those people that isn't true about everybody else? What else was different or is today different about these southern Europeans? Their family life? No. They have five wives at once, and we have them one at a time.

I knew my father and my mother; I knew two of my grandparents; back of that I have only heard; I know nothing further. How far can you go back and still know that pure Nordic blood is running in your veins? Why, we are mixed with all the animal species. Did you ever take out your blood, drop by drop, and say, "Here is a drop of English blood; here is one of Swedish; I am sorry, but here is some Italian blood." And one time, to be a Roman was to be greater than to be a king. Can you sort it out? I don't think so. If I could, I would turn out the Nordic.

There is no such thing as a race. There are people who are isolated in certain communities for a long time and they take on particular characteristics, but spread them out over a long period of time and they vanish. What do we know about the origin of things, anyhow?

Let us look at the history of the world. First the Chaldeans, then the Babylonians, then the Egyptians. Coming down to the modern world, we get a great deal from the Greeks—perhaps the greatest people who ever lived. Of course the Nordics would have been greater if they had lived then. And then the Romans, the Italians whom we speak of so lightly; the great colonizers and empire builders. Then we come down to the English; and now the Americans. Where are we going? We are probably on our way. Soon we shall land in the dust heap and something else will take our places.

When you try to interfere with the working out of the laws of nature, you get hurt, and for our puny minds to say that this is good and that is bad, and that this is better and that is worse for the short time we shall be here on earth is just foolishness. . . .

I may say that my friend seems to meet this issue squarely, but it seems that there is no discrimination. Is the present law which discriminates against the southeastern European a good policy? If there is no question, then what is this all about?

Just because somebody comes here and raises more food, should that make me poorer? No; it ought to make me richer. There is no excuse for a poor man in America. And yet Secretary Davis estimates that eighty-five per cent of the people in America are poor. Well, they didn't all vote for Al Smith; some of them voted for the high-priest of efficiency—because of prosperity. These folks are not poor because America is over-populated. If our population were reduced to ten million, eighty-five per cent of them would be poor. If it were increased to five hundred million, still eighty-five per cent of them would be poor.

I do not know why my friend is interested in the unborn millions who have a right to be born. These millions of unborn Americans consist of the trillions of cells in the future women of the race down the course of perhaps a million years, and the septillions of male cells that might possibly happen to fertilize those particular cells if certain accidents should turn out that way. I never asked to be born; that isn't the way we got here. Now you are here; what are you going to do about it? We all have some intelligence. We have a little common idealism to let other people live, and about all we can do to settle a question rightly is to settle it upon what little light we have.

We drove the Indian out because there wasn't room here for both races, and the Indian was already becoming crowded. What right had we to say to the people of the rest of the world that they can't come? Why can't they come? Because away down the course of time, perhaps a million years hence, the unborn babies are struggling to get born in America.

Now I have one kind of imagination; my friend has another.

I can't for the life of me understand anybody who is worrying about what is going to happen to him in five hundred thousand years. There won't be any America to me in fifteen years; perhaps a little less. I have looked up the obituary tables. Why should I worry about what is going to happen in America a thousand years from now? I don't. I have children, but they must take their chances with all the other children of the world. They need expect no pile of money to be left by me. I can help them best by trying to make the world decent so that every child who lives may have a chance.

There is no excuse for poverty, especially in America, and there is no use for it anywhere else. Is England poor? Why? Because a few people own all of it. Need France or Germany be poor, barring a war they have just been through? Why have they been poor? Just for the same reason that a few people in the world take it all. Are the people of China poor? Yes. The older a country is and the more thoroughly organized it is, the poorer the people are.

If an old Italian comes to America and gets three dollars a day, does that make you poorer? It is not production that causes poverty; it is lack of distribution. If we ever get to the point where the captains of industry turn their attention to the distribution of things instead of production, this question will be solved.

I have done everything about labor except work. I have tried many of their cases, and I sympathize with them on account of their conditions of labor. Have you ever a time when working men seeking higher wages or better conditions were not met by the combined wealth of the rich, or by a machine? The rich never did care, and they never will care; they are interested in keeping America for the Americans, and to keep out bolshevist ideas. They don't even know what these words mean. They say the same old fool things over and over again, without a single thought as to what the words mean. They are all organized for a common purpose—to keep things as they are.

I am not in favor of keeping things as they are; I would like to make them better, but I do not like to make them better by forgetting the poor of other lands, by injustice, by oppression, by wrong. I don't think justice can ever grow on injustice; I don't believe that kindness and humanity can ever come from selfishness. I do not believe that because we get to a place first where there is plenty of room, that we should say to others like ourselves, "You can't come."

Are these men afraid of Russian working men or Russian ideas? Are they afraid of Russian laborers or Russian Jews? Why is it, if American machinery is equal to three billion men, that we can't live in comfort and plenty? There is just one reason, that's all—the horrible injustice of an unfair division of wealth. We have forgotten all about it; we have lost all sense of proportion; we have lost all sympathy with our fellow-men.

Isn't that a fine picture here in America? With our great natural resources we can produce enough to feed the whole world. Here in America, and we must keep everyone else out because of the unborn millions. Germany, France, and England are doing the same thing. What is it? Is it anything less than the backsweep of a great war that carried with it all the human feeling that man has acquired? All over the world we find that the war for democracy made everybody cruel and hard. We told everybody to fight for democracy, and now we are fighting for the spoils.

I find again that nothing will pay in the long run unless it meets our feelings of kindness, of humanity, of universal sympathy, of the brotherhood of man which Christians talk about on Sunday but whose gates they close up on Monday.

Why, if Jesus Christ, as the story has been told, should land in Wilmington tomorrow, he would be deported. He would be lucky if he got off with that.

I tell you, this world has grown soggy and cruel since the Great War. I was a near-patriot myself. I believed in the war, and fought for it with oratory, if this is oratory, but I am beginning to realize that I was not quite logical in my arguments. I see the direct result that comes to every country on the earth—tyranny, oppression, filled jails, prohibition, and every other plague that infested Egypt.

Now let us see if we can't settle this question. Are you going to have less because somebody else comes here and works? If you do, something is wrong with distribution, isn't it? I remember when that green statesman, the inspired president who was given to the United States as a direct act of the Almighty, Calvin Coolidge, had his attention called to the troubles the southern farmers were having about the price of cotton. He said, "Well, we will try to do something for you, but you mustn't raise so much again." The same is true of the farmers in the West. But when the manufacturers are stumped on account of over-production they don't have any trouble. They own the mills, and they can shut them down until the demand catches up. The trouble with our world is that we are suffering from too much.

There isn't any need for poverty. There is room on the earth for all the people who are here. Although population may overtake the food supply, it hasn't done so yet. And we may be able to make food out of the primary elements more cheaply than we can raise it. We may be able to make everything we need, and much more cheaply than at present. If the work of three billion people can be done by the machines invented in the last generation, what difference can be made in our economic organization by having one Italian or Russian Jew come over here?

There are such people as descendants of Nordics; they are hounds for the Nordics. And now we have a law, unjust in every way you look at it, dated back to 1890 because at that time the southern European hadn't come in such great numbers.

Why is an Englishman so much better than an Italian? The Italians have produced wealth on the old abandoned New England farms. I suppose they will own New England some day; and I know they will be more tolerant than the Puritans ever were. Why should we cut out anybody? Isn't one as good as another?

I suppose I am a Nordic. I am not bragging about it; I am apologizing for it. Of course, I am not a Puritan in much. I believe in taking a drink; I believe in letting everybody else take a drink. But I am broadminded about it; I don't believe in forcing a Puritan to take a drink if he doesn't want it. And I am of Puritan stock, but from so far back that I can't trace it.

Men can't be separated on kinds of blood any longer. As you know, all kinds of blood circulate in all human beings who live. We go back to Europe; they go back to Asia; for a million years men have been tramping up and down over the face of

America. I can't know all my ancestors; I can't know all the kinds of blood that are mixed in me.

Who am I to say that my kind alone shall come to America and all the rest must stay away? I believe this earth is big enough for all the human race. When it gets so crowded that they can't all live, if I am here I will be willing to cast lots to decide who shall die and who shall stay, and give everybody an even break.

Suggestions for Further Reading

The Drive for Internal Security

William Preston, Jr., *Aliens and Dissenters: Federal Suppression of Radicals, 1903–1933* (1963)*; Melvin Dubofsky, *We Shall be All: A History of the Industrial Workers of the World* (1969); Theodore Draper, *The Roots of American Communism* (1957)*; Robert K. Murray, *Red Scare: A Study in National Hysteria, 1919–1920* (1955); Robert L. Friedheim, *The Seattle General Strike* (1964); Stanley Coben, *A. Mitchell Palmer* (1963); George L. Joughin and Edmund M. Morgan, *The Legacy of Sacco and Vanzetti* (1948)*; Paul L. Murphy, "Sources and Nature of Intolerance in the 1920's," *Journal of American History*, vol. 51 (1964), pp. 60–76.

The Heyday of Racism

John Higham, *Strangers in the Land . . . American Nativism, 1860–1925* (1955)*; William S. Bernard, *American Immigration Policy* (1950); David M. Chalmers, *Hooded Americanism . . . the Ku Klux Klan* (1965)*; Charles C. Alexander, *The Ku Klux Klan in the Southwest* (1965)*; Emma Lou Thornbrough, "Segregation in Indiana during the Klan Era of the 1920's," *Mississippi Valley Historical Review*, vol. 47 (1961), pp. 594–618; Kenneth T. Jackson, *The Ku Klux Klan in the City 1915–1930* (1967)*.

The Indians

William T. Hagan, *American Indians* (1961)*; Henry L. Fritz, *The Movement for Indian Assimilation* (1963); Randolph

C. Downes, "A Crusade for Indian Reform, 1922–1934," *Mississippi Valley Historical Review*, vol. 32 (1945), pp. 331–354.

The Black Man

August Meier, *Negro Thought in America, 1880–1915* (1963)*; Samuel R. Spencer, *Booker T. Washington* (1955)*; W.E.B. Du Bois, *Dusk of Dawn* (1940)*; Francis L. Broderick, *W.E.B. Du Bois* (1959)*; Elliott M. Rudwick, *W.E.B. Du Bois* (1960)*; Louise Kennedy, *The Negro Peasant Turns Cityward* (1920); James Weldon Johnson, *Black Manhattan* (1930)*; Gilbert Osofsky, *Harlem: The Making of a Ghetto* (1966)*; Allan H. Spear, *Black Chicago: The Making of a Negro Ghetto* (1967)*; Robert A. Bone, *The Negro Novel in America* (1965)*; Stephen Bronz, *Roots of Negro Racial Consciousness: The 1920's* (1964); E. David Cronon, *Black Moses: The Story of Marcus Garvey* (1955)*; Richard B. Sherman, "The Harding Administration and the Negro . . . ," *Journal of Negro History*, vol. 49 (1964).

Religious Crisis in Modern America

Paul A. Carter, *The Decline and Revival of the Social Gospel . . . 1920–1940* (1956); Robert M. Miller, *American Protestantism and Social Issues, 1919–1939* (1958); Donald B. Meyer, *The Protestant Search for Political Realism, 1919–1941* (1960); Kenneth K. Bailey, *Southern White Protestantism in the Twentieth Century* (1964); William G. McLoughlin, *Billy Sunday Was His Real Name* (1955); Norman F. Furniss, *The Fundamentalist Controversy, 1918–1931* (1954); Ray Ginger, *Six Days or Forever? Tennessee v. John Thomas Scopes* (1958)*; Lawrence W. Levine, *Defender of the Faith, William Jennings Bryan . . . the Last Decade, 1915–1925* (1965)*.

Prohibition

James H. Timberlake, *Prohibition and the Progressive Movement, 1900–1920* (1963); Charles Merz, *The Dry Decade* (1931); Andrew Sinclair, *Prohibition, the Era of Excess* (1962)*.

Four negroes hung to death.

Tri-City Social Club.

All photos on this page, courtesy of Culver Pictures, Inc.

"It seems there was a negro and an Irishman and a Jew—"

From *Judge* magazine, August 16, 1924.
Courtesy of Culver Pictures, Inc.

Treasury agents wrecking a bar. Courtesy of Brown Brothers.

Calvin Coolidge campaign headquarters in Minneapolis, 1924.
Courtesy of the Minnesota Historical Society.

Listening to auto radio, 1922.
Courtesy of Culver Pictures, Inc.

Traffic practice.
Courtesy of the Minnesota Historical Society.

Chapter Four

The Politics of Normalcy

"Four-fifths of all our troubles in this life would disappear," mused President Calvin Coolidge in the Twenties, "if we would only sit down and keep still." For over five laconic years, "Silent Cal" sat still, confident that he had little to do in the White House, since as he put it tersely, "the business of America is business." Businessmen, untrammeled by government controls or labor unions, knew what was best for the country they had built, he thought, and therefore they deserved to run it. A generation earlier, another Republican president, Theodore Roosevelt, espousing the Progressive view, voiced contrary sentiments. "The more I see of the wealthy," he had maintained, "the more profoundly convinced I am of their entire unfitness to govern the country. . . ." By the 1920s Roosevelt's view became passé.

The Eclipse of Progressivism

Progressivism declined in the 1920s, a victim of internal weaknesses. A vague, amorphous coalition, more a frame of mind than a movement, held temporary control of both political parties by catering to widespread fear that unchecked private power condemned millions to poverty, corrupted government, despoiled natural resources, and crushed the initiative of independent businessmen and farmers. The middle classes who cheered Roosevelt and Wilson feared social convulsions and

176

backed politicians who promised to curb private power. Progressives claimed to have risen above class interest. They searched for ways to stabilize a turbulent society and replace group conflict, such as that which had burst forth so violently in the late nineteenth century, with more rational and equitable means of making decisions. They sought a more cohesive, peaceful and just society—one in which, incidentally, they would have greater power.

Progressive results fell far short of progressive aspirations. Despite modest successes, two decades of reform did not equalize power and end privilege. A few persons still monopolized the nation's wealth; Big Business had not been tamed; the economy remained vulnerable to the boom and bust cycle; and millions of Americans still lived in squalor with little prospect, no matter what they did, of improving their conditions. By 1916 Progressivism seemed exhausted politically. Wilson barely won a second term; the standpatters whom Theodore Roosevelt had checked regained control of the Republican party and Progressivism floundered, lacking clear direction. The eagerness to achieve reform ebbed among the middle classes. Many believed their purposes accomplished with the adoption of Wilson's New Freedom in 1913 and parts of the New Nationalism in 1916. The much-feared explosion of the downtrodden never materialized and the humanitarians comforted themselves by believing that life for the have-nots was improving as a result of the social gospel, settlement work, labor legislation, and the slow growth of labor unions.

In the end Progressives failed to achieve reform because they did not understand clearly the realities of power, and they were not willing to push for fundamental changes in the structure of society without which stability, cohesion and social justice were impractical goals. Regarding themselves as a disinterested class, eager to avoid conflict, Progressives failed to mobilize the underdogs, their "charges," the only effective way to counter the entrenched power of conservatism. Still wedded to individualism, still fearful of lodging too much power in the hands of government, and still suspicious of labor, Progressives relied excessively on private, voluntary instruments for reform and on goodwill to solve social problems. Progressives did enlarge the scope of government, but such characteristic Progressive goals as tariff reduction, antitrust laws, and the purification of politics were aimed primarily at increasing opportunity for themselves. Progressives took tentative steps toward welfare statism—such as workmen's compensation, tenement house reform, and minimum wage laws for women—but they failed to press for comprehensive measures that would assure a minimum decent standard of living for all Americans.

Nothing revealed the shallowness and confusion of Progressivism more graphically than its uncertain grappling with the trusts. In the campaign of 1912, Wilson had promised to destroy monopolies; as president he reassured businessmen by loading the Federal Reserve Board and Federal Trade Commission with pro-business appointees. LaFollette, unsullied by power, remained a consistent crusader against "monopoly" but produced no alternative to the large corporation; and Theodore Roosevelt, who accepted bigness as inevitable and beneficial so long as the titans of industry consulted him or men like him, ended his career by returning to the party he had abandoned as a hopeless captive of reactionaries and a saber rattler in foreign affairs.

For Roosevelt, as for so many other Progressives, the First World War came as a great relief, and he rushed to offer his military services. "The American nation needs the tonic of a serious moral adventure," advised Herbert Croly, theoretician of the New Nationalism. Croly, like other Progressives, saw the war as an opportunity to provide new outlets for the reform impulse. Going to war to make the world safe for democracy enabled Progressives to substitute for the confusion at home a grandiose enterprise abroad.

The Role of the War

At first the war justified Progressive expectations. Fighting a war required national unity. Americans would have to stop quarreling among themselves and cooperate to reach common goals. War offered the possibility, therefore, of achieving that long-sought sense of American community as people sacrificed personal interest to achieve the noble aims Wilson proclaimed in 1917.

The national emergency also justified resorting to coercive means for achieving unity, not only through propaganda and repression of dissenters, but through unprecedented direction and coordination of national resources by the government. The first step toward central economic planning arose from the need to make the nation's industrial machine serve the war effort more efficiently. Thus, following a gigantic bottleneck on the railroads, the federal government took over management of the industry. Shortages of food and raw material led to federally directed rationing. Private shipbuilders did not turn out ships rapidly enough so the government tried its hand. Wheat farmers received federal subsidies to stimulate production and relieve the shortage of grain, and coal producers got minimum-price guarantees that expanded output. Big Business no longer had to worry about the antitrust laws and the federal government encouraged unionization, especially in industries dependent on government contracts. In the short run, federal controls succeeded in gearing the economy to war production. The Wilson administration adjusted tax policy so that a proportionally greater burden fell on the more prosperous classes than on low-income families, though the new rates fell far short of "soaking the rich." Many people grumbled about wartime economic policy, but businessmen and other conservatives acquiesced to temporary controls during an emergency. Besides, the war meant prosperity.

The return of peace brought the immediate termination of government's wartime planning and control. The transition to a peacetime economy proved vexing. Demand declined and prices fell; the war boom gave way to an economic recession.

The war had stimulated an expansion in production in the United States but when peace returned overseas markets contracted. Since Europe no longer depended so heavily on the United States, a serious imbalance developed between supply and demand. Farmers were especially hard hit. A nationwide recession in 1921–1922 caused widespread unemployment and numerous bankruptcies. But eventually the economy adjusted and climbed steadily to produce prosperity during the rest of the decade.

The Democrats lost heavily in the 1918 Congressional elections. Wartime controls and postwar economic distress turned voters against the party in power. All the anxieties generated by the war began to surface and people blamed the Democrats. Wheat farmers, mostly midwestern Republicans, accused the Democrats of giving special favors to cotton farmers, mostly southerners. Midwestern shippers charged that federal railroad rates discriminated against them in favor of the Northeast. Businessmen became alarmed by the rapid wartime gains of organized labor and the attempt to extend unionization to heavy industry which resulted in the Great Steel Strike of 1919.

At the same time, the peace settlement mocked the noble ideals for which Wilson said he led the country into war, and did much to discredit the Progressive view, even among the true believers. As the victors picked over the spoils at the Versailles conference, Wilson seemed helpless to bring about the magnanimous and lasting settlement he had promised. Progressives grew cynical and disillusioned. The war had made great fortunes at home and had ended in the triumph of imperialism abroad. And it had unleased a spirit of intolerance and repression among Americans that divided the country more than ever.

The war, explained the professional reformer, Frederic C. Howe, finally opened his eyes to reality, after a life spent trying first to reform Ohio and then the world. "My class did not see beyond its own interest," he confessed, "I had not been a realist but a moralist. I came to realize that reform was only possible from labor, not from my own class. I thought my class, its intelligence properly applied, would save the world. I wanted equal opportunity; my class did not."

Progressivism did not vanish altogether in the 1920s, however. The quest for social stability continued, but under the leadership of conservatives and the business community. The Progressives had singled out the power of concentrated wealth as the most acute social problem. By the 1920's, however, many came to accept the existence of mammoth corporations as necessary, inevitable, and beneficial. The first three decades of the twentieth century were relatively prosperous, marked only briefly by recessions. People enjoyed cars, radios, and movie houses—

all proof of a rising standard of living created by the American business system. As long as most people shared in the gains, it seemed unimportant that a few reaped the largest share. Organized labor, after great gains during the war, declined as workers proved unresponsive to unionization and employers turned hostile. Farmers, who fared less well in the 1920s than other groups, remained politically too divided and weak to obtain anything but marginal government aid.

For a dozen years after 1918, conservative Republicans dominated American politics. But in 1929, "Republican Prosperity" collapsed, and with it faith in the leadership of businessmen and conservatives. The country plunged into the worst depression in its history and searched desperately for new leadership. For a decade, however, the Republicans had confidently ruled, unaware of what lay ahead.

Republican Supremacy, 1920–1928

Despite the strains Progressivism placed on the party system, especially on the Republicans, the electoral patterns that had emerged in the 1890s remained largely intractable through the 1920s. The South was still Democratic territory but the rest of the country went either solidly Republican or leaned toward the GOP. Wilson's two victories represented deviations from the norm and owed much to the split between conservatives and progressive Republicans. Since the Republicans were normally the majority party, control of the GOP proved crucial. By the 1920s the progressive Republicans became an isolated minority. Many had abandoned the party to follow Roosevelt into the Progressive party in 1912, but after its failure many drifted back to a GOP firmly in the grip of the standpatters.

Well before the 1920 presidential elections, the GOP smelled victory. A powerful group of conservative Republican senators blocked the candidacy of men they thought less pliable than their man, Senator Warren G. Harding of Ohio. "People are rather tired of great ability," explained a midwestern businessman, "they've seen enough of that sort of thing in the Jews. What they want is a good, plain, common sense man of the people." Harding fit the bill perfectly. He climbed the ladder of Ohio politics with a devastating combination of a third-rate mind, laziness, and lack of ambition. His hard-working wife helped to make a success out of his languishing newspaper in Marion, and then a group of clever friends helped him win state office. Harding's success owed much to his lack of deep conviction and to his need to be popular, traits which led him to act as conciliator among the warring factions of the Ohio GOP. Harding himself had coined a word to describe his editorial and political approach, inoffensivism." Later, as a member of the United States Senate, he preferred playing golf to attending roll calls, but when he did vote he generally sided with conservative Republicans and party regularity earned him choice committee appointments.

A handsome man with silver-grey hair and a good physical presence, Harding outwardly fit the presidential image, though some dismissed him as "a waxwork Adonis." Senator Boies Penrose, an architect of his nomination, made no great claims for the man. "Harding," he admitted, "is not as big a man as I thought he was, he should have talked more about the tariff and not so much about playing cymbals in the Marion brass band." Yet it was precisely his identification with an older America which preferred brass bands to jazz bands that so endeared the Ohioan to the average voter.

The same was true of his oratory, which said nothing but sounded eloquent to the ears of Main Street. "We have not only wrought the most liberty and opportunity for ourselves at home," he once intoned with a straight face, "but the firmament of the earth, occident and orient, is aglow with shining suns of new republics, sped to the orbs of human progress by our example." The cynical journalist H. L. Mencken expressed a strictly minority view when he said that Harding's speechmaking reminded him of a string of wet sponges. Democrat William G. McAdoo claimed a Harding speech reminded him of "an army of pompous phases moving over the landscape in search of an idea; sometimes these meandering words would actually capture a straggling thought and bear it triumphantly, a prisoner in their midst, until it died of servitude and overwork." But middle America ignored such criticism of their hero.

Saddled with the burden of defending the unpopular Wilson administration, and losers in the fight for American participation in the League of Nations, the gloomy Democrats sent James M. Cox, former governor of Ohio, and his running mate, Franklin D. Roosevelt, to an embarrassing defeat in 1920. Much of the big-city ethnic vote, traditionally Democratic, deserted the party. Irish-Americans, for instance, who supported Ireland's fight for independence against Britain complained that the peace settlement left the British Empire stronger than ever and thus Irish freedom even more remote. German-Americans, whose loyalty had been questioned, turned on the party that had declared war against the Kaiser. Only the South remained loyal. The basic issue of the campaign, Senator Penrose explained, was "Americanism," though when asked what that meant, the Pennsylvania Republican boss replied: "How the hell do I know. But it will get a lot of votes." Harding won 60 percent of the vote and entered the White House a hero, promising to return the country to "normalcy."

Normalcy proved disastrous. Harding once confided to a journalist that he was just "a man of limited talents from a small town. . . . Often times, as I sit here, I don't seem to grasp that I am President." Many of the issues that came across his desk puzzled him. "I can't make a damn thing out of this tax problem," he confessed. "I listen to one side and they seem right, and then—God—I talk to the other side and they seem just as right. . . . I know somewhere there is a book that will give me the truth, but hell! I couldn't read the book." Though he sensed his many inadequacies, Harding surrounded himself with cronies from Ohio with whom he could indulge two of his favorite pastimes, drinking and poker playing. He appointed a few able men to his cabinet, such as Secretary of State Charles Evans Hughes and Secretary of Commerce Herbert Hoover, but he also named friends who proved his undoing. "The Ohio Gang, as they came to be known," writes one historian, "were a bunch of old-fashioned spoilsmen, political shysters, and just plain crooks who used public office for private gain." They sold protection to bootleggers, pardons to criminals, and favors to businessmen. The most notorious scandal involved the illegal transfer by Secretary of the Interior Albert B. Fall of the government's Teapot Dome oil reserves, worth millions, in exchange for bribes.

When facts began to leak out, some of the guilty left immediately for Europe; a few committed suicide. Harding began to panic, although early in 1923 only a scandal in the Veterans' Administration had been made public. But he knew that further disclosures were coming, and his wife had learned about his relations with his mistress, Nan Britton. Looking none too well, the president left for a tour of Alaska and the Northwest. Ptomaine poisoning struck him in San Francisco, and he died soon after of pneumonia. The circumstances had been clouded enough to create rumors that his wife had poisoned him; but the specific infirmities and lack of the will to live were more than enough to kill him.

The Harding administration symbolized much more than it accomplished. Here was a man from the heartland of America, a "just folks" sort of person; a hand-shaking, good guy of average abilities, with whom millions of Americans could identify; someone like themselves who could be relied on to restore "normalcy" after two decades of exhausting crusades at home and abroad.

Though Harding disappointed his admirers, they did not give up their desire to restore the past. Vice President Calvin Coolidge, the rock-ribbed and sour Yankee from New England who succeeded to the presidency, proved more reliable. Born in Vermont, he rose through the ranks of the Republican party in Massachusetts to become governor. He gained a national reputation in 1919 when he broke the Boston Police Strike. A man of considerable political skill, he had the confidence of Big Business without appearing to be their front-man. Coolidge was a man of few words and Spartan habits (Theodore Roosevelt's daughter said he had been "weaned on a dill pickle"). He refused for instance to buy an automobile. Editor William Allen White called him "a perfect throwback to the primitive days of the Republic." His conception of the presidency was that of a housekeeper who guarded the national treasury against undue expenditures, kept his administration free of scandal, and resisted efforts to enlarge the federal government's operations. He probably slept more than any other occupant of the White

House and he kept healthy in a job that broke Wilson and Harding physically, he explained, "by avoiding the big problems."

Coolidge moved swiftly to clean up Harding's mess. He sternly instructed the head usher at the White House: "I want things as they used to be—*before*." Coolidge thus undercut the corruption issue in preparation for his reelection campaign in 1924.

The Democrats approached the 1924 elections divided and at a loss to deal with the prosperity issue, which was Coolidge's strongest card. Disillusionment over the war and the campaign for 100 percent Americanism proved traumatic for the Democrats and brought the final collapse of Wilsonian Progressivism. The immigrant masses, mainly Catholic, dominated the Democratic party in the cities. But the party had also relied on the votes of rural Protestants in the South and West. Conflict in the 1920s between the old stock and the new, between urban and rural cultures that revealed itself in Prohibition, the resurgence of the Klan, Protestant fundamentalism, repression of aliens, and racist immigration legislation, converged to tear apart the already weakened Democratic party. The Democrats, more socially heterogeneous than the Republicans, were more vulnerable to factionalism under the pressures of the 1920s.

Ethno-cultural, sectional and status rivalries have shaped the character of American politics and mitigated against extreme polarization along economic and class lines. Cultural conflict divided farmers and working classes and caused suicidal rifts within the Democratic party. For instance, Irish-Catholics had been loyal Democrats for generations; powerful in the inner councils of the party, they nevertheless rarely aspired to major public office except in overwhelmingly Irish constituencies. In the 1920s, the Irish and other groups began to seek greater political recognition. The issue exploded at the 1924 Democratic Convention. The big-city Democrats backed Al Smith, an Irish-Catholic who had risen from a clerkship in the Fulton Fish Market in Manhattan to the governorship of New York. Smith was the ablest politician the newer Americans had yet produced. Though a product of a big-city machine—New York's Tammany Hall—his was more than just an urban, Catholic candidacy. He supported labor and welfare legislation which benefitted his working class constituency, of course, but he also extended his appeal to old-stock Progressives by working for administrative reform and defending civil liberties during the Red Scare.

Rural Democrats from the South and West backing William G. McAdoo blocked Smith's candidacy. Al Smith affronted the most cherished values of Democrats like William Jennings Bryan. Smith was a "wet" and he symbolized the metropolis which the small-town old stock sought to contain. The Smith forces demanded that the party publicly condemn the Klu Klux Klan; the southern and western Democrats refused. The convention deadlocked, after 95 votes, and as humorist Will Rogers warned the delegates: "New York invited you people here as guests, not to live." The exhausted party finally nominated John W. Davis, a Wall Street lawyer who stirred little enthusiasm among either the urban masses or the Bryan Democrats in the South and West.

With neither of the two parties offering a choice, remnants of the Progressive coalition rallied behind Wisconsin's Senator Robert LaFollette who ran on the ticket of a new Progressive party. The eclipse of Progressivism left a small isolated minority in the Republican party with a voice in Congress through spokesmen like the aging LaFollette, but with a power base confined largely to the midwestern grain belt. LaFollette tried to assemble a Progressive coalition by appealing to discontented farmers, labor, middle-class reformers, and Socialists (whose candidate in 1920, Eugene V. Debs, had polled nearly a million votes while in prison for antiwar protest activity). He also appealed to the postwar isolationist spirit and to the German-Americans, for he had been the most prominent opponent of American involvement in the First World War.

The Coolidge campaign concentrated its fire on LaFollette and tried to smear the Progressive party as socialistic and a threat to prosperity. "If we could discover the three people who disgraced our district by voting for LaFollette," said the wife of a midwestern Republican businessman, "we'd certainly make it hot for them." In a light turnout of only half the eligible voters, LaFollette polled nearly five million votes, cutting into Democratic strength in the northeastern cities and running well in former centers of progressive Republicanism in the Midwest. Coolidge, however, won with more votes than both his opponents combined, further disheartening progressive Republicanism and making the Democrats even more cautious about disputing the reigning Republican philosophy that "the business of America is business."

Business Supremacy

As the American economy and stock market boomed, President Coolidge, who disapproved of gambling, became concerned about the speculation in securities. He summoned Harvard economist W. Z. Ripley to Washington and listened to the expert describe how "prestidigitation, double-shuffling, honey-fugling, hornswoggling, and skullduggery" helped to sustain the Great Bull Market on Wall Street. In thé end, however, the president declined to act to curb speculation or openly counsel moderation, since he thought businessmen knew best. Government, the president insisted, must properly act as a servant, not a watchdog of business.

During the Progressive era, business had been on the defensive as a result of rivalry among business interests and widespread fears of concentrated economic power. By the 1920s, however, banking, railroad, and tariff reforms had muted many of the differences which had previously divided businessmen. More important, the performance of Big Business, especially well-known firms like Ford and GM, did much to diminish popular hostility toward the large corporation. Now businessmen and their spokesmen explicitly claimed the right to rule. Free enterprise, they argued, made America great and had produced the highest standard of living in the world.

Driven by the profit motive, businessmen had supposedly done more for the good of mankind than all the do-good reformers put together. "The Carnegie who made steel and millions of dollars was a hero," argued an advocate of business control, "but the Carnegie who gave medals to heroes and built libraries was just a sweet old lady." Another put it more bluntly: "The 100 percent American believes in the doctrine of selfishness, although he is often ashamed to admit it." The majority of people had limited ability and were easily fooled by radical troublemakers and vote-seeking politicians. Power should be left in the hands of the nation's natural elite, the businessman. The majority must be kept busy at work because leisure was dangerous. Any man who wanted a forty-hour work week "should be ashamed to claim citizenship in this great country." Inequality was inevitable, desirable, and necessary: inevitable because people differed in ability and talent, desirable because the chance to earn great wealth spurred creative engergies, and necessary because the fear of destitution was the only thing that kept people working hard.

Government in the 1920s generally gave businessmen what they wanted: a free hand to run their own affairs and special privileges. The Wilson administration had granted businessmen virtual immunity from the antitrust laws. The Republicans in the 1920s expanded that policy to encourage the "New Competition." In certain industries, such as steel, autos, tobacco, and meat packing, a few firms dominated, divided the market and fixed prices.

In industries with many small producers, however, cut-throat competition proved troublesome. The Federal Trade Act, designed to curb "unfair" competition, established a Federal Trade Commission which President Wilson staffed with pro-business commissioners. Republicans in the 1920s went further, turning the regulatory agencies into tools of the industries they were established to regulate. Government, especially the Department of Commerce, under Secretary Herbert Hoover, gave its blessing to this new method of limiting competition, thus legitimizing business practices that otherwise might provoke criticism.

The Transportation Act of 1920 represented yet another victory for business consolidation. The railroad unions demanded that government keep control of the railroads after the war. The railroads, aided by other businessmen and by midwestern Progressives who complained that government control had discriminated against the interests of their region, defeated nationalization. Instead, the railroads received permission to consolidate into a few large systems with immunity from antitrust prosecution. At the same time, the ICC received greater power over rates. The booming new electric power industry also came under regulation by the Federal Power Commission (1920) but this agency proved an equally ineffective watchdog of the public interest.

Successful in making government "regulation" serve their interests, businessmen also pushed for lower taxes. During the war the government imposed personal and corporate income taxes that fell most heavily on those with the greatest ability to pay. In the 1920s, under the leadership of Secretary of the Treasury Andrew Mellon of the Aluminum Company of America (and a member of one of the country's wealthiest families), the federal government economized on expenditures and cut taxes. Progressive Republicans and Democrats fought to preserve the progressive tax structure, but by the mid-1920s Mellon pushed through Congress substantial tax relief for the well-to-do.

At the same time conservatives and businessmen fought welfare programs to help working people, such as health insurance and old-age pensions. They did so on the premise that only "rugged individualism" created prosperity, yet all the while they sought handouts and special favors for themselves. Secretary Fall gave away valuable federal oil reserves. Progressive senators, however, got wind of bribery in the executive branch and exposed the Teapot Dome corruptionists. Led by Senator George Norris of Nebraska, Progressives also blocked another giveaway to private industry of huge hydroelectric works built by the government during the First World War to produce nitrates at Muscle Shoals, Alabama. This preserved, for possible future public development, the water power resources of the Tennessee Valley.

Businessmen were more successful in increasing tariff rates. In 1921 and in 1922, Congress reversed the tariff reductions of the Progressive years. This satisfied businessmen who wanted protection against foreign competition, and it also pleased farmers caught in a postwar agricultural depression, though higher tariffs did them little real good. The high duty on imported reindeer meat, for example, did not help raise the price of wheat.

Despite conservative opposition to increased government spending, the budgetary trend moved markedly upward between 1900 and 1930. Government's share of national income in 1920 stood at just below 10 percent but it had grown 60 percent since the first decade of the twentieth century. Education took the largest share of public revenues, about 20 percent. While funding for other public services—welfare, sanitation, water, and police—lagged because of conservative opposition, ambitious, publicly financed highway programs made possible an automobile-based economy and represented a gigantic subsidy to industry which the public supported because it also benefitted from better roads.

The Supreme Court

As in the 1890s, the Supreme Court reflected the conservative temper of the twenties. Progressives had tried to promote social justice by adopting legislation on behalf of lower income groups. Reformers argued that industrialism subjected people to hazards they could not cope with individually. They therefore recognized the need for such collective protections as trade unions, and laws limiting child labor, setting maximum hours and minimum wages, and providing security against industrial accidents, unemployment and impoverishment in old age. These ideas did manage to make inroads, but many businessmen reacted negatively to Progressive solutions to the labor question. In the 1920s the judiciary came to the aid of conservatives by declaring national welfare legislation unconstitutional and ruling repeatedly against labor unions.

One of the progressives' strongest points of attack, the crusade against child labor, twice fell victim to judicial vetoes. Before the First World War the Supreme Court had allowed states to regulate the working conditions of certain types of laborers—women and children, or men with particularly dangerous jobs like miners. But judicial approval in a handful of cases did not create overall state policy. Progressives campaigned for a federal law which would outlaw child labor. In 1916 Congress barred the shipment of goods in interstate commerce made by children under the age of fourteen, or if made by children, between ages fourteen and sixteen who worked more than eight hours a day. Two years later, in *Hammer* v. *Dagenhart* (1918), the Court used an extremely narrow definition of the federal commerce power to declare that Congress could not regulate manufacturing, a state concern, however laudable its intent to put an end to child labor.

Congress, refusing to give up, then placed a tax of 10 percent on the profits of any company using child laborers. Again the Court, in *Baily* v. *Drexel Furniture Company* (1922), declared the law void on the grounds that Congress could not use the federal taxing power to regulate a matter reserved to the states. Chief Justice Taft warned: "The good sought in unconstitutional legislation is an insidious feature, because it leads citizens and legislators of good purpose to promote it without thought of the serious breach it will make in [the Constitution] the ark of our covenant." Taft spoke for judicial restraint, but it should be noted that the Supreme Court's liberals, Holmes and Brandeis, both supported the Taft position in the *Bailey* case, though in the first child labor case Holmes had dissented, arguing that if the nation could prohibit alcohol, it could just as well prohibit "the products of ruined lives."

Previously, the Court had upheld certain state limitations on the hours of labor on the grounds that a state could protect the health and safety of workers, and that limiting the workday might reasonably aid in achieving that desirable end. Progressives had hailed these decisions as landmarks, since they appeared to overrule the hated *Lochner* v. *New York* opinion (1905) which invalidated a New York law prohibiting a workday of more than ten hours' work for bakers. In that case the Court held that the New York statute deprived both employers and employees of freedom of contract, a guarantee of the due process clause of the Fourteenth Amendment.

In the years after *Lochner* the Court seemed to soften. Before joining it, Louis D. Brandeis, the country's leading Progressive lawyer, argued and won several regulatory cases before the Supreme Court. One involved Oregon's attempt to ease working conditions for women, and Brandeis in presenting his case observed wryly: "Experience has taught us that harsh language addressed to a cow impairs her usefulness. Are women less sensitive than beasts in these respects?" Tentative Progressive victories created the false impression that the Court might enter a sustained liberal phase after World War I; but the Court would soon agree with one of its staff members who snorted: "Brandeis has got the impudence of the devil to bring his socialism into the Supreme Court."

In 1923 the Court struck another blow against the beginnings of the welfare state. It revived the doctrine of substantive due process in *Adkins* v. *Childrens' Hospital* (1923), declaring unconstitutional a minimum wage law passed by Congress for the District of Columbia. Felix Frankfurter had argued the case for regulation, presenting a Brandeis-type sociological legal brief, but this time the Court would not accept it. Justice Sutherland, then starting his service to judicial conservatism declared: "We cannot accept the doctrine that women of mature age require . . . restrictions upon their liberty of contract." So the scrubwomen at Childrens' Hospital were "free" to accept whatever wages the trustees saw fit to pay them. Chief Justice Taft, this time one of the dissenters, protested that the majority wanted to "hold congressional acts invalid simply because they are passed to carry out economic views which the Court believes to be unwise or unsound." The cartoonist John Kirby was blunter: "This decision," he told working women, "affirms your constitutional right to starve."

At the same time that the Court invalidated legislation to protect unorganized workers, it made it harder for labor to protect itself through trade union activity. Unions had welcomed the Clayton Act (1914), thinking it had granted immunity from the antitrust laws, previously used to break strikes. In the 1920s, however, the Supreme Court interpreted the Clayton Act in a way which again brought unions under the provisions of the antitrust laws. The Court also struck down an Arizona law which barred injunctions against picketers, claiming it denied employers equal protection of the law. Whatever the legal basis for this decision, and it was hotly debated, the justices had made their antilabor bias apparent. Chief Justice Taft explained that trade unions were dangerous institutions which "we have to hit every little while."

The Decline of Organized Labor

During the Progressive era, unions had experienced their greatest growth up to that time, aided by prosperity and a favorable climate of opinion. During the First World War, with labor in short supply, unions almost doubled their membership, reaching five million in 1920. This union growth alarmed employers who launched counteroffensives through such organizations as the National Association of Manufacturers. In the 1920s employers stepped up their antilabor drive with considerable success. By the end of the decade union membership had fallen to less than three and a half million workers.

Employers capitalized on the postwar antiradical hysteria to smear unions as socialistic and un-American. The bosses' "American Plan" called for outlawing the "closed shop," a device which made union membership a condition of employment. Businessmen insisted that closed shops deprived workers of the right to work, and thus violated the tenets of rugged individualism, though in fact unorganized workers were powerless to influence the conditions of employment. The open-shop movement was an attempt to restore to employers a monopoly of power wherever unions had intruded. Aided by antilabor judges, politicians, and the press, resorting to the use of labor spies and hired toughs, employers created an atmosphere hostile to union growth. They were also helped by modest advances in real wages, tangible improvements in living standards, and substantial unemployment during the first half of the 1920s, which made workers more docile and less susceptible to unionization. The great citadels of the open shop were the mass-production industries, such as steel and automaking, which remained impervious to unionization.

At first, unions tried to fight back, but strikes against coal mines, railroads, and steel failed. The American Federation of Labor, therefore, altered its strategy on the assumption that labor could not grow through struggle as it had in the past. The AFL tried to convince business that unions were desirable because they promoted harmony and efficiency. The unions joined conservatives in attacking radicalism and supporting a high tariff in the hope of gaining respectability. But, although tariff rates went up, businessmen remained hostile.

Instead, some advanced "welfare capitalism" as a means of assuring labor peace. Leaders of big corporations such as Procter and Gamble, General Motors, and General Electric wanted a stable, pliable labor force. They recognized that labor had real grievances. Workers not only wanted decent wages, fair hours, and good working conditions, but protection against unemployment, the insecurity of old age, and arbitrary treatment in the factory as well. Welfare capitalism assumed that business could satisfy these needs through company unions which gave workers the illusion they could redress grievances. Several large corporations also tried to provide year-round employment, others established pension plans, built company housing, and offered employees stock purchasing plans.

But the most important legacy of welfare capitalism was the development of personnel administration as a "scientific" method of managing labor. The industrial relations movement of the 1920s was one of the main thrusts of "scientific management." As the modern, bureaucratic corporation evolved, businessmen rejected the older, informal methods of management, which relied heavily on trial and error. Corporations such as General Motors, DuPont, Sears Roebuck, and Standard Oil of New Jersey found it necessary to develop new administrative techniques for more efficient production, planning, and marketing as well as the control of labor.

The father of "scientific management" was an engineer named Frederick W. Taylor. Taylor wanted to replace conflict between labor and management with rational cooperation. He thought it possible to determine scientifically the most efficient way to do a job through careful study. This in turn would permit engineers to determine rationally what constituted a fair day's work and would enable companies to regard workers according to performance. Taylor thought labor productivity would increase if employers shared profits with workers through a system of wage incentives geared to gains in efficiency. In theory, "scientific management," with its faith in "rational" solutions devised by "impartial" experts, was a typically Progressive approach to a social problem.

In practive, however, Taylor found employers unwilling to accept limitations on their authority, whether dictated by experts or by labor unions. But employers did see the value of adopting a philosophy of "industrial partnership" as a means of maintaining a docile labor force. They hired personnel officers to recruit loyal workers and weed out troublemakers. Industrial psychologists discovered that workers wanted to be treated like human beings, not as cogs in a machine, and that poor morale caused absenteeism, high turnover, and low productivity. The more sophisticated businessmen experimented with this "human relations" approach to labor. It also enabled businessmen to insist that voluntary programs eliminated the need for government action. Actually, very few workers received pensions or enjoyed stable employment, but as long as prosperity continued, welfare capitalism seemed plausible. The Great Depression (1929–1941), however, destroyed that illusion just as it convinced people that the basic problems of farm and factory required massive government intervention.

The Dilemma of Agriculture

In the two decades after the collapse of Populism, American farmers prospered. As urbanization enlarged domestic markets and the end of the frontier limited the amount of new acreage coming under cultivation, demand finally caught up with supply. This brought higher prices and a shift by farmers from protest to economic organization that would enable them to reap some of the advantages of new business methods. Like workers who joined unions and manufacturers who formed trade associations, farmers were learning that in modern America it was "organize or perish."

Agricultural cooperatives numbered 12,000 by 1921. Dairy farmers, for instance, found that it was more efficient to set up cooperatives to manufacture butter and cheese so they could concentrate on the production of milk. Grain farmers thought they could cut middlemen's costs and assure fair grading by marketing through cooperative grain elevators. Through cooperatives, farmers acquired better knowledge of markets and learned that scientific methods meant higher profits.

Farmers also established other organizations through which they hoped to advance their interests. The American Society of Equity limited output to raise prices but proved impractical without government control. The Farmers Union set up its own fertilizer and farm implement factories and went into the insurance business. In the winter wheat belt of the Dakotas and Minnesota, the Non-Partisan League emerged after 1914 with a program of state aid for agriculture. The League gained control of the dominant Republican party in North Dakota, elected its own candidates to office, and established state-owned grain elevators and a state bank to aid farmers.

But the most powerful farm organization proved to be the American Farm Bureau. The Farm Bureau grew out of efforts to encourage farmers to adopt modern scientific and business methods. Early in the twentieth century the boll weevil plagued southern cotton growers. Backed by the Department of Agriculture and business, experts induced farmers to try new techniques of fighting the pest. Experimental farms convinced other farmers, a naturally conservative group who clung to old methods, to follow the advice of experts. A network of county agents, financed by the government and by businessmen, participated in agriculture extension programs in the state universities. When farmers stubbornly resisted new methods, local merchants and bankers refused them credit. Dominated largely by the wealthiest farmers, the bureaus were ostensibly private organizations, but they were often managed by paid government officials.

The American Farm Bureau solidified its position in the 1920s when agricultural prosperity gave way to a chronic agricultural depression. Dwindling overseas outlets after the war sent prices plunging, and farmers groped for solutions. Conservative Republicans offered higher tariffs but midwestern farmers found that tariffs did not help, since few faced competition from foreign producers. Farmers placed increased emphasis on cooperatives, but these proved no more effective in shoring up sagging prices than tariff juggling.

Farmers then turned to the McNary-Haugen plan, under which the government would make up the difference between the market price and a politically fixed "fair exchange value." With support from farm implement manufacturers and other businessmen in the Midwest and Far West, farmers under the leadership of the American Farm Bureau eventually pushed the scheme through Congress. Eastern Republicans, however, opposed a subsidy to farmers and President Coolidge vetoed the bill. Yet despite defeat, the Farm Bureau and other such organizations had developed a powerful farm bloc that linked southern and western farmers to those businessmen directly dependent on agricultural prosperity in a common cause.

In the end, however, farmers found themselves too isolated from other interests to master the power necessary to obtain relief from government. Hostile to organized labor, seeking only to advance its own interests, the Farm Bureau was doomed to frustration until the Great Depression found allies for the farmers outside of agriculture. Confident of their political supremacy, eastern Republicans ignored agrarian demands. President Coolidge, thinking perhaps about his native state's hard-scrabble agriculture, philosophized: "Well, farmers never had made money. I don't believe we can do much about it. But of course we will have to seem to be doing something; do the best we can and without much hope." Thus Coolidge accepted the politics of normalcy with its reliance on free enterprise and its hostility toward government intervention. But his successor, Herbert Hoover, caught in the crisis of the Great Depression, could not continue the Coolidge policy of avoiding the big problems and relying on the uncontrolled operation of the free market.

The End of Normalcy

Perhaps Calvin Coolidge sensed that danger lay ahead when he announced he would not run for reelection in 1928. The Republicans then turned to Herbert C. Hoover, "the Great Engineer." Hoover was not the professional politician's choice but he seemed the best Republican available. An orphan,

Hoover had a meteoric rise before the First World War as a mining engineer and a self-made millionaire. He then won fame directing relief efforts to Belgium and elsewhere during the war. To millions of Americans he came to symbolize the Progressive businessman, a man who had harnessed his administrative and organizing talents to humane purposes.

As Secretary of Commerce from 1921 to 1928 he brought advanced business thinking to Washington. In place of conflict between capital and labor, Hoover favored both welfare capitalism and unions; instead of cutthroat competition, he favored trade associations and business cooperation; in place of negative government, he believed government should actively encourage all economic sectors to organize into associations to promote prosperity and social stability. "We are passing from a period of extreme individualistic action," he once said characteristically, "into a period of associational activities." As one of the most articulate exponents of this "New Individualism," a man people regarded as a disinterested public servant rather than as a professional politician, Hoover seemed equipped with the vision and the technical expertise a complex modern society required. In this sense, Hoover symbolized a shift in American politics from figures like Harding and Coolidge whose popularity owed much to their ability to evoke nostalgia for an earlier, simpler time. In contrast, Hoover thoroughly identified with the idea that America had in the 1920s entered a New Era in which the genius of the American business system had created unprecedented affluence and permanent prosperity. Four more years of Republican rule, Hoover and his party promised, would bring the country near the day when it would achieve final victory over poverty. "The poor house is vanishing," he assured.

Hoover's Democratic opponent, Governor Alfred E. Smith of New York, ran with several handicaps. He was the first representative of the Newer Americans, the first Roman Catholic, and the first poor boy from the big city to run for president. He was also an open foe of Prohibition. In 1924 southern and western rural Democrats had blocked Smith's nomination. Four years later many deserted their party: "You *felt* with Smith or you *felt* with Hoover," recalled one observer. Feeling ran so high that for the first time since Reconstruction, Republicans cracked the Solid South as Democrats voted for Hoover to save America, they thought, from a Catholic takeover following Smith's election. The more paranoid Bible-Belters thought Catholics would "hang, waste, boil, flail, strangle and burn alive" Protestants and "rip up the stomachs and wombs of their women and crush infants' heads against the wall."

Conflicts between two cultures which had divided the country throughout the decade dominated the 1928 campaign, though it is doubtful that *any* Democrat (even a Methodist bishop) could have beaten Hoover that year. During the campaign, old-stock Protestants met on the streets, wrote one of them, and told each other: "We cannot live if Hoover is not elected." And when Hoover won they exulted: "We are saved! . . . this great Country, its presence lying out there in the vast darkness, like a soft thing enveloped in the sweet misty night, immense but one in purpose for the Clean Man, the Free Man," —Herbert Hoover of West Branch, Iowa.

Hoover won the election of 1928 impressively. He benefitted from continued "Republican prosperity" and from the normal GOP majority.

Yet the extent of Hoover's victory temporarily obscured important shifts in voting behavior which would have long-term consequences. Smith ran unusually well in the traditionally Republican midwestern farm belt, a clear sign of farm discontent with the GOP. He proved even more popular in big cities with large ethnic populations. For the first time, Newer Americans could identify with a candidate for the presidency. Smith's origins betrayed him with every word he uttered. His New York (Noo Yawk) accent and manners evoked laughter and contempt among the Protestant native-born but the immigrants accepted him as one of their own. Newer Americans who had previously voted Republican or had not bothered to vote thus trooped to the polls for Al Smith and shifted many big cities to the Democratic column.

Hoover's triumph soon turned sour. In October 1929, the booming stock market collapsed and for the remaining three years, "the Great Engineer" wrestled unsuccessfully with the worst depression in American history. Even before the Wall Street debacle, several business indicators pointed to trouble. The auto and residential construction booms had levelled off and agricultural depression clouded the economy throughout the Twenties. At first people minimized the stock market crash. "There has been a little distress selling on the Stock Exchange," explained a senior partner in the firm of J. P. Morgan & Co. "I see nothing . . . in the present situation that is either menacing or warrants pessimism," opined Secretary of the Treasury Andrew W. Mellon. The American productive system, President Hoover reassured the country, remained sound; the difficulties in the stock market were temporary disturbances. Events soon turned these assurances into graveyard whistling.

The Roots of Collapse

Hoover and most other hopeful experts proved dead wrong. The crash in Wall Street touched off a chain reaction that sent the economy spiralling downward and prostrated the nation. Within three years, 75 percent of the paper value of securities vanished. In 1929, 659 banks failed, wiping out $250 million in deposits; two years later another 2,294 banks and $1.7 billion dollars met a similar fate. Industrial production in 1932 dropped 50 percent from the 1929 level and unemployment grew from four million in October 1930 to seven million the next year and to eleven million by the fall of 1932. During the first three years of the Depression, farm income decreased by half, paralleling a decline in national income from $88 billion in 1929 to $40 billion in 1933.

Some pinned the blame on excesses in the stock market. Banks loaned funds for speculation too easily and the government had failed to control security issues. Investors, for instance, could buy stocks without putting down much cash. The boom in securities rested in part on the solid performance of the economy in the latter half of the 1920s. But the lopsided distribution of national income that placed huge sums in the hands of corporations, banks, and wealthy investors fed the speculative impulse. The upper middle classes joined in the spree in unprecedented numbers, seeking a quick killing on Wall Street.

As investors bid up the prices, security values reached levels far greater than warranted by reality. The speculative frenzy that had set the market soaring, tripling the values of stocks on the New York Stock Exchange between 1925 and 1927, was highly vulnerable to any unfavorable economic change. Millions of investors, sensing an inflated market, were likely to sell if they suspected a break. When that break occurred in October 1929, everyone rushed to sell before prices plummeted further and wiped out profits.

Yet the market crash would not have been so devastating had not profound structural weaknesses existed in the economy. The Federal Reserve System had only limited powers to control the shaky banking system and regulate the credit supply; and even these it failed to exercise energetically. The banks had gone into the securities retailing business and, by liberally extending credit for speculation, they had helped to create the Great Bull Market and the crash.

Equally serious was the precariousness of the international economy. The First World War made the United States the world's banker. European nations liquidated investments in the United States to finance war purchases and as they exhausted these resources the United States had to grant large loans. As a result Europe emerged from the war deeply in debt to the United States, a condition which placed heavy burdens on its economy.

The worldwide postwar economy depended on the export of American capital to enable other countries to meet their debt payments. American loans to Germany helped finance reparations payments to France and Great Britain, which were thus able to meet their obligations to the United States. Maintaining high tariffs and exporting more than it imported, the United States made it doubly difficult for foreign countries to pay their debts. And when the flow of capital from America to Europe tapered off in the late 1920s, the international financial structure crumbled. As the Depression engulfed Europe, it disrupted world trade and worsened conditions in the United States.

Yet even more important than the shakiness of the international economy were structural imbalances at home, where Americans sold most of their goods. The economy showed signs of sagging as early as 1927. National income was very unequally distributed. The top 20 percent of the nation's families and unattached individuals received 54 percent of the income, while the bottom 40 percent received only 12 percent. Had income been more equitably apportioned, millions of Americans would have had effective purchasing power. But instead of passing along gains in productivity to workers in the form of higher wages, or to consumers through lower prices, corporations increased their profits. Billions of dollars in corporate profits were either retained or went to finance speculation instead of being invested in productive activities that generated jobs and economic growth. Finally, the chronic difficulties of agriculture and other depressed sectors during the 1920s hung like a dead weight on the American economy.

The richest country in the world now staggered through an economic catastrophe that reduced millions to destitution and many to despair. "We are the first nation in the history of the world," Will Rogers announced, "to go to the poor house in an automobile." In Kingstown, Ohio, the local newspaper reported:

FATHER OF TEN DROWNS SELF;
JUMPS FROM BRIDGE, STARTS TO SWIM
GIVES UP, OUT OF WORK TWO YEARS

"We are about to lose our home," sobbed the widow of a jobless steel worker who had worked for Republic Steel for twenty-seven years. In an Illinois coal town of 1350 people, only two miners still had jobs in 1931. By 1932 one out of every three wage and salary workers was out of a job. In that year, 100,000 Americans applied for work in Communist Russia, where they had heard everybody had a job.

Mass unemployment (12.6 million, or 25 *percent* of the work force, was out of work by 1933) resulted in mass malnutrition and unprecedented hunger. New York City had an average of 31 breadlines a day in 1931. Near Danbury, Connecticut, in 1932, police found a mother and her 16-year-old daughter starving in the woods, huddled under a strip of canvas tied from a boulder to the ground; the woman had moved from town to town to seek work without success after her husband deserted.

Here and there food riots broke out. In Minneapolis in 1931, "Several hundred men and women in unemployment demonstrations late today stormed a grocery and meat market in the Gateway district, smashed plate glass windows and helped themselves to bacon and ham, fruit and canned goods." None suffered worse than children. In Pennsylvania 27 percent of the school children were undernourished. In a coal-mining town a teacher noticed that a little girl looked sick. "No, I'm all right," she explained, "only I'm hungry." The teacher told her to go home and get some food but the child refused: "It won't do any good . . . because this is sister's day to eat." In Philadelphia, a family lived exclusively on stale bread for eleven days. In the nation's richest city in 1931 the hospitals reported the deaths of dozens of persons weakened by malnutrition.

Tens of thousands lost their homes and farms. By 1933 a million men and women were on the road without a place to live. Dozens met their death stealing rides on the railroads. Because Chicago's city shelter was too small, hundreds of "women of good character," reported the Commissioner of Public Welfare, slept in the parks in the fall of 1931. Shantytowns sprung up around the cities on empty lots constructed of whatever flotsam and jetsam the homeless could find for a shelter, creating communities which the embittered residents called "Hoovervilles."

Some farmers took the law into their own hands to block foreclosure sales. In Iowa dairymen declared a milk holiday. "All roads leading to Sioux City were picketed," reported *Harper's Magazine*. "Trucks by hundreds were turned back. Farmers by hundreds lined the roads. They blocked the roads with spiked telegraph poles and logs. They took away a sheriff's badge, his gun, and threw them in a cornfield. Gallons of milk ran down the road ditches. Gallons of confiscated milk were distributed free on the streets of Sioux City."

In the spring of 1932, nearly 12,000 veterans marched on Washington to demand immediate payment of a veterans' bonus not yet due. Building a shantytown near the Capitol, the Bonus Marchers sang:

Mellon pulled the whistle,
Hoover rang the bell,
Wall Street gave the signal,
And the country went to hell.

The president reacted nervously. A riot which resulted in two deaths, and reports of Communist activity among the marchers, caused him to order the U. S. Army to evict the protesters. In an excess of zeal, the troops under General Douglas MacArthur used gas to disperse the veterans and burned down this newest Hooverville in the nation's capitol.

Yet such outbursts and protests by the distressed were not the general rule. Most Americans silently, stoically accepted hard times, bewildered by the unexpected, paralyzed about how to respond. So many had believed in the myths of the New Era that their explosion left them dazed and floundering. Hoover realized that the country expected Washington to lead. "The Great Engineer" tried his best but failed, for Hoover like almost everybody else did not fully understand the causes of the Depression.

Herbert Hoover and the Great Depression

However people explained the collapse, they looked to President Hoover for leadership. Conventionally minded businessmen like Secretary of the Treasury Andrew Mellon advised a hands-off policy. They regarded depressions as natural phenomena which cured themselves after a period of belt tightening. In economics, as in physics, they said with well-heeled resignation, whatever goes up must come down. Hoover disagreed. Neither his social philosophy nor political realities would allow him to maintain a do-nothing policy as had earlier presidents confronting hard times. As leading prophet of the "New Individualism," Hoover believed that the cooperation of business, labor, and agriculture could turn the economy around without unduly enlarging the powers of government at the expense of individual freedom.

Restoring business confidence became his chief goal. Traditionally, businessmen cut expenses at signs of recession in hopes that by reducing prices and wages, and by cutting investment, they could insulate themselves from disaster. But retrenchment only worsened the deflationary spiral. Determined to avoid the mistakes of the past, Hoover summoned representatives of business and labor to Washington. Industry promised to maintain existing wage levels, stabilize employment and expand investment. Hoover also urged the states and cities to speed up public works to offset the decline in private construction. To restore confidence in banking, Hoover called on the strong banks to help shore up the weaker ones and to loosen credit. Even before the Crash, Hoover had pushed through Congress the Agricultural Marketing Act (1929), his solution to the farm depression. The new law encouraged cooperative marketing and gave a Federal Farm Board $500 million to buy agricultural surpluses that were depressing farm prices.

None of Hoover's schemes worked. Relying on farmers voluntarily to curtail production, the Federal Farm Board kept on buying and prices kept on falling as farmers piled surplus on top of surplus. The board quickly suffered losses of over $350 million. Voluntarism worked no better with the bankers. The Federal Reserve Board loosened credit in the hope that banks would expand loans. Instead they used the new funds to decrease their indebtedness so they might survive should conditions worsen. The National Credit Corporation, established in 1931 by the bankers at Hoover's urging, proved a fiasco, since the strong banks refused to aid the weak ones. For a while, manufacturers made serious efforts to maintain employment and prices but as the Depression deepened these efforts also collapsed. The radio commentator Elmer Davis concluded that Hoover's strategy had failed: "It is easier to believe that the earth is flat than to believe that private initiative alone will save us."

The failure of voluntarism pushed the president reluctantly toward direct federal intervention. For a decade he had preached the theory of countercyclical finance: when business spending declined, government spending should increase to take up the slack. When the Depression hit, Hoover tried to follow his policy but the sharp drop in government revenue limited the funds available for public works. Hoover believed that a budget deficit due to greater public spending would undermine business confidence, the key to recovery. Under pressure from business for relief, the president agreed however to depart from voluntarism and establish the Reconstruction Finance Corporation (1932), a federal agency with another $500 million to lend to business and agriculture. When the RFC immediately went to the rescue of J. P. Morgan & Co. and other business giants, criticism mounted, especially in view of Hoover's failure to come up with a plan to help millions dependent for survival on public relief.

Ordinarily, private charities took care of the destitute. But mass poverty in the Depression revealed the hopelessness of relying on voluntarism despite efforts to raise more funds for charity. The burden of relief now fell on local government, whose resources were so strained that many cities and counties verged on bankruptcy. The president, despite his reputation for humanitarianism, *seemed* indifferent to the plight of the unemployed. The administration had no accurate information on the number without jobs, the magnitude of the relief problem, or the financial ability of local government to shoulder the burden. Nor did Hoover present a realistic alternative to the collapse of local relief efforts. He ruled out federally funded relief because, said Senator David I. Walsh of Massachusetts, "Whatever the emergency, whatever the appeal, whatever the cry that comes from the suffering people of this country, he does not propose to levy one dollar more in increased taxes. . . ." But how could he, when informed opinion held that cutting government spending was the essential first step to restore business confidence?

Hoover found himself trapped by his own assumptions. Yet he was not alone. Most of the country's leaders agreed that government could or should do very little. "The main trouble," explained economist George Soule, "is not that business is in the saddle; the trouble is that nobody is in the saddle." The failure of voluntarism left Herbert Hoover without a policy and left the country without a leader. As unemployment grew worse and suffering spread, Will Rogers warned, "If our big men in the next year can't fix that—well, they just ain't big men, that's all." The "big men" failed and in 1932 the voters decided they "just ain't big men." In that year, Americans elected a new president, a physically handicapped man with an assured manner who made vague promises of a new deal.

Document: The Politics of Boobocracy
H. L. Mencken on Politics in the 1920s

Born in Baltimore of German stock in 1880, Henry L. Mencken received his apprenticeship as a journalist on the Baltimore Sun, *and later edited the* Smart Set *and the* American Mercury. *In their pages Mencken became a relentless and devastating critic of Middle America—its literature and art, its manners and mores, its politics and business ethic. "Who knows," asked social philosopher Walter Lippman, "having read Mr. Mencken and Mr. Sinclair Lewis, what kind of world will be left when all the boobs and yokels have crawled back in their holes and have died in shame?"*

With his rapier-sharp pen and wit, his instinct for the jugular, Mencken became a virtuoso hurler of scorn and invective against all the conventional pieties the new generation of intellectuals and artists rejected. Mencken was the champion of urban America against rural America, cosmopolitanism against provincialism, literary naturalism against the tepid evasions of the Genteel Tradition. A skeptic, he roasted William Jennings Bryan's defense of the old-time religion in the Monkey Trial at Dayton, Tennessee; a beer-lover of German ancestry, he hated Prohibition with a furious passion; a champion of artistic innovation, he defended Theodore Dreiser against the censors.

At bottom, Mencken was a critic of mass society. He did not believe that the majority was either morally or intellectually competent to be entrusted with unlimited power. Freud's discovery of the irrational only confirmed his view, based on observation, that men were often caught in the grip of dark passions and self-destructive bigotries. Of the American farmer, supposedly the solid foundation of the Republic, he wrote: "No

*more grasping, selfish, and dishonest Mammal, indeed, is known
to students of the Anthropoidea." "To hell with this prehensile
moron," he exploded. As for America's Anglo-Saxon majority,
confident it was the superrace, Mencken erupted:*

> The Anglo-Saxon of the great herd is, in many important
> respects, the least civilized of men and the least capable of true
> civilization. His political ideas are crude and shallow. He is
> almost wholly devoid of aesthetic feeling; he does not even make
> folklore or walk in the woods. The most elementary facts about
> the visible universe alarm him, and incite him to put them
> down.

*No one was better at putting down those he scorned than
the "Sage of Baltimore." In the 1920s, Mencken flourished as
never before. "Every Babbitt read him gleefully and pronounced
his neighbor a Babbitt," explained literary historian Alfred
Kazin. "Mencken's technique was simple: he inverted conventional prejudices. To a Protestant America, he proclaimed himself a Nietzschean; to a moral American, an atheist; to the
Anti-Saloon League Mind, a devotee of the fine art of drinking;
to a provincial America, a citizen of the world. . . . In a culture
aching for emancipation from the Prohibition mind, from vul-
garity and provincialism and conventionality, Mencken was a
source of light."*

*The following samples of Mencken's commentaries on
American politics in the 1920s characteristically give off a good
deal of heat but they also shed light on the politics of cultural
conflict in that decade.*

(In Praise of Gamaliel)
October 18, 1920

The learned *Freeman* calls attention to something that
must have long since wrung the hearts of right-thinking Republicans, to wit, the fact that the candidates and fuglemen of their
party are strangely silent about certain great moral issues that
lie temptingly under their noses. For example, the Hog Island

Source: *A Carnival of Buncombe*, Malcolm Moos ed. (Vintage Books,
1960) Copyright © 1960 by The Johns Hopkins Press. Reprinted by permission.

issue: who hears anything about the herculean stealing that
went on down there during the war? Again, the Debs-O'Hare
issue: what Republican boob-bumper has ever sobbed and bellowed over the continued caging of dear old Gene? Yet again:
the Hard-Boiled Smith issue: who of the Grand Old Party lifts his
voice against the mad riot of courts-martial that went on during
the war? Several months ago Hard-Boiled himself was paroled
after serving half of his light sentence; meanwhile, the military
dungeons are still full of boys jailed under the Zuluesque system
that he adorned. But does Gamaliel moan and beat his breast?
He does not.

The *Freeman* hints that he is silent because every blast of
indignation would come back, boomerang-like, and singe his own
withers. All such great moral enterprises, in fact, were managed
upon a strictly bi-partisan basis. Every time a Democratic patriot,
whether capitalist or honest toiler, got an easy dollar at Hog
Island, a Republican patriot was given another dollar. Every
time a German factory was sold at 10 cents on the dollar to a
deserving Democrat, a German mill was sold at 11 cents on the
dollar to a Republican full of exalted rage against the Hun. And
every time a Democratic judge and a Democratic state's attorney
railroaded a Socialist to jail, or a Democratic judge advocate
demanded 30 years for some bewildered doughboy accused of
failing to salute a major in the Quartermaster's Department, a
Republican judge and state's attorney railroaded two Socialists
and a Dunkard, and a Republican judge advocate demanded
100 years for some doughboy accused of sticking out his tongue
at a lithograph of General Pershing. In brief, it was a brotherly
and amicable business, and the Republicans had a fair whack at
the loot and the fun. If Gamaliel and his whoopers went into the
matter, the matter would explode in their hands. They must let
it alone, as the committees of investigation appointed by a
Republican House of Representatives had to let it alone. It is far
safer to set up a din about the League of Nations, which is fortunately unintelligible, and hence not loaded. The worst that can
happen is that Woodrow calls someone a liar, and someone calls
Woodrow another.

So far the estimable *Freeman*. Unluckily, it too has to be a bit wary—it too has to avoid monkeying with a buzzsaw. That buzzsaw is its naïve and charming belief in the intrinsic integrity and passion for justice of the great masses of plain men—its laudable superstition that an unveiling of the facts would send them into tantrums of indignation, and so cause them to set down both Cox and Gamaliel as agents of the devil, and to cast their virtuous votes for Debs, and if not for Debs, then for Christensen, the grand worthy exalted supreme archon. This belief, as I say, is charming and laudable, but that is all I care to say in favor of it at the present time. To argue that it is sound, it seems to me, is to spit boorishly into the very eye of the facts.

In other words, there is actually no such nobility in the public breast, and not all the yelling and tear-squeezing of Gamaliel, imagining him reckless enough to take a chance, would suffice to plant it there. No loud demand for light upon all those gaudy satanries has ever issued from the awful depths of the boob conscience. There has come, once or twice, a demand for the hides of the scoundrels who put up the price of sugar, flour, potatoes and hog-meat, and there will come anon an even more raucous demand for the hides of those who prepare to sell a mixture of 10% anthracite and 90% cobblestone at $20 a ton, but there has never been any authentic rage against the merry men who robbed, not the consumer, but the Government and the enemy. It is not a crime, by American ethics, to rob the Government, either in peace or in war. On the contrary, it is an evidence of normalcy, the act of an intelligent and patriotic man. All of the chief operators at Hog Island were eminent patriots, and for two long years anyone who attacked them stood in danger of getting 10 years under the Espionage Act.

Nor is there any settled public horror of cruel and unusual punishments, as in the case of Debs and company and that of the victims of Hard-Boiled Smith. The only persons who demand that Debs be released today are (a) Socialists, and (b) a few sentimental Liberals, of whom I am surely not one. The plain fact is that the great masses of the plain people, in all such melodramatic affairs, are almost unanimously on the side of the prosecution, and that it is impossible to interest them in the case of the defense, save by turning it into a super-prosecution. This was not done in Hard-Boiled's case for obvious reasons, and so he has been released without protest, and no one bawls about his poor victims. The mob likes a cruel and bloody show; the prosecution gives the show. Every intelligent district attorney with an eye upon the Federal bench prays nightly that God will deliver a Debs, a Leary or a Kate O'Hare into his hands. Nearly half of the eminent men mentioned for the Presidency during the past eight or ten years became eminent by trying to get some conspicuous victim or victims into jail. I name a few: Hughes, Folk, Palmer, Whitman, Heney, Johnson, Wood.

Thus Gamaliel is silent about all the atrocities mentioned by the *Freemen*. On the one hand, he knows that agitation of the matter would hurt him as much as it aided him, and on the other hand he knows that public interest in it would be feeble and transient. In brief, he is a sound politician, a man with a talent for boob-bumping. But has he anything else? Is there any further reason for voting for him? There is. Gamaliel has the very rare virtue (in American politics) of being relatively honest —of being almost as honest, in fact, as the average porchclimber, detective or seller of Mexican oil stock. He pulls the noses of the plain people in little ways, for they like to have their noses pulled, but when it comes to the capital issues he exposes himself in the altogether. He does not pretend falsely to be a Progressive when everyone knows that he is not. He does not say one thing to the wets and another thing to the drys. He does not fill the air with a babble about brummagem ideals that he doesn't believe in, and is secretly preparing to drop down the nearest sewer. He does not bawl for liberty, and make ready to stuff more jails with Debses. He doesn't take money from his millionaire backers, and then caress the proletariat with vague and windy libels upon capitalism. He does not blow hot and think cold. He doesn't seek votes by false pretenses.

It seems to be that here is sufficient reason to vote for him —that here is the reason the overwhelming majority of Americans are going to vote for him. They tire, after twenty years, of a steady diet of white protestations and black acts; they are weary of hearing highfalutin and meaningless words; they sicken of an idealism that is oblique, confusing, dishonest and ferocious. The thing began under Roosevelt, the bogus Progressive. It has continued *ad nauseam* under Wilson, the bogus Liberal. Today no sane American believes in any official statement of national policy, whether foreign or domestic. He has been fooled too often, and too callously and impudently. Every idea that has aroused him to sentimental enthusiasm and filled his breast with the holiest of passions has been dragged down into the mud by its propounders, and made to seem evil and disgusting. He wants a change. He wants a renaissance of honesty—even of ordinary, celluloid politician's honesty. Tired to death of intellectual charlatanry, he turns despairingly to honest imbecility.

But all this, you may say, is a reason for voting for Debs, not for the Marion stonehead. Such is the eloquent argument of the Hon. Jesse Lee Bennett, my suffering colleague. But *is* it? I think not. Debs is honest too, but his notions are hopeless. His whole case is predicated upon the theory that capitalism is sick unto death, and will presently give way to something new and worse. This theory is nonsense, at all events in America. Capitalism may be down with salaam convulsions in Russia, it may show an appalling albuminuria in Italy, and it may be covered with urticaria in England and Germany, but in the United States it was never more vigorous. It will outlive you and me, fair friends. The war did not weaken it; the war enormously strengthened it. We'll live under capitalism until we die, and on the whole we'll be reasonably comfortable. Gamaliel represents this capitalism, openly and unashamed. He is not a fraudulent Progressive like Cox, but a frank reactionary. Well, if we are to have reaction, why not have it willingly and without any attempt to disguise it? Why not hand over the conduct of the state to an honest reactionary? Why take on more idealism in place of the idealism that we are getting rid of? Why try to cure fraud with more fraud?

(Gamalielese)
March 7, 1921

On the question of the logical content of Dr. Harding's harangue of last Friday I do not presume to have views. The matter has been debated at great length by the editorial writers of the Republic, all of them experts in logic; moreover, I confess to being prejudiced. When a man arises publicly to argue that the United States entered the late war because of a "concern for preserved civilization," I can only snicker in a superior way and wonder why he isn't holding down the chair of history in some American university. When he says that the United States has "never sought territorial aggrandizement through force," the snicker arises to the virulence of a chuckle, and I turn to the first volume of General Grant's memoirs. And when, gaining momentum, he gravely informs the boobery that "ours is a con- stitutional freedom where the popular will is supreme, and minorities are sacredly protected," then I abandon myself to a mirth that transcends, perhaps, the seemly, and send picture postcards of A. Mitchell Palmer and the Atlanta Penitentiary to all of my enemies who happen to be Socialists.

But when it comes to the style of a great man's discourse, I can speak with a great deal less prejudices, and maybe with somewhat more competence, for I have earned most of my liveli- hood for twenty years past by translating the bad English of a multitude of authors into measurably better English. Thus quali- fied professionally, I rise to pay my small tribute to Dr. Harding. Setting aside a college professor or two and half a dozen dipso- maniacal newspaper reporters, he takes the first place in my Valhalla of literati. That is to say, he writes the worst English that I have ever encountered. It reminds me of a string of wet sponges; it reminds me of tattered washing on the line; it reminds me of stale bean-soup, of college yells, of dogs barking idiotically through endless nights. It is so bad that a sort of gran- deur creeps into it. It drags itself out of the dark abysm (I was about to write abscess!) of pish, and crawls insanely up the top- most pinnacle of posh. It is rumble and bumble. It is flap and doodle. It is balder and dash.

But I grow lyrical. More scientifically, what is the matter with it? Why does it seem so flabby, so banal, so confused and childish, so stupidly at war with sense? If you first read the inaugural address and then heard it intoned, as I did (at least in part), then you will perhaps arrive at an answer. That answer is very simple. When Dr. Harding prepares a speech he does not think it out in terms of an educated reader locked up in jail, but in terms of a great horde of stoneheads gathered around a stand. That is to say, the thing is always a stump speech; it is conceived as a stump speech and written as a stump speech. More, it is a stump speech addressed primarily to the sort of audience that the speaker has been used to all his life, to wit, an audience of small town yokels, of low political serfs, or morons scarcely able to understand a word of more than two syllables, and wholly unable to pursue a logical idea for more than two centimeters.

Such imbeciles do not want ideas—that is, new ideas, ideas that are unfamiliar, ideas that challenge their attention. What they want is simply a gaudy series of platitudes, of threadbare phrases terrifically repeated, of sonorous nonsense driven home with gestures. As I say, they can't understand many words of more than two syllables, but that is not saying that they do not esteem such words. On the contrary, they like them and demand them. The roll of incomprehensible polysyllables enchants them. They like phrases which thunder like salvos of artillery. Let that thunder sound, and they take all the rest on trust. If a sentence begins furiously and then peters out into fatuity, they are still satisfied. If a phrase has a punch in it, they do not ask that it also have a meaning. If a word slides off the tongue like a ship going down the ways, they are content and applaud it and wait for the next.

Brought up amid such hinds, trained by long practice to engage and delight them, Dr. Harding carries over his stump manner into everything he writes. He is, perhaps, too old to learn a better way. He is, more likely, too discreet to experiment. The stump speech, put into cold type, maketh the judicious to grieve. But roared from an actual stump, with arms flying and eyes flashing and the old flag overhead, it is certainly and brilliantly effective. Read the inaugural address, and it will gag you. But hear it recited through a sound-magnifier, with grand gestures to ram home its periods, and you will begin to understand it.

Let us turn to a specific example. I exhume a sentence from the latter half of the eminent orator's discourse:

I would like government to do all it can to mitigate, then, in understanding, in mutuality of interest, in concern for the common good, our tasks will be solved.

I assume that you have read it. I also assume that you set it down as idiotic—a series of words without sense. You are quite right; it is. But now imagine it intoned as it was designed to be intoned. Imagine the slow tempo of a public speech. Imagine the stately unrolling of the first clause, the delicate pause upon the word "then"—and then the loud discharge of the phrase "in understanding," "in mutuality of interest," "in concern for the common good," each with its attendant glare and roll of the eyes, each with its sublime heave, each with its gesture of a black-smith bringing down his sledge upon an egg—imagine all this, and then ask yourself where you have got. You have got, in brief, to a point where you don't know what it is all about. You hear and applaud the phrases, but their connection has already escaped you. And so, when in violation of all sequence and logic, the final phrase, "our tasks will be solved," assaults you, you do not notice its disharmony—all you notice is that, if this or that, already forgotten, is done, "our tasks will be solved." Whereupon, glad of the assurance and thrilled by the vast gestures that drive it home, you give a cheer.

That is, if you are the sort of man who goes to political meetings, which is to say, if you are the sort of man that Dr. Harding is used to talking to, which is to say, if you are a jackass.

The whole inaugural address reeked with just such non-sense. The thing started off with an error in English in its very first sentence—the confusion of pronouns in the *one-he* combination, so beloved of bad newspaper reporters. It bristled with words misused: *Civic* for *civil, luring* for *alluring, womanhood* for *women, referendum* for *reference,* even *task* for *problem.* "The *task* is to be *solved*"—what could be worse? Yet I find it twice. "The expressed views of world opinion"—what irritating tautology! "The expressed conscience of progress"—what on earth does it mean? "This is not selfishness, it is sanctity"—what intelligible idea do you get out of that? "I know that Congress and the administration will favor every wise government policy to aid the resumption and encourage continued progress"—the resumption of what? "Service is the supreme *commitment* of life"—*ach, du heiliger!*

But is such bosh out of place in a stump speech? Obviously not. It is precisely and thoroughly in place in a stump speech. A tight fabric of ideas would weary and exasperate the audience; what it wants is simply a loud burble of words, a procession of phrases that roar, a series of whoops. This is what it got in the inaugural address of the Hon. Warren Gamaliel Harding. And this is what it will get for four long years—unless God sends a miracle and the corruptible puts on incorruption. . . . Almost I long for the sweeter song, the rubber-stamps of more familiar design, the gentler and more seemly bosh of the late Woodrow.

(The Impending Plebiscite)
October 22, 1923

The connoisseur of the higher political mountebankery cannot fail to yield his veneration to the great talents of the Hon. J. Calvin Coolidge, the present First Chief of the Republic. How much shrewder he is than his illustrious predecessor, the Martyr Harding! Harding, at the time the Reds did him to death, was rocking his own boat so violently that many of his most faithful partisans were coming down with *mal de mar*. The more he searched and felt about for issues, publicly and clumsily, the more he alarmed the great masses of the plain people. No less than three times he tried to heat them up with his unintelligible scheme for a World Court in which the leading burglars should sit upon the bench, and no less than three times he saw them blanch, tremble and go cold. If, at the time he fell a victim to his patriotism, he was gradually abandoning all such disturbing issues and concentrating his passion for Service upon Prohibition, then it was surely not due to any interior vision, but simply to the force of events. With the Ohio Anti-Saloon League pushing and the plain people themselves pulling, he had to go that way or blow up altogether.

Dr. Coolidge is far more adept and realistic. He sees very clearly that, in the struggle ahead of him, issues that are perplexing can only do him damage, and so he is avoiding them with magnificent assiduity. No more is heard about World Courts. There will be no economic conference. The coal strike was shoved off on Pinchot, who will remain a hero until the coal bills come in; *i.e.,* until about the time the Coolidge campaign really gets under weigh. Harding, given the word to recognize Mexico, would have tried to 'rouse the rabble over it; Coolidge performed the business *pianissimo*, well knowing that Mexico, if talked of too much, could only lose him votes. His whole appeal, it appears, will be based upon a clarion demand for law enforcement and respect for the Constitution, which is to say, for Prohibition. The issue will be clear, single, simple and familiar. More, it will win.

But it is a fact, then, that a majority of the people of the United States are still in favor of Prohibition? I doubt that anyone knows; I doubt, indeed, that anyone can say with assurance that a majority of them were *ever* in favor of it. But that is not the point. The point is that Dr. Coolidge doesn't have to convince a majority of the voters in order to be reëlected; all he has to do is to convince such a number as, added to the horde of job-holders and other safe men, will make a majority. It seems to me that it will be enormously easier for him to do this by embracing prohibition, a tried and well-understood issue with a great body of organized opinion already behind it, than it would be by endeavoring, like the late Harding, to manufacture a new issue, and so run the risk, like Harding again, of arousing only suspicion and alarm.

By declaring for moonshine and Christian Endeavor the learned and distinguished candidate will not only solidify the rural Methodists of the North and West, most of whom are Republicans anyhow; he will also stand a good chance of making even further inroads upon the rural and Methodist South than Harding made. The South, of course, was never wetter than it is today, but whoever believes that the great geysers of bad booze now spouting down there indicate that the low-caste Confederates have lost their enthusiasm for Prohibition is surely an unpracticed student of the Methodist-Baptist, or Ku Klux mind. The very fact, indeed, that the sub-Potomac yokels have plenty to drink themselves only augments their yearning to make the

Jews, Catholics, fugitive Moors and other Reds of the big cities
dry. Lynching is their sport; not suicide. They are Democrats,
true enough, but before they are Democrats they are Christian
idealists—and Dr. Coolidge, with great skill and delicacy, has
got a strangle hold upon the best keg of Christian idealism ever
on tap. They will vote for a Democrat if he is as dry as or drier
than Coolidge, but—

Here, indeed, is where the eminent candidate reveals the
full horse-power of his sagacity; by jumping aboard the water-
wagon so early in the race he leaves the Democrats almost helpless. If they could find a safe and incurable wet of national
reputation and had the courage to nominate him boldly and
make the campaign on a beer-wagon, they might have a chance
to win; certainly they would carry all of the big cities and most of
the so-called key States almost unanimously. But they have
neither the candidate nor the courage. The Hon. Al Smith is
obviously hopeless; the day he was nominated the Methodist
Ku Kluxers of every State south of the Potomac would begin
building forts along the coast to repel the Pope. To make the
attempt with any other leader would be still worse; he could be
jammed through the convention only by nailing the Southern
delegates to the floor, and the whole gang would go home as
despondent as the gang which nominated Cox at San Francisco.

Thus the Democrats, lacking a candidate of any heft or
beam and facing an issue forced upon them, will have to do
either one of two things: they will have to swallow the issue
themselves and so reduce the contest to a mere sham battle, or
they will have to pussyfoot. If they do the latter, both wets and
drys will suspect them, and Dr. Coolidge will have a walk-over.
And if they do the former he will have a walk-over almost as
easy, for their cowardice will lose them all the wet States of the
North without gaining them anything save the Ku Klux States of
the South, most of which are bound to stick to them anyhow. In
politics, the first candidate who grabs an issue always gets the
best of it. The plain people distrust the trailer, particularly if his
vacillations have been public, and their distrust has a sound
instinct under it. Whoever is nominated by the Democrats will

be a palpable fraud. No even half-honest man has any more chance of getting the nomination than a Chinaman. . . .

(The Clowns March In)
June 2, 1924

At first blush, the Republican National Convention at Cleveland next week promises to be a very dull show, for the Hon. Mr. Coolidge will be nominated without serious opposition and there are no issues of enough vitality to make a fight over the platform. The whole proceedings, in fact, will be largely formal. Some dreadful mountebank in a long-tailed coat will open them with a windy speech; then another mountebank will repeat the same rubbish in other words; then a half dozen windjammers will hymn good Cal as a combination of Pericles, Frederick the Great, Washington, Lincoln, Roosevelt and John the Baptist; then there will be an hour or two of idiotic whooping, and then the boys will go home. The LaFollette heretics, if they are heard of at all, will not be heard of for long; they will be shoved aside even more swiftly than they were shoved aside when Harding was nominated. And the battle for the Vice-Presidency will not be fought out in the hall, but somewhere in one of the hotels, behind locked doors and over a jug or two of bootleg Scotch.

A stupid business, indeed. Nevertheless, not without its charms to connoisseurs of the obscene. What, in truth, could more beautifully display the essential dishonesty and imbecility of the entire democratic process. Here will be assembled all the great heroes and masterminds of the majority party in the greatest free nation ever seen on earth, and the job before them will be the austere and solemn one of choosing the head of the state, the heir of Lincoln and Washington, the peer of Caesar and Charlemagne. And here, after three or four days of bombarding the welkin and calling upon God for help, they will choose unanimously a man whom they regard unanimously as a cheap and puerile fellow!

I don't think I exaggerate. Before the end of the campaign, of course, many of them will probably convince themselves that Cal is actually a man of powerful intellect and lofty character, and even, perhaps, a gentleman. But I doubt seriously that a single Republican leader of any intelligence believes it today. Do you think that Henry Cabot Lodge does? Or Smoot? Or any of the Pennsylvania bosses? Or Borah? Or Hiram Johnson? Or Moses? Or our own Weller? These men are not idiots. They have eyes in their heads. They have seen Cal at close range. . . . But they will all whoop for him in Cleveland.

In such whooping lies the very soul and essence of humor. Nothing imaginable could be more solidly mirthful. Nor will there be any lack of jocosity in the details of the farce: the imbecile paralogy of the speeches; the almost inconceivable nonsense of the platform; the low buffooneries of the Southern delegates, white and black; the swindling of the visitors by the local apostles of Service; the bootlegging and boozing; the gaudy scenes in the hall. National conventions are almost always held in uncomfortable and filthy places; the one at San Francisco, four years ago, is the only decent one I have ever heard of. The decorations are carried out by the sort of morons who arrange street fairs. The hotels are crowded to suffocation. The food is bad and expensive. Everyone present is robbed, and everyone goes home exhausted and sore.

My agents in Cleveland report that elaborate preparations are under way there to slack the thirst of the visitors, which is always powerful at national conventions. The town is very well supplied with bootleggers, and regular lines of rum ships run into it from Canadian ports. Ohio has a State Volstead act and a large force of spies and snoopers, many of them former jail-birds. These agents of the Only True Christianity, no doubt, will all concentrate in Cleveland, and dispute with the national Prohibition blacklegs for the graft. I venture the guess that bad Scotch will sell for $15 a bottle in the hotels and at the convention hall, and that more than one delegate will go home in the baggage car, a victim to methyl alcohol.

Ohio is run by the Anti-Saloon League, and so the city of Cleveland will be unable to imitate the charming hospitality of the city of San Francisco, four years ago. The municipality there ordered 60 barrels of excellent Bourbon for the entertainment of the delegates and alternates, and charged them to the local smallpox hospital. After the convention the Methodist mullahs of the town exposed the transaction, and proved that there had not been a patient in the hospital for four years. But the city officials who were responsible, when they came up for reëlection soon afterward, were re-elected by immense majorities. Despite Prohibition, the people of San Francisco are still civilized, and know the difference between entertaining human beings and entertaining horned cattle.

The managers of the Hon. Mr. Coolidge's campaign are apparently well aware that the nomination of the Hon. Al Smith by the Democrats would plunge them into a very bitter and serious fight, and so they are trying to weaken Al by weakening Tammany Hall. One of the principal arguments used to bring the Democratic convention to New York was that Tammany would see that the delegates and alternates got enough sound drinks at reasonable prices to keep pleasantly jingled—an unbroken tradition at Democratic national conventions since the days of Andrew Jackson. Now the Coolidge managers have hurled hundreds of Prohibition agents into Manhattan, and a desperate effort is under way to make the town bone-dry. The Dogberries of the Federal bench, as usual, lend themselves willingly to the buffoonery: dozens of injunctions issue from their mills every day, and some of the principal saloons of the Broadway region are now padlocked.

But all the New Yorkers that I know are still optimistic. There are, indeed, so many saloons in the town that all the Federal judges east of the Mississippi, working in eight-hour shifts like coal miners, could not close them completely in the month remaining before the convention opens. Every time one saloon is closed two open. Meanwhile, the 12-mile treaty with England seems to have failed absolutely to discourage bootlegging from the Bahamas. On the contrary, the price of Scotch has declined steadily since it was signed, and the stuff now coming in is of very excellent quality. It is my belief that the theory that it is heavily adulterated is spread by Prohibitionists, who are certainly not noted for veracity. I have not only encountered no bad Scotch in New York for a year past; I have never heard of any. All the standard brands are obtainable in unlimited quantities, and at prices, roughly speaking, about half those of a year ago.

Moreover, very good beer is everywhere on sale, and nine-tenths of the Italian restaurants, of which there must be at least two thousand in the town, are selling cocktails and wine. Along Broadway the difficulty of concealing so bulky a drink as beer and the high tolls demanded by the Prohibition enforcement officers make the price somewhat high, but in the side streets it is now only 60 per cent above what it was in the days before the Volstead act. The last time I went into a beer-house in New York, two or three weeks ago, the *Wirt* greeted me with the news that he had just reduced the price 10 cents a *Seidel*. His place was packed to the doors.

I am thus inclined to believe that the efforts of M. Coolidge's artisans to employ the Eighteenth Amendment against M. Smith will fail. When the white, Protestant, Nordic delegates from the Christian Endeavor regions of the South and Middle West arrive in the big town, their tongues hanging out, they will get what they have dreamed of all these months. It will cost them somewhat more than the dreadful corn liquor of their native steppes, but they will quickly get too much aboard to bother about money. In brief, I formally prophesy that the Democratic National Convention will be as wet as Democratic national conventions have always been, and that the Prohibitionist delegates, as always, will do more than their fair share of the guzzling. The soberest men in the hall, no doubt, will be the Tammany delegates and their brethren from the other big cities of the East. To these cockneys drinking has vastly less fascination than it has for the hinds of the hinterland; decent drinks are always under their noses, and so they are not tortured by the pathological thirst of the rural Ku Kluxers. Moreover, they will have a serious job in hand, and so they will avoid the jug. That job will be to get the bucolic Baptists drunk, and shove Al down their gullets before they recognize the flavor.

(Twilight)
October 17, 1927

Having pussy-footed all his life, it is highly probable that Dr. Coolidge will go on pussy-footing to the end of the chapter. There is nothing in the known facts about the man to indicate any change of heart. He was born with that pawky caution which is one of the solid qualities of the peasant, and he will hang on to it until the angels call him home. It has made life comfortable for him, as the same quality makes life comfortable to a bishop or a mud turtle, but what it will cost him in the long run! The verdict of history upon him is not hard to forecast. He will be ranked among the vacuums. In distant ages his career will be cited as proof of the astounding fact that it is possible to rise to the highest places in this world, and yet remain as obscure as a bookkeeper in a village coal-yard. The present age has produced other examples: King George of England, that King of Italy whose name I forget, and perhaps six of the nine judges of the Supreme Court of the United States.

Dr. Coolidge, if he had any enterprise and courage in him, would be the most enviable man in the world today. For he faces nearly a year and a half of almost imperial power—and no responsibility whatever, save to his own conscience. If, as I believe, he is honest in his withdrawal from the race for his own shoes, then he is free to do anything he pleases, and nothing can happen to him. He could, if he would, force almost any conceivable legislation upon Congress. He could bring irresistible pressure to bear upon the Supreme Court. He could clear out the frauds and imbeciles who infest the high offices of government, and put in decent men. He could restore the Bill of Rights.

All these things he could do in his seventeen months, and without going outside his constitutional prerogatives. But there is not the slightest chance that he will do any of them, or that doing them will so much as occur to him. He has been plodding along in the goose-step too long for him to attempt any leaping and cavorting now. He will pass from the Presidency as he came into it—a dull and docile drudge, loving the more tedious forms of ease, without imagination, and not too honest.

When I speak of honesty, of course, I mean the higher forms of that virtue—the honesty of the mind and heart, not of the fingers. I suppose that, in the ordinary sense, Dr. Coolidge is one of the most honest men ever heard of in public life in America. True enough, he did his best to hush up the Daugherty scandal, and connoisseurs will recall that a great deal of lying had to be done to hush up his hushing up. But no one ever alleged that he was personally corrupt. The Ohio Gang never took him into its calculations. If he went to its rescue, it was not to protect thieves, but simply to prevent *scandalum magnatum*—a more dangerous thing, in an inflammable democracy, than a little quiet stealing. His motives, one may say, even transcended the partisan; they were, in a certain sense, almost patriotic.

But of intellectual honesty the man apparently knows nothing. He has no taste for cold facts, and no talent for grappling with them. There is no principle in his armamentarium that is worth any sacrifice, even of sleep. Human existence, as he sees it, is something to be got through with the least possible labor and fretting. His ideal day is one on which nothing whatever happens—a day sliding into a lazy afternoon upon the *Mayflower*, full of innocent snores. There is no record that he has ever thought anything worth hearing about any of the public problems that have confronted him. His characteristic way of dealing with them is simply to evade them, as a sensible man evades an insurance solicitor or his wife's relatives. In his speeches, though he knows how to write clear English, there is nothing that might not have occurred to a Rotarian, or even to a university president.

All his great feats of derring-do have been bogus. He kept out of the Boston police strike until other men had disposed of it: then he echoed their triumphant whoops in a feeble falsetto. He vetoed the Farm Relief bill because he couldn't help it—because signing it would have made trouble for him. He opened fire upon poor Daugherty only after the man was dead and the smell of his carcass unbearable. He intrigued for a third term until it became obvious that he couldn't get it without a fight, and then he fled ignominiously, leaving his friends upon a burning deck.

There is something deeply mysterious about such a man. It seems incredible that one with such towering opportunities in this world should use them so ill. The rest of us sweat and struggle for our puny chances, and then wreck ourselves trying to turn them into achievements. But here is one who seems content to pass by even great ones: he appears, indeed, to be scarcely conscious of them when they confront him. During his years in the highest office among us the country has seen a huge slaughter of its ancient liberties, a concerted and succesful effort to convert every citizen into a mere subject. He has done nothing to stop that, and he has said nothing against it. Instead, he has devoted himself to puerile bookkeeping. The man who had a million in 1923 now has, perhaps, a million and a quarter.

But who, in the long run, will give a damn? Of what use are such achievements to the progress of the human race? Who knows what the tax-rate was in 1847, or who benefited by it, or who was in favor of it or against it? History, it seems to me, deals with larger issues. Its theme, when it is not written by mere pedants, besotted by names and dates, is the upward struggle of man, out of darkness and into light. Its salient men are those who have had a hand in that struggle, on one side or the other. What will such history say of Coolidge? It will say even less, I believe, than it says of John Tyler, who at least had the courage to take himself off the scene in a blaze of treason.

Laws multiply in the land. They grow more and more idiotic and oppressive. Swarms of scoundrels are let loose to harass honest men. The liberties that the Fathers gave us are turned into mockeries. Of all this Dr. Coolidge seems to be almost unaware, as he is apparently unaware of any art or science save party politics. He has to be sure, adverted to the subject in an occasional speech, but only in weasel words. What has he done about it? He has done absolutely nothing.

What he could do if he wanted to, even in the short time remaining to him, is almost past calculation. He could stop the grotesque crimes and oppressions of the Prohibition blacklegs with a stroke of the pen. He could bring a reasonable sanity and order into the whole Prohibition question, and open the way for its candid reconsideration. He could clear out the Department of Justice, and return it to common decency. He could prepare and advocate an intelligent plan for the national defense, and put an end to the disingenuous and dangerous debate which now goes on. He could restore our dealings with foreign nations to frankness and honesty. He could improve the Federal bench by appointing better men. He could shame Congress into some regard for the honor of the nation.

All these things a man of diligent enterprise and laudable ambition could do—and if not all of them, then at least most of them. It might take some fighting, but he would win that fighting, for all men of any decency would be with him. He could turn the flow of national events back to the sound principles upon which the Republic was founded, and get rid of the follies and dishonesties that have displaced those principles. He could confound rogues and hearten honest men. He could leave behind him, win or lose, the memory of an honorable and useful life. He could make it something, once more, to be an American.

But he will do nothing of the sort. The year and a half ahead of him, like the years behind him, will be years of ignoble emptiness. He will keep on playing the politics of the village grocery. The best men of his time will continue to lie beyond his ken, and he will continue to recreate himself with the conversation of cheap-jacks and ignoramuses. There will be the familiar reports of his brave intentions, and the familiar disappointments. He will eat so many more meals, make so many more trips on the *Mayflower* with rogues and bounders, hear so many more reports from herders of votes, and make so many more hollow speeches. The stove will be spit on regularly. The clock will be wound up every night. And so, at last, he will pass from the scene, no doubt well rewarded by those who admire him with intelligent self-interest—an empty and tragic little man, thrown by fate into opportunities beyond his poor talents, and even beyond his imagination.

(The Impending Combat)
May 28, 1928

All the political seers and sourcerers seem to be agreed that the coming Presidential campaign will be full of bitterness, and that most of it will be caused by religion. I count Prohibition as a part of religion, for it has surely become so in the United States. The Prohibitionists, seeing all their other arguments destroyed by the logic of events, have fallen back upon the mystical doctrine that God is somehow on their side, and that opposing them thus takes on the character of blasphemy. At Charleston, W. Va., not long ago, some of them were gravely discussing whether or not Jesus should be reprimanded *post mortem* for the miracle at Cana. And others had frequently maintained that violators of the Volsteadian rumble-bumble should be publicly executed, as heretics were executed in mediaeval Europe.

These earnest men, led by their appointed pastors, will make a violent fight against the nomination of the Hon. Al Smith, LL.D., at Houston, and if they fail to head him off, as seems likely, they will continue that fight before the country. Henry M. Hyde, who was lately in attendance upon the great Baptist convention at Chattanooga, Tenn., the Jerusalem of the Fundamentalist Holy Land, tells me that all the Baptist evangelists are preparing to take the stump against Al and the Harlot of the Seven Hills, and that they are already in a lather of spiritual zeal. More, they will be joined by hundreds of pastors who now serve cures: these cures will be abandoned for the duration of the campaign.

There is even a great deal of wild talk in the South about bolting the ticket, and the experts in political pathology attached to the Washington bureau of the *Sunpaper* seem inclined to take it more or less seriously. Myself, I view it lightly, for I believe that the Democrats of the South are far dumber than anyone has ever suspected, even in Boston or Harlem. They would vote for the Pope himself if he were nominated at Houston. But though they will fall into line in November, they will undoubtedly do a great deal of hard sweating before its first Tuesday dawns, and the evangelists who plan to operate upon them will find it easy to fever and alarm them, and incidentally to gather in their mazuma.

If Al is undone, either at Houston or at the polls, it will not be because he is a Tammany man, nor even because he is wet, but simply and solely because he is a Catholic. The issue grows clearer every day. His defeat will be a smashing affront to all Catholics, who will be notified thereby that the majority of their fellow-citizens do not regard them as sound Americans. And if he is nominated and elected it will be a no less smashing affront to those millions of Protestants who believe in all sincerity that Catholicism is inimical to free government, and that the election of a Catholic President will sound the death-knell of the Republic.

In either event, the result is bound to leave much bitterness. The campaign itself, as I have said, will be extraordinarily bitter. There will be absolutely no way to compromise the leading issue. The Catholics and their allies will stand pat, and the anti-Catholics and their allies will stand pat. Each side will have at the other with all the ferocity of so many Liberty Loan orators, vice crusaders or D.A.R. beldames. For religion is the greatest inspirer of hatred the world has ever seen, and it shows no sign of losing that character in its old age. Every effort to make the warring sects lie down together has failed. They quarrel incessantly, and they will keep on quarreling to the end of the chapter.

Why this should be so I don't know, but so it seems to be. The enmities set up by nationalism are as nothing compared to those set up by religion. A few hours after the formal conclusion of a bloody war the soldiers of the opposing armies are friends, and only those who stayed at home keep up the bawling. But when religion gets into a difference it is fought out to the death, and there is never any treaty of peace. Consider again, Prohibition. It used to be discussed good-humoredly, and the two sides kept up a certain show of politeness to each other. Even such violent partisans as Carrie Nation were viewed tolerantly. But the moment the Baptist and Methodist pastors began taking jobs with the Anti-Saloon League the contest became a bloody riot, and now it has come to such a pass that murder is a daily incident of it. Naturally, it is wets (and innocents) who are being murdered, for the pastors are on the side of the drys.

I recite these lamentable facts, not to deplore them, but to say that I do *not* deplore them. Life in America interests me, not as a moral phenomenon, but simply as a gaudy spectacle. I enjoy it most when it is most uproarious, preposterous, inordinate and melodramatic. I am perfectly willing to give a Roosevelt, a Wilson, a Fall, an Elder Hays, an Andy Mellon or a Tom Heflin such small part of my revenues as he can gouge out of me in return for the show that he offers. Such gorgeous mounte-

banks take my mind off my gallstones, my war wounds, my public duties and my unfortunate love affairs, and so make existence agreeable. I'd rather read the *Congressional Record*—or,
failing that, any good tabloid—than go to see a bishop hanged.

This show is good at all times, but it is best when some
great combat is in progress, and I can think of no combat more
likely to be violent and hence thrilling than one in which religious
zealots are engaged. However trivial its actual issues, it is bound
to show all the savagery of a dog fight. In the present case that
savagery will be there, but the issues will not be trivial. The
question to be decided, indeed, will be of capital importance—
that is, to the extent that any political question can be important. By their votes the massed morons of America will be called
upon to determine whether the unwritten law of a century and a
half, that no Catholic shall sit in the White House, shall be abandoned forever, or whether it shall be reaffirmed and given a new
force and authority.

This is the first time that the question has come squarely
before the so-called people, and no one can say how they will
answer. But the very fact that there is a doubt will give the struggle an added fury. Thus I look for entertainment of the first
calibre, exactly to my taste in all its details, and as a sworn neu-
tral in theology I shall view it with the advantage of not caring a
hoot which side wins. If Al wins there will be a four years' circus.
And if he loses there will be a circus too.

Personally, I hope to vote for him. It will be the duty of
every lifelong Democrat. More, it will be a pleasure. For he is,
I believe, an honest and worthy man, and it will be interesting
to observe how he deals with the great problems sure to confront the next President—for example, the question of Prohibition. No matter what he does or says there will be roars of rage.
If he tries to restore the Bill of Rights by appointing Federal
judges unacceptable to the Anti-Saloon League, the Baptist par-
sons will yell that the Pope is upon us. And if he lets fall the
slightest hint that the Eighteenth Amendment is also in the Constitution, the wets will bawl that he has betrayed them, and is an
ingrate, a traitor and a *Schuft*.

I do not envy Al, but neither do I envy any of the other

gentlemen who make of Our America the greatest show since Rome caved in. There is such a thing as sitting in the audience without getting stage-struck, as going to bull fights without wanting to be either the màtador or the bull. After all, it is the spectator who has the fun, not the clown. The clown has to daub himself with unpleasant paint, get into an absurd costume, and then expose his stern to the blows of the slapstick. Not infrequently, I daresay, they hurt. When the show is over he has to wash up, hunt for his collar-buttons, and paint his bruises with arnica. The spectator, by that time, is snoring in bed, or sitting comfortably in some quiet beer house, deploring the decay of art.

But the art of political buffoonery is surely not decaying, at least in the Federal Union. On the contrary, it seems to be improving year by year. When I was a boy, in the last century, Presidential campaigns were still corrupted by serious purpose. The candidates were such grave and learned men as Cleveland and Harrison, and the issues were of such character that they engaged political economists and statisticians. But now all that is happily past. The combat ensuing will keep to the level of a debate on Darwinism between a hedge pastor and the village atheist, with music by the United Brethren choir. It will break up in a fist fight, with ears torn off and teeth knocked out. It will be a good show.

(The Eve of Armageddon)
November 5, 1928

It has been, by God's will, a very bitter campaign, which is to say, an unusually honest one. Every effort to conceal the real issues—and both sides moved in that direction at the start—has gone to pot. If Al wins tomorrow, it will be because the American people have decided at last to vote as they drink, and because a majority of them believe that the Methodist bishops are worse than the Pope. If he loses, it will be because those who fear the Pope outnumber those who are tired of the Anti-Saloon League.

No other issue has got anywhere, nor will any other swing any appreciable number of votes. Al and Lord Hoover seem to be at one on the tariff, both say they are for economy, and both

promise relief to the farmer though neither says how he is going
to achieve it. When Hoover denounced Al as a Socialist it fell
flat, for everyone knows that he is not, and when Al tried to
hook up Hoover with Fall and Doheny it fell flat, for Americans
are not opposed to corruption. Both sides have appealed alike to
Negroes and Negro-baiters, and neither knows which way either
group is going to jump. Labor, foreign policy, water power—all
these questions are off the board.

There remain only Prohibition and religion, or more accurately, only religion, for Prohibition, in the dry areas, has long
ceased to be a question of government or even of ethics, and has
become purely theological. The more extreme drys, real and
fake, simply refuse to discuss it. Throughout the Bible country
belief in it has become a cardinal article of faith, like belief in
the literal accuracy of Genesis. Men are denounced as traitors
for so much as arguing that it ought to be discussed. Practically
every one in those wilds guzzles more or less, as explorers quickly
discover, but to suggest that Prohibition has failed and that
something better is imaginable is as grave an indecorum as it
would be to suggest to a Catholic theologian that the question
whether the wine is really turned into blood at mass be sub-
mitted to a committee of chemists. In such fields *Homo sapiens*
scorns and abominates human evidences. Challenged, he merely
howls.

I daresay the extent of the bigotry prevailing in America,
as it has been revealed by the campaign, has astounded a great
many Americans, and perhaps even made them doubt the testi-
mony of their own eyes and ears. This surprise is not in itself
surprising, for Americans of one class seldom know anything
about Americans of other classes. What the average native
yokel believes about the average city man is probably nine-tenths
untrue, and what the average city man believes about the average yokel is almost as inaccurate.

A good part of this ignorance is probably due to the powerful effect of shibboleths. Every American is taught in school that
all Americans are free, and so he goes on believing it his whole
life—overlooking the plain fact that no Negro is really free in
the South, and no miner in Pennsylvania, and no radical in any

of a dozen great States. He hears of equality before the law, and he accepts it as a reality, though it exists nowhere, and there are Federal laws which formally repudiate it. In the same way he is taught that religious toleration prevails among us, and uncritically swallows the lie. No such thing really exists. No such thing has ever existed.

This campaign has amply demonstrated the fact. It has brought bigotry out into the open, and revealed its true proportions. It has shown that millions of Americans, far from being free and tolerant men, are the slaves of an ignorant, impudent and unconscionable clergy. It has dredged up theological ideas so preposterous that they would make an intelligent Zulu laugh, and has brought the proof that they are cherished by nearly half the whole population, and by at least four-fifths outside the cities. It has made it plain that this theology is not merely a harmless aberration of the misinformed, like spiritualism, chiropractic or Christian Science, but the foundation of a peculiar way of life, bellicose, domineering, brutal and malignant—in brief, the complete antithesis of any recognizable form of Christianity. And it has shown, finally, that this compound of superstition and hatred has enough steam behind it to make one of the candidates for the Presidency knuckle to it and turn it upon his opponent—basely to be sure, but probably wisely.

Certainly something is accomplished when such facts are exposed to every eye, and with overwhelming reiteration. It may be uncomfortable to confront them, but it is surely better to confront them than to be ignorant of them. They explain many phenomena that have been obscure and puzzling—the rise to power of the Anti-Saloon League, the influence of such clowns as Bishop Cannon, the Rev. John Roach Straton and Billy Sunday, and, above all, the curious and otherwise inexplicable apparition of the Klan, with its appalling trail of crime and corruption.

All these things go back to one source, and that source is now known. The problem before the civilized minority of Americans is that of shutting off its flow of bilge-water. Can that be done? I am not so sure. The majority of rural Americans, with the best blood all drained to the cities, are probably hopelessly uneducable. Sound ideas make no more appeal to them than decent drinks. They prefer nonsense to sense as they prefer white mule to Burgundy. Abandoned for years to the tutelage of their pastors, they have now gone so far into the darkness that every light terrifies them and runs them amuck.

But though the job of enlightening them may be difficult, it should be worth trying. And if, in the end, there is only failure, then the way will be open for other and more radical remedies. For in the long run the cities of the United States will have to throw off the hegemony of these morons. They have run the country long enough, and made it sufficiently ridiculous. Once we get rid of campmeeting rule we'll get rid simultaneously of the Klan, the Anti-Saloon League and the Methodist Board of Temperance, Prohibition and Public Morals. We'll get rid of the Cannons and Heflins, the Willebrandts and Wayne Wheelers. And we'll get rid, too, of those sorry betrayers of intelligence who, like Hoover and Borah, flatter and fawn over the hookworm carriers in order to further their own fortunes.

It seems to me that Dr. Hoover has been exposed in this campaign as no candidate for the Presidency ever was before, not even the ignoramus Harding or the trimmer Davis. He went into it as a master-mind, a fellow of immense and singular sagacies; he comes out of it a shrewd politician, but nothing more. His speeches have been, on the one hand, so disingenuous, and, on the other hand, so hollow, that even his most ardent followers now take refuge behind the doctrine that he will, at all events, be safe—that he will not invite the Pope to Washington, or monkey with such divine revelations as the tariff and Prohibition, or do anything to alarm stock speculators, or make any unseemly pother about stealing.

Hoover, since the day he abandoned mine-stock promoting for Service, has always had the help of a good press. He knows how to work the newspapers. The Washington correspondents, in large majority, dislike him, but still they fall for him, for he is adept at the art of taking the center of the stage and posturing there profoundly. In the past his futilities were only too often overlooked, in the blinding light of his publicity. He went to the Mississippi in all the gaudy state of a movie queen, but came back with no plan to stop the floods there. He issued tons of reports of dull subjects, but said nothing. But always he got lavish press notices.

In the campaign, however, his old devices failed. His original plan, obviously, was to look wise and say nothing. His speech of acceptance was a mass of windy platitudes, almost worthy of Coolidge. But gradually Al forced him into a corner and he had to talk. What has he said? I defy anyone to put it into reasonable propositions. No one, to this moment, knows what he really proposes to do about the tariff, or about Prohibition, or about foreign affairs, or about water power, and in the matter of farm relief he has simply passed the buck. Theoretically an abyss of wisdom, he has chattered like a high-school boy. Once he muttered three sentences against religious intolerance. But the bigots kept on supporting him, and they will support him tomorrow, and he knows it and is counting on it.

(Autopsy)
November 12, 1928

Al Smith's body lies a-mouldering in the grave, but his soul goes marching on. He fought a good fight, and he was right. So far as I have been able to make out, not a man or woman who voted for him regrets it today. The phenomenon is almost unique in American politics. Usually, after a disastrous failure, the standard-bearer is heaved into Coventry and has to bear a lot of the blame. It was so with the pussyfooting Davis. It was so with the preposterous Cox. It was even so with Roosevelt: his last days, as everyone knows, were lonely and bitter. But no one blames Al. He made a gallant and gaudy campaign against tremendous odds, and he went down to defeat with every flag flying and the band playing on deck. He was, is, and will remain a man. There are not many in public life in America. They are so few, indeed, that the American people have got out of the habit of looking for them, and of following them when found. The standard-model statesman of today is a far more limber and politic fellow. Avoiding ideas as dangerous—which they unquestionably are—he devotes himself to playing upon emotions and sentimentalities. He may be himself an ignoramus, like Harding, or he may be a bright lad with a pushing spirit and an elastic conscience, like Hoover. In either case he has immense advantages over any frank, earnest, candid and forthright man.

I incline to believe that Hoover could have beaten Thomas Jefferson quite as decisively as he beat Al. He could have knocked off Grover Cleveland even more dramatically. His judgment of the American people was cynical but sound. Whenever he fed them it was with the mush that is now their pet fodder. He let Al bombard them with ideas, confident that the ideas would only affright and anger them. Meanwhile he did business behind the door with all the professional boob-squeezers, clerical and lay. His victory was a triumph of technique, of sound political engineering. It did credit to his gifts as a politician. But Al hogged all the glory as a statesman and a man. . . .

Suggestions for Further Reading

General

Karl Schriftgiesser, *This Was Normalcy* (1948); Arthur M. Schlesinger, Jr., *The Crisis of the Old Order* (1957)*.

The Eclipse of Progressivism

Herbert F. Margulies, *The Decline of the Progressive Movement in Wisconsin, 1890–1920* (1968); Arthur S. Link, "What Happened to the Progressive Movement in the 1920's?" *American Historical Review*, vol. 64 (1959), pp. 833–851; Russel B. Nye, *Midwestern Progressive Politics* (1951); Paul W. Glad, "Progressives and the Business Culture of the 1920's," *Journal of American History*, vol. 53 (1966), pp. 75–89; Donald C. Swain, *Federal Conservation Policy, 1921–1933* (1963); Preston J. Hubbard, *Origins of the TVA: The Muscle Shoals Controversy, 1920–1932* (1961)*; George W. Norris, *Fighting Liberal* (1945)*.

The Role of the War

Selig Adler, "The War-Guilt Question and American Disillusionment, 1918–1928," *Journal of Modern History*, vol. 23

236   *The Politics of Normalcy*

(1951), pp. 1–28; Harold and Margaret Sprout, *Toward a New Order of Sea Power . . . 1918–1922* (1940); D. F. Fleming, *The United States and World Organization, 1920–1933* (1938).

Foreign Policy

John Chalmers Vinson, *The Parchment Peace . . . the Washington Conference 1921–1922* (1955); L. Ethan Ellis, *Frank B. Kellogg and American Foreign Relations 1925–29* (1961); Robert H. Ferrell, *Peace in Their Time: The Origins of the Kellogg-Briand Pact* (1952); William A. Williams, "The Legend of Isolationism in the 1920's," *Science and Society*, vol. 18 (1954), pp. 1–20; Herbert Feis, *The Diplomacy of the Dollar* (1950)*; Joseph Brandes, *Herbert Hoover and Economic Diplomacy . . . 1921–28* (1962).

Republican Supremacy

Wesley M. Bagby, *The Road to Normalcy* (1962)*; Andrew Sinclair, *The Available Man . . . Warren Gamaliel Harding* (1965)*; Robert K. Murray, *The Harding Era* (1969); Burl Noggle, *Teapot Dome: Oil and Politics in the 1920's* (1962)*; William Allen White, *A Puritan in Babylon . . . Calvin Coolidge* (1938)*; Donald R. McCoy, *Calvin Coolidge* (1967); Edmund A. Moore, *A Catholic Runs for President: The Campaign of 1928* (1956); Ruth C. Silva, *Rum, Religion, and Votes: 1928 Re-examined* (1962); Paul A. Carter, "The Campaign of 1928 Re-examined: A Study in Political Folklore," *Wisconsin Magazine of History*, vol. 46 (1963), pp. 263–272; Oscar Handlin, *Al Smith and His America* (1958)*; David Burner, *The Politics of Provincialism: The Democratic Party in Transition 1918–1932* (1968); J. Joseph Huthmacher, *Massachusetts People and Politics, 1919–1933* (1959)*.

Business Supremacy

James Prothro, *Dollar Decade: Business Ideas in the 1920's* (1954)*; Morrell Heald, "Business Thought in the Twenties . . . ," *American Quarterly*, vol. 13 (1961), pp. 126–139.

The Supreme Court

Alpheus T. Mason, *William Howard Taft: Chief Justice* (1965); Stanley Kutler, "Chief Justice Taft, National Regulation and the Commerce Clause," *Journal of American History*, vol. 51 (1965), pp. 651–668; S. J. Konefsky, *The Legacy of Holmes and Brandeis* (1956); J. F. Paschal, *Mr. Justice Sutherland: A Man Against the State* (1951); Alpheus T. Mason, *Harlan Fiske Stone* (1956); R. G. Fuller, *Child Labor and the Constitution* (1929); Edward Berman, *Labor and the Sherman Act* (1930).

The Decline of Organized Labor

Irving Bernstein, *The Lean Years: A History of the American Worker, 1920–1933* (1960)*; Philip Taft, *The A. F. of L.* (2 vols., 1957–1959); David Brody, *Steelworkers in America: The Nonunion Era* (1960); Allen M. Wakstein, "Origins of the Open Shop Movement, 1919–1920," *Journal of American History*, vol. 51 (1964), pp. 460–475; Milton J. Nadworny, *Scientific Management and the Unions, 1900–1932* (1955).

The Dilemma of Agriculture

James H. Shideler, *Farm Crisis, 1919–1923* (1957); Gilbert C. Fite, *George N. Peek and the Fight for Farm Parity* (1954); Theodore Saloutos and John D. Hicks, *Twentieth Century Populism: Agricultural Discontent in the Middle West* (1951)*; Robert L. Morlan, *Political Prairie Fire: The Nonpartisan League, 1915–1922* (1955).

The End of Normalcy

Giulio Pontecorvo, "Investment Banking and Security Speculation in the Late 1920's," *Business History Review*, vol. 32 (1958), pp. 166–191; Robert Sobel, *The Great Bull Market* (1968)*; John K. Galbraith, *The Great Crash* (1955)*.

Hoover and Depression

Harris G. Warren, *Herbert Hoover and the Great Depression* (1959)*; Albert U. Romasco, *The Poverty of Abundance:*

Hoover, the Nation, and the Depression (1965)*; Carl N. Degler, "The Ordeal of Herbert Hoover," *Yale Review*, vol. 52 (1963), pp. 563–583; Robert H. Ferrell, *American Diplomacy in the Great Depression* (1957)*; Broadus Mitchell, *Depression Decade . . . 1929–1941* (1947)*.

Sacco-Vanzetti sympathizers with banners at Union Square, August 9, 1927.
Courtesy of Wide World Photos.

Clarence Darrow (left) and William Jennings Byran (right) at the
John Scopes Trial.
Courtesy of Brown Brothers.

The "Spirit of St. Louis."
Courtesy of Culver Pictures, Inc.

The poet, Robert Frost at stone cottage, 1921.
Courtesy of Yankee magazine.

New York Times headline on Stock Market slump, October 29, 1929.
Courtesy of Brown Brothers.

Sign on the New York Bank Co., February 15, 1913, protesting the Stock Exchange rule which forbid the listing of any securities except those engraved by certain companies which were affiliated. (insert). Courtesy of Culver Pictures, Inc.

Index

243